BUILDING SET APPLICATIONS
FOR SECURE TRANSACTIONS

MARK S. MERKOW
JIM BREITHAUPT
KEN L. WHEELER

WILEY COMPUTER PUBLISHING

JOHN WILEY & SONS, INC.
New York • Chichester • Weinheim • Brisbane • Singapore • Toronto

Publisher: Robert Ipsen
Editor: Robert M. Elliott
Managing Editor: Brian Snapp
Editorial Assistant: Brian P. Calandra
Text Design & Composition: Pronto Design & Production, Inc.

Designations used by companies to distinguish their products are often claimed as trademarks. In all instances where John Wiley & Sons, Inc., is aware of a claim, the product names appear in initial capital or ALL CAPITAL LETTERS. Readers, however, should contact the appropriate companies for more complete information regarding trademarks and registration.

This book is printed on acid-free paper. ∞

Published by John Wiley & Sons, Inc.

Published simultaneously in Canada.

This publication is designed to provide accurate and authoritative information in regard to the subject matter covered. It is sold with the understanding that the publisher is not engaged in professional services. If professional advice or other expert assistance is required, the services of a competent professional person should be sought.

Library of Congress Cataloging-in-Pubilcation Data:

0-471-28305-3

Printed in the United States of America.

10 9 8 7 6 5 4 3 2 1

TABLE OF CONTENTS

ACKNOWLEDGMENTS

From Mark S. Merkow, CCP:

Books are never written in a vacuum. As such, a virtual cast of hundreds is required to pull information together into a semblance of form and fitness.

There aren't enough "Thank You's" on the planet to express the gratitude to the following people for any and all combinations of assistance, support, encouragement, patience, discussions, reassurance, and unconditional solace. Thanks to David Armes, Pete Bennett, Mike Boland, Amy Bohlman, Don Brown, Richard Cole from GlobeSet, Laurie Doescher, Dr. James Dzierzanowski, Jennifer Killian from IBM, Wally Lake, Joe Lesko, Dr. David P. Skinner, and Jennifer Sloan.

A hearty thank you to my co-authors Jim Breithaupt and Ken Wheeler for the dedication it takes to make a good book a great one.

Tremendous gratitude goes to Bob Elliott at Wiley for his belief and effort in making this book a success. Special thanks to Brian Calandra and Brian Snapp at Wiley for their endless hard work and dedication they demonstrated in continuous improvements to the manuscript you hold before you.

Particular thanks to Carole McClendon at Waterside Productions for her tenacity in bringing what you're now holding in your hands to fulfillment.

Last of all, but far from least of all, I'd like to thank my two children— Joshua and Jasmine Merkow—for putting up with yet-another adventure into book publishing. If all gratitude could be accumulated into one place, it would still be insufficient to repay them for their endurance, patience, and support during this project.

From Jim Breithaupt:

The only thing tougher than working on a book is writing the acknowledgment—at least, this is my experience. I owe thanks first of all to Mark Merkow for asking me to contribute to this project and for the excellent job he has done shepherding this book along. His unflagging enthusiasm and optimism almost made a convert out of me. I also want to give thanks to the many people at Wiley who have given close and constructive consideration to our words.

On the home front, I thank my wife Margaret for her encouragement, support, and perhaps most importantly, her patience with my late night rantings and ravings at the keyboard. She has seen the worst of my moods and yet was still willing to celebrate our fifth wedding anniversary with me. To my children Faye and Bo, who already appreciate the power and mystery of words and inspire me to imagine, I give you my undying love and support.

Finally, but not necessarily in any pecking order, I salute my lost parents for their gift of life and language, to my brothers, especially Dave, who challenges me to write, and to old Shep, the greatest dog that ever lived.

From Ken Wheeler:

I'd like to thank Mark Merkow, who asked me to join in this endeavor and was always there to assist me when I struggled. Without his experience and guidance this project would have been unachievable.

Thanks also go out to Amber Pommerening and my two children—Cassie and Marc Wheeler—for supporting me throughout, especially during those times when I was pre-occupied with this project. I'd also like to thank Claudia Duncan and Bill Group at IBM for pointing me in the right direction to assistance within IBM.

INTRODUCTION

*"A big inhibitor to commerce on the Internet is security . . .
whether real or perceived."*

—BILL CAMPBELL, VICE PRESIDENT OF
MERCHANT SERVICES FOR BANK OF AMERICA

Is It Safe?

An IBM TV commercial begs the question as wary consumers discuss their fears of entering credit card information on the Internet. Any use of credit cards—whether face-to-face, by phone, mail order, or through a proxy—carries some degree of risk, but, through the Internet, the perception of risk is far more frightening.

Horror stories of Internet credit card fraud and deception abound. Criminal-launched Internet sites appear innocent enough, yet have one purpose—stealing credit card information. Often, the alarm isn't sounded until your billing statement arrives. By then, the perpetrators have cashed in and moved on to other victims. Card companies understand these risks, and generally protect consumers when thefts are reported. Merchants aren't quite so fortunate. Their choices come down to absorbing the fraud or raising prices.

Enter the Secure Electronic Transaction (SET) Standard: the future for on-line payments, specifically and cooperatively developed to protect buyers and sellers in conducting "card-not-present" transactions via the Internet.

With this book, you hold a single source of information to help you build successful, secure, and robust SET-enabled shopping sites. *Building SET Applications for Secure Transactions* takes you through all points of view related to charge processing to help you deliver your customers the high assurances of security, reliability, and privacy that they demand.

In *Building SET Applications for Secure Transactions,* you'll learn how to transform SET's features into real-life benefits that save you money, encourage new revenues, reduce your fraud losses, and pave the road to leading-edge business opportunities that only the Internet can offer.

While many readers will possess deep technical knowledge about payment card and POS technologies, and others are well-versed in the language of cryptography, few will be accomplished in both disciplines. To bridge that gap, this book offers substantial detail to help implement POS systems rooted in cryptography. No prior knowledge of either is assumed for the readers of this book, but those who'll gain the most should possess a good working knowledge of the Internet, be familiar with distributed processing concepts, and work comfortably around Web-based technologies.

The ultimate goal of the book is to help business owners—large and small alike—in "bolting on" SET to their existing or new Merchant Commerce sites. In addition, this book helps company webmasters and systems administrators with the work related to implementing SET throughout the entire system's development life cycle.

Chapters are categorized as follows:

Introduction. Chapter 1 looks at the motivation to develop SET, its roots, its features and benefits, and how SET fits into the Web buying experience. Chapter 2 provides a comprehensive look at payment cards and associated systems and processing, defines terms and concepts, then illustrates how SET emulates in the on-line world what occurs in the non-Internet world. Chapter 3 introduces the concept of digital certificates and describes what participants in a SET payment card transaction might expect.

Cryptography. Chapter 4 offers a high-level overview of cryptography, paving the way to SET's application of principles and understanding the notation of SET message pairs, covered in Chapter 5. Chapter 6 looks at various choices to render cryptographic processing on Merchant Commerce Systems.

SET Digital Certificates. Chapter 7 describes the Tree of Trust that SET establishes to provide the highest possible degrees of security and protection of sensitive and private information. Chapter 8 looks at how SET key management principles maintain that security for the long haul. Chapter 9 looks at the software for SET that Cardholders will use when buying from your site. Chapter 10 surveys several SET POS Systems that "bolt on" to Web-based Merchant Commerce environments.

SET Protocols and Message Pairs. Chapter 11 illustrates how through combining SET messages, POS and certificate management services are performed. Chapter 12 breaks each SET message pair down into its elementary components to help you understand how your back-office systems will need to interface to the system for transaction processing. Chapter 12 also serves as a reference chapter for anyone interested in SET message details.

Implementation. Chapter 13 starts out with some planning steps needed for your project's success. Chapter 14 leads you through the analysis work required for full understanding of the road ahead. Chapter 15 helps you through some design choices for the hardware and software required to implement SET. Chapter 16 helps you work through the installation and configuration steps, while Chapter 17 helps you through the testing and certifying steps for your new operation. Chapter 18 takes a look at the daily activities required to maintain security and overall operation.

Extending SET's Reach Outward. Chapter 19 reviews intranet and extranet technologies and looks at how SET might be used for internal and external corporate purchasing. Chapter 20 further surveys the commercial procurement landscape and introduces the Open Buying on the Internet (OBI) protocol for high-volume, low-dollar business-to-business purchases. Chapter 21 looks to see where SET is headed, and how its future will be affected by international e-commerce and SmartCards. Finally, we wrap up with a discussion of SET interoperability and some challenges that lie ahead.

At the end of the book, you'll find an appendix of Web resources for additional information and ways to contact SET vendors. You'll also find links to resources on cryptography, security, credit card fraud, and other topics that we discuss.

Behind the Web Resources Appendix, you'll find the Glossary, which will aid as a quick reference as you move through the book.

WHAT'S AT STAKE?   1

S ecure Electronic Transactions (SET) will help make the new "industrial revolution" a reality in the 21st century, this time without smokestacks or assembly lines.

Why SET?

Consumer concern about the security of business conducted over the Internet is the single most important issue facing electronic commerce today. Whether this perceived threat is real or imaginary makes no difference. The fact is, SET now provides the mechanism to unleash explosive and unlimited global commerce the likes of which the world has never before seen. Everyone from the home shopper who purchases garden tools from QVC to Supervox (a European "do-it-yourself" wholesaler) will conduct their business safely and securely under the new shopping paradigm. The Internet coupled with the SET technology will rewrite the old business equations.

The issue of security looms large when you look at projected volumes of business via the Internet over the next few years. Industry experts such as the Forrester Research group estimate that the value of goods and services traded over the Internet could exceed $8 billion annually by the year 2002. Other numbers released from International Data Corporation claim that as much as *$220 billion* will be spent over the Internet by 2002. SET, incorporated into the on-line buying model, promises to turn these predictions into reality. The U.S. Government states that global trade involving the sale of software, financial and professional services, entertainment products, information services, and technical information accounted for over $40 billion of U.S. exports

Tough Lessons to Learn

In an on-line *New York Times* article, Peter Wayner tells the story of how James Kantor, the president of Eastern Avionics, an international aviation company, had decided to develop a company Web site only to learn the importance of security on the Internet the hard way:

"Plugging his company's name into a general search engine, Kantor discovered that his company's Web site was already finished and on-line. Any item from the catalog could be ordered with a click of a button and a credit card number.

"'Lo and behold!' Kantor said, 'I found I was already on the Internet.'

"The frightening truth caught up with him after he called Capstone Studio, the company designing his site. Their work wasn't finished, they told Kantor, and whoever had launched the Eastern Avionics site was probably masquerading as his company to steal credit card numbers."

Wayner reported that Capstone Studio found at least thirty-five additional bogus Web sites whose sole purpose was to steal credit card numbers. After contacting the FBI, Capstone had the site taken down. The FBI treated the crime of setting up the rogue site as simple wire fraud because no one had actually broken into Eastern Avionics computers to steal their data.

Unfortunately, Eastern Avionics is not alone. Other unscrupulous people have built everything from Web sites pretending to belong to political candidates set up by their opponents, trying to smear them, to sites in which individuals attempt to defame organizations. One such site masquerading as People for the Ethical Treatment of Animals (PETA) set up their PETA site for People Eating Tasty Animals. The scope of such activity is unknown, partly because bogus Web sites can go undetected for a considerable period of time before someone in authority notices. The result? A nation of wary consumers who won't trust electronic communications. Obviously, such stories drive consumers and businesses away from using the Internet for credit card purchases, creating an unacceptable situation in the eyes of many big businesses, as well as to such promoters of the Internet as the IETF (Internet Engineering Task Force) who want to assuage the public's fears.

alone during the past decade. This growth is not without pain or the risks associated with securing private and confidential information while it traverses the vast networks of the public and insecure Internet.

These risks, entrusted to the private sector to solve, require the development of technology necessary to secure electronic business along with the guidelines and policies that enforce its responsible uses.

SET is that solution.

Even with the absence of an Internet-based credit card security standard, 1996 on-line business reached almost $25 million, or roughly $2.50 for each of the million or so Internet users at the time. The predicted growth in volume of credit card transactions over the Internet demands a protocol that protects consumers and Merchants alike, allowing each to verify the identities of the other parties without unnecessarily revealing credit card information. This level of authentication simply does not exist in other cryptography-based protocols such as the Secure Sockets Layer (SSL).

With SET, on-line window shoppers are persuaded to become buyers via the Internet because payment card processing couldn't be any safer. According to a survey of over 23,000 Internet users conducted by the University of Michigan and Georgia Tech, security is an imperative in the minds of many Internet users. Simply put, the more users learn about the Net, the greater their concerns over safety and security. Figure 1.1 shows the ratio of on-line browsers to buyers.

Figure 1.1 Browsers vs. buyers.

1. How much money have you spent through Internet transactions overall?

Answer:	Count:	%:	0 50 100
None	302	31.39%	
$1-$50	179	18.60%	
$51-$500	321	33.36%	
Over $500	160	16.63%	

Few of those surveyed trust the Internet enough for large dollar purchases. Even though roughly 50 percent dabble in small purchases, that still leaves close to a third of them who didn't attempt to purchase anything at all.

To help introduce SET, we'll look at a few of the earlier approaches to securing electronic communications, then move into an overview of SET. Some of the topics include:

- The motivation for SET

- SET's roots and the SET Consortium

- Features and benefits of SET

- SET's role in on-line payment processing

Web Trends: Less Hype, More Hyperspeed

Studies continue to show that the Internet turns the traditional business cycle—including communication, marketing, and direct sales—on its ear. *Activmedia*'s semi-annual report on the Web's "Real Numbers" shows business trends for companies moving to the Web. In the current report, Activmedia illustrates how companies, especially those selling products and services other than advertising, begin to turn real profits the longer they are on the Web, as shown in Figure 1.2. The longer a company maintains their Web presence, the better off they become financially, as news of their presence and positive experiences by consumers collect and spread throughout the Internet buying communities.

Activmedia has identified some current trends in Web success:

- Despite a sevenfold increase in the number of new commercial Web sites, three out of ten existing sites remain profitable.

- Web sites generating revenue have increased from one in three to three in five from 1996 to 1997.

- The number of Web sites generating advertising revenue (one in six) has tripled over the past year.

Figure 1.2 Web experience translates into profitability.

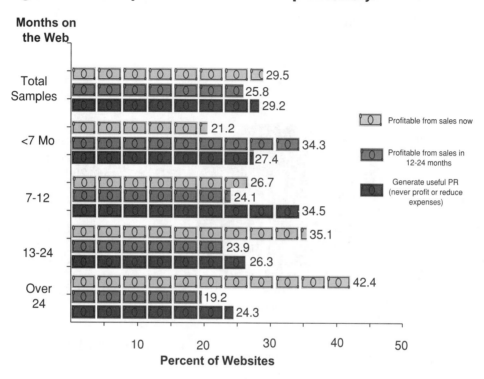

One in ten Web sites now generate more than $10,000 a month in income. Top producers earn more than $1 million a month in income, representing 90 percent of all Web revenues today.

As companies gain experience selling and advertising on the Web, they can expect to see greater increases in their share of Web spending (see Figure 1.3). Since 1986, Activmedia asked executives whether their sites were already profitible and, if not, when they believed they would be profitable. Those already profitable command a 65 percent share of all Web-generated revenues.

The numbers produced by groups like the Forrester Group and Activmedia show an unmistakable trend: businesses both large and small continue to move to the Web and embrace it as the "new economy." As their

Figure 1.3 Turning a profit.

Share of Total Web-Generated Revenue By Profitability
(March 1997)

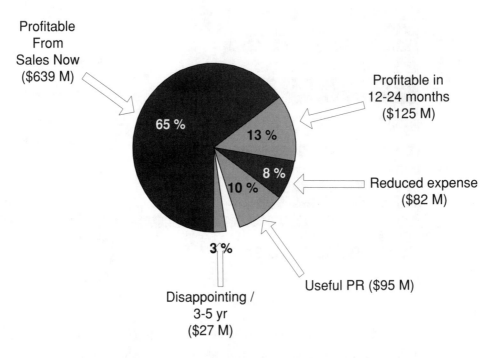

experience selling on the Internet grows, so will their profits and expectations. And SET figures into that equation: businesses will demand a higher level of security on the Internet, and consumers will continue to flock to their sites knowing that SET has made the Internet a safe place to shop.

By securing the Internet for electronic commerce, SET helps *level the playing field,* allowing any company, regardless of size, to create an electronic global selling presence. This market-driven impulse will push the technology into areas where it previously did not exist, and out of this new spirit of competition arises new opportunities for innovation, expanded services, a broader participation of businesses, lower prices with improved customer service, and heightened customer satisfaction.

The Internet, coupled with SET technology, revolutionizes retail and direct marketing enterprises. Consumers can shop for a wide range of products and services across the globe. They can access more extensive product and technical information, visualize what the product looks like or how it might work, make product inquiries through e-mail or in chat rooms, order, and pay for their choices electronically—with far less manual effort on everyone's part.

SET also revolutionizes business-to-business commerce. "Middlemen" may one day become an anachronism, as companies reduce inventory-on-hand while lowering costs and improving customer service. Businesses that offer round-the-clock service will gradually see a decline in phone and fax orders, freeing up sales people to focus more on the customers rather than on the processing of their orders.

The scope of the protection provided by SET is not limited to transactions involving hard goods. Sales of intellectual property are also protected. Although SET can't vouch for the quality of the products or services offered over the Internet, it does authenticate the consumer to the Merchant and vice versa and guarantees that no one alters any transactions anywhere along the line.

All of this underscores the need for stable, scalable, and secure platforms that encourage rather than stifle the development and promotion of new and innovative ways to do business on the Internet.

Back in the early 1990s, when the Web was first thought to be a marketer's Holy Grail, banks refused to accept or process charges originating on it and required Merchants to use existing infrastructures for charge authorizations, point-of-sale, phoned-in requests, and batch processed requests. These same banks, led by pressures on two sides, from both Merchants and consumers, began pressing Visa and MasterCard to develop a secure standard for using credit cards over any insecure channel, such as the Internet.

The Roots of SET

Visa and Microsoft responded to their cry with a standard they released in September 1995. The *Secure Transaction Technology* (STT) specification was posted to the Visa Web site for download by interested parties. At the same time, Microsoft announced that it would develop STT implementation tools for Windows 95 and Windows NT that could be licensed by developers. Tools for other desktop platforms would be developed by Spyglass Technology.

Meanwhile, MasterCard and its allies, Netscape, IBM, Cybercash, and GTE, had developed the *Secure Electronic Payment Protocol* (SEPP) as a proposed specification and posted it to the MasterCard Web site for a public comment period. MasterCard had hoped that SEPP could be in use for Internet transactions as early as April 1996.

STT and SEPP generated such heated debate and finger-pointing between the two opposing factions that the entire industry was at odds as to which way to turn. Both sides claimed their standard was defined with "openness in mind" and was designed in cooperation with the Internet standards-setting bodies, the W3 Consortium, the Internet Engineering Task Force (IETF), CommerceNet, and the Financial Services Technology Consortium. The IETF, however, claimed that neither side was going to win any merit badges for openness.

> *Jeffrey I. Schiller, the Internet Engineering Steering Group's Area Director for Security, said both parties came to the IETF looking for an endorsement, but neither got one, since IETF won't endorse work done outside its internal standardization processes. According to Schiller, "Both sides are welcome to contribute their technology to the IETF open process, but that means that their work would be scrutinized and potentially changed. Neither side has expressed a willingness to do that."*

Industry and financial services observers at the time believed that STT and SEPP were similar, yet different enough to render them incompatible. This meant that separate implementation efforts were required, and all parties desiring to support Visa and MasterCard products needed two separate processing facilities.

Not So Different under the Hood

In fact, STT and SEPP attempted to achieve the same objectives, but did so from different directions. Those objectives included

- Changing banker's treatment of Internet-based credit card transactions from the risky *card-not-present* scenario (such as mail order/telephone order transactions) to the less risky *card-present* situations (such as retail shopping and eateries) to reduce the chances of fraud, and increase the potential to lower the fees that Merchants must pay for maintaining Merchant accounts. By using the same risk models that are used in card-present transactions, Internet transactions would be treated under the same set of conditions and similar risks.

- Requiring all parties in a transaction (customer, Merchant, credit card processor, and bank) to possess digital certificates that establish their identities and their authority to conduct transactions.

- Requiring that public key certification agencies (Certificate Authorities) manage the certificate distribution processes on behalf of the card association or member banks.

- Using industry-standard public key cryptography techniques, as developed by Ron Rivest, Adi Shamir, and Leonard Adelman (RSA Data Security).

- Encrypting only credit card numbers and transactional data rather than encrypting the entire browser and shopping sessions.

- Concealing credit card data from all Merchants to prevent Merchant-initiated fraud.

- Enabling use of *any* type of credit card product, regardless of issuer. The card associations, however, reserved the right to specify that only *their* protocol be permitted for transactions with their cards.

By the latter part of 1995, banks that issued both Visa cards and MasterCards were up in arms over the attempt to require two separate standards to accomplish the same task. The banks persisted, and finally forced Visa and MasterCard to work together on a *single* standard.

In February 1996, the announcement rocked the Internet community:

> *Visa and MasterCard Combine Secure Specifications for Card Transactions on the Internet into One Standard*

> *"This is the first step in making cyberspace a profitable venture for banks and merchants. A single standard limits unnecessary costs and builds the business case for doing business on the Internet. Further, our work with Master- Card demonstrates our unwavering commitment to address the needs of our member financial institutions, and their merchants and cardholders," said Edmund Jensen, presi- dent and CEO of Visa International.*

The SET Consortium

Upon the agreement, Visa and MasterCard, along with GTE, IBM, Micro- soft, Netscape Communications Corp., SAIC, Terisa Systems, VeriSign, and RSA Data Security, formed the SET Consortium. Their goal was to resolve the differences and conflicts between STT and SEPP and develop a new uni- fied standard.

The development of SET, a relatively quick response to an explosive growth of the Internet (although some consider it an eternity in Web-years), arose not so much from the spirit of mutual cooperation as from the inter- vention of major banks who saw the industry giants, Visa and MasterCard, heading in separate directions. Obviously, for any pragmatic solution to the problems of electronic commerce to succeed, a single, standard approach, both flexible and platform-independent, was absolutely essential.

SET Consortium's work, the Secure Electronic Transaction (SET), was released to developers in draft form on June 24, 1996. The draft release, embodied in three separate documents, was intended to be used for testing and to elicit comments from outside experts. These books contained suffi- cient preliminary specifications that developers could use to build components that would "bolt on" to existing Cardholder browsers, Merchant commerce servers, and financial institution credit authorization systems. SET Version 0.0 appeared as:

Book 1. The business description containing background information and processing flows. It was intended as a primer on software that interfaces with payment systems and employs public-key cryptography.

Book 2. The programmer's guide containing the technical specifications for the protocol intended for use by software developers who wish to build Cardholder and Merchant software components.

Book 3. The formal protocol definition, intended for use by cryptographers analyzing SET's security aspects, writers producing programming guides for toolkits or components, and system programmers developing cryptographic and messaging primitives.

Upon its initial release, SET Version 0.0 was placed under formal change control with a January 1997 deadline for enhancement requests to Version 1.0, and March 1997 for proposed corrections to the testing version. On April 21, 1997, SET Version 0.2 was released to the public containing those requests for enhancements that satisfied the additional needs of non-Visa/MasterCard issuers, such as American Express, Japan Commerce Bank (JCB), and Novus/Discover.

On May 31, 1997, SET Version 1.0 was released to the public.

SET Global Acceptance

Integral to the success of SET is its acceptance in the marketplace as an open standard for conducting electronic commerce on the Internet.

To this end, the SET business definition outlines these noble pursuits:

- Gain worldwide acceptance through its ease of implementation, with as little disruption as possible to the Merchants and Cardholders

- Provide "bolt-on" implementation of the SET protocol to existing client applications

- Minimize the change in the relationship between acquirers and Merchants, and Cardholders and card issuers, leaving the current business models intact
- Minimize the impacts to Merchant, acquirer, and payment system applications
- Provide a protocol that is efficient for financial institutions

Demonstrated Commitment to the New Gospel

In July 1997, SET moved one step closer to becoming a global standard when 20 technology companies showcased their products at the *Promise of SET* event, co-hosted by Visa International and MasterCard International.

Former MasterCard senior vice-president of electronic commerce Steve Mott had this to say at the event: "Today's participants play a crucial role in the acceptance of SET as the global payment standard of choice for shopping on the Internet, providing financial institutions, merchants and consumers a secure means of electronic commerce at a time of dramatic growth."

Steve Herz, senior vice-president of Internet Commerce—Visa International, also shared in the fanfare, claiming: "The SET Consortium has undertaken a huge task to replicate in the virtual world the trust system which exists in the payment system in the physical world today. SET addresses one barrier of electronic commerce and that is trust." The next steps for the SET Consortium were also announced at the Promise of SET Conference. They included:

- The creation of a SET software compliance process to validate vendor software against the SET specification and manage use of the SETMark
- The creation of a Root Key Authority to manage and issue the SET digital certificates to the payment brands, thus establishing the SET Tree of Trust (discussed in Chapter 7)
- Validation of vendor software against the 1.0 specification and the deployment into the global market

Figure 1.4 The SETMark.

- Roll-out of pilot and production uses through financial institutions, Merchants, and Cardholders

As visible proof of long-term commitment, the Secure Electronic Transaction Mark was also unveiled. Its purpose is to indicate successful SET certification of vendor software and Merchant Web sites, thus providing consumers with the comfortable knowledge that they're transacting using SET. The SETMark, shown in Figure 1.4, will be licensed to any vendor or payment brand that's certified as SET compliant.

SET's Objectives

Like its predecessors, STT and SEPP, SET addresses seven major business requirements:

- Provide confidentiality of payment information and enable confidentiality of order information that is transmitted along with the payment information

- Ensure the integrity of all transmitted data

- Provide authentication that a Cardholder is a legitimate user of a branded payment card account

- Provide authentication that a Merchant can accept payment card transactions through its relationship with an acquiring financial institution

- Ensure the use of the best security practices and system design techniques to protect all legitimate parties in an electronic commerce transaction

- Create a protocol that neither depends on transport security mechanisms nor prevents their use
- Facilitate and encourage interoperability among software and network providers

Since payment cards and their systems have been around since the 1950s, banks and issuers have had plenty of time to decide how to secure their processing. The vast private networks developed for the purpose, using leased-lines and dial-up connections, helped in assuring their safety and security, building Merchant and consumer confidence. SET does the same using insecure public communication channels, such as the Internet.

To better understand how SET achieves this privacy and security, think of its operation using the following context. Take a secret, write it down on a piece of paper, seal the paper in an envelope, place the envelope in a safe, place the safe in a vault, and ship the vault to your recipient using a common-carrier.

While it's possible that your secret could be discovered en route, what are the chances that this will happen? SET secures information so thoroughly that the costs to discover it far outweigh the benefits of knowing it. That's the basic principle of all security systems—protect your belongings just a *little* better than your neighbor protects theirs, making them less attractive for a thief to pursue (takes longer than desired, requires more efforts, etc.). SET, however, takes that concept much further, essentially wrapping up every secret within an impenetrable fortress of cryptography.

With SET's official release as a standard, work toward its implementation continues across the globe with pilot testing between and among dozens of software developers, hardware developers, financial services companies, and a handful of pioneering Merchants.

SET's Features Make It Happen

The features of the SET standard are described as separate components, but they are not intended to function independently. To achieve compliance with the specification, all security functions *must* be implemented.

- Confidentiality of information is required to assure Cardholders that their payment information is safe and readable only by the intended recipient. SET's use of message encryption ensures the confidentiality of information.

- Integrity of data guarantees that message contents are not altered during the transmission between the originator and the recipient. SET provides for digital signatures to ensure the integrity of payment information.

- Cardholder account authentication offers Merchants a means to verify that a Cardholder is a legitimate user of a valid branded payment card account. SET uses digital signatures and Cardholder certificates to ensure the authentication of such accounts.

- Merchant authentication offers Cardholders a means to confirm that a Merchant has a relationship with a financial institution that allows that Merchant to accept payment cards. SET uses digital signatures and Merchant certificates to ensure authentication of the Merchant.

- Interoperability permits SET compliance across a variety of hardware and software platforms without preferential treatment for any combinations. SET is built using specific protocols and message formats that provide the degree of interoperability desired.

Once a Merchant has established a SET-enabled Web site, he can immediately enjoy the benefits of doing business on the Internet regardless of the size of his business.

SET's Benefits Know No Bounds

Those who stand to benefit the most from SET are the "little guys" who are determined enough to win big in the world of e-commerce. Amazon.com, Inc., a Seattle-based on-line-only bookseller, is one such example. Drawn by SSL-only payment information protection and a highly effective marketing machine, people flock to Amazon.com to peruse its extensive list of more than two million titles, few of which are stored at its modest "brick-and-mortar" warehouse operation. Amazon.com tracks a buyer's purchases and recommends other titles that might be appealing. The company can also help the buyer search for out-of-print or otherwise hard-to-find titles. Orders are processed on-line, typically at a discount to the buyer, since Amazon.com deals directly with its distributors, and most titles are shipped within a week of the order date.

Integrating SET into Merchant Web Site Operations— Loose or Tight?

E-commerce stands at a crossroads. Till now, what many companies call an e-commerce channel is little more than an extension of existing manually intensive processing, with little or no direct linkages into back office systems. More than a few "order entry" Web sites are out there that capture input from a customer and receive it in e-mail or other simple forms. Operators then print the contents and re-key every piece of information onto a data entry terminal.

SET shatters this model most completely. SET not only encourages a full integration into existing processes, it practically mandates and presupposes that it will be operated as such. Those older "data capture" services won't hold up to the transactional nature of SET processing.

Those of you unprepared to commit to that level of integration required to make SET work as it's intended may want to reconsider migrating. SET is not for the lazy or the faint of heart. While the long road to SET leads to fortunes, all shortcuts lead to disaster.

On the other hand, if you're considering shelving those orphaned, outdated, or otherwise problem systems related to back office order entry and fulfillment, SET may well be your best bet. SET is a new technology employing the most contemporary of system architectures; your choice to use SET may lead you to better office solutions, too.

Forewarned is forearmed. The choice is yours!

Securing transactions over the Internet means that businesses will spend less time processing orders and more time improving their product line and marketing strategies. They will necessarily place more emphasis on bridging the gap between marketing and development, on integrating existing services, and on developing new strategies for creating an even larger global market. Transactions are likely to become increasingly complex as Merchants, suppliers, and buyers exercise their options.

As Robert Marczak, president of Marczak Business Services in Sharon Springs, New York, says, "Once secure transactions become more prominent, the Web will be for people of this century what the Sears Roebuck catalog was for consumers in the last century."

Where SET Stands

Integral to the success of SET is its acceptance in the marketplace as an open standard for conducting electronic commerce on the Internet. SET's uses are specific to certain phases of a shopping and buying transaction, and its processing is identified to support only those phases of the e-shopping model. In the next section we outline the steps in a common electronic payment transaction. We'll elaborate on this model in Chapter 2.

SET's Role in On-line Shopping and Payment Processing

Of the eight defined phases of e-shopping in the following list, SET is active in phases 4, 5, 6, and 8. All the phases are further detailed in Chapter 2 and referenced throughout the book:

Phase 1. Cardholder browses for items via the Web, through a CD-ROM-based catalog, or through a mail-order paper-based catalog.

Phase 2. Cardholder selects items for purchase.

Phase 3. Cardholder completes an order form, including total costs, shipping, handling, and taxes (if any). This form may be presented, already filled-in electronically via the Web, or may be created off-line on the Cardholder's PC.

Phase 4. Cardholder selects the form of payment card to use for the order. SET is initiated at this point.

Phase 5. Cardholder sends completed order form and payment instructions to the Merchant. SET is used to sign these order forms and payment instructions digitally using the Cardholder's digital certificate to prove they came from the Cardholder and no one else.

Phase 6. Merchant requests payment authorization from the Issuer of the payment card using its Merchant account through its Acquirer's payment system. SET wraps these messages in cryptography to assure their privacy and confidentiality.

Phase 7. Merchant ships goods or performs requested services based on the order.

Phase 8. Merchant requests to capture the payment that was previously approved for processing in Phase 6. SET wraps these messages in cryptography, to ensure their privacy and confidentiality. Those phases not included under SET are considered out-of-band (or out of scope) activities, and their implementation is left up to the involved parties. In addition, those interfaces to systems required for using SET are also out-of-band to the specification. SET provides open and robust data structures and corresponding security to handle virtually any type of order processing. It establishes an infrastructure for banks and Merchants to plug into using software they customize to meet infrastructure requirements. How that software is developed, and any affected systems, remain outside of SET's definition.

In Chapter 2, we take a close look at the payment card industry to establish the context for SET's enablement. There you'll learn how SET opens the Internet to the otherwise closed world of Point-of-Sale (POS) payment card processing, and helps you along the road to your custom implementation.

PAYMENT SYSTEMS 101

With today's technology of intelligent Point-of-Sale (POS) devices, high-speed communication networks, and hidden back-end host systems, charge processing appears simple to the uninitiated, but in fact the constituent involvement and the steps of processing are rather complex.

Nothing is obvious or intuitive about the processing that goes on, either. Between the sheer number of systems involved and the high volume of charges, trying to follow a charge through all its steps, from start to finish, is enough to make your head spin.

To aid in building an understanding of how SET serves the industry, this chapter first explains what the industry is. Topics covered here include:

- A brief history of payment cards and how they operate
- Some basic terminology
- Running the payment process on-line with SET

Charge It!

Credit cards, charge cards, bank cards, payment cards—no matter what you call them, all relate to a family of payment options that involve relationships rooted in trust and good faith.

You trust that the financial institution that issued you a card will pay the Merchant for the goods and services you purchase. Merchants trust that the card issuers will pay them reasonably quickly, and the card issuers trust that you'll pay your bill on time each month to reimburse the money they're advancing on your behalf.

Credit or Charge, What's the Difference?

Although they're thought by some to be the same, credit and charge cards differ in how they work and in the agreements associated with each.

In general, a *credit* card is a payment card that carries a preset spending limit established by the issuer based on a line of credit (either signature or secured line of credit) obtained at the time of issue. In addition, the account balances revolve around the line of credit that may be paid in full or financed over time. Finance charges apply to unpaid balances left at the end of the month, at fixed Annual Percentage Rates (APR) that are set at the time of issue and may or may not change over time. Visa cards and MasterCards are the most prevalent examples of credit cards that are issued by specific banks or other financial institutions; these institutions license the use of Visa and MasterCard trademarks from the brand associations.

Charge cards, like the American Express Personal (Green), Gold, and Platinum Cards, carry no preset spending limits, are due in full at the end of the month, are not tied to revolving lines of credit, and do not accumulate interest or finance charges under normal uses.

A Brief History of Payment Cards

The general-purpose payment card industry will celebrate its Golden Anniversary in 2001. Diners Club was the first general-use *charge* card, born in March 1951 as the brainchild of Frank McNamara, who once ran out of cash and couldn't pay his tab at a New York restaurant. He and his partners set out to create a universally accepted card, primarily for use at restaurants.

Building on the ideas behind the success of department store charge cards, which were firmly in place at the time, Diners Club's bylaws established that its Cardholders receive an interest-free 30 day float (loan) for their charges as long as they paid their balances in full each month. Diners Club considered its Cardholders as Members who paid an annual membership fee for the privilege. The growth of the Diners Club franchise made it the first successful Travel and Entertainment (T&E) card, with 250,000 members by 1956.

In 1957, American Express decided to enter the payment card business as a natural extension of their money order and travelers check lines of business. Through significant marketing, by the time the American Express Card launched in October 1958, they had already built up a network of 17,500 Merchants, and 250,000 card members ready to shop, travel, and spend. Like Diners Club, American Express charged an annual fee: $5.00— $2.00 more than Diners Club—with a special appeal of prestige to the traveling and affluent segments of the public.

Also launched in 1958, BankAmericard, from the Bank of America, appeared on the scene as the first general-use *credit* card. Throughout the 1960s, Bank of America licensed the use of the BankAmericard brand to banks across the United States. During this time, member bank associations began to form both within and outside the United States. In 1966, fourteen eastern U.S. banks formed the Interbank Card Association (ICA) and absorbed the Master-Charge Bank Association, which later became MasterCard International, Inc. Meanwhile, Bank of America renamed the BankAmericard the Visa Card, and what became Visa International was formed as a result of banking associations from the western United States. Later on, MasterCharge was renamed Master-Card, and its name remains today.

Open vs. Closed Loops

When a financial institution serves as a broker between the user of its cards and the Merchants who accept its card via transaction processing, they're called *closed loop systems*. American Express, Discover, and Diners Club are examples of closed loops. There is one American Express franchise, one Diners Club franchise (now owned by CitiBank), and one Discover Card company.

When a Cardholder with a bankcard from Bank A uses her card to transact with a Merchant whose account is at Bank B and their transaction is processed through a different third party, it's called an *open loop system*. Bankcard systems using Visa and MasterCard are examples of open loops.

In reality, neither the Visa nor the MasterCard companies issue credit cards directly to consumers. Rather, they rely upon their member banks to establish the lines and set the terms for consumer credit within their own portfolios. They also rely on the banks to offer the Merchant services to enable retailers to accept their cards as forms of payment. Typically a Merchant's bank will provide such services in addition to the other banking services retailers need.

Visa and MasterCard serve as Brand Association authorities that establish and maintain the *by-laws* that frame the uses of their logos and the accompanying agreements *between* their member banks. Both Visa and MasterCard claim they have over 20,000 member banks throughout the world that form their franchises.

Payment Cards Today

Over the years, several other payment card brands appeared, including Carte Blanche, Discover Card, and Optima Cards (American Express's revolving credit card products). International cards have also appeared in the United States, including ones from the Japan Commerce Bank (JCB).

By 1992, U.S. consumer credit, primarily from credit cards, stood at 15% of the 1992 Gross National Product (GNP), or $799 billion. Today, credit cards are as pervasive as cash registers. Visa International claims that 600 million cards carry the Visa brand label or one of their acceptance marks (Visa InterLink or Visa Electron). They further claim that 14 million locations accept their brand, which led consumers to purchase more than $1 trillion in goods and services in the 12 months ending in March 1997.

Other payment products have also appeared to support the needs of corporations for business uses. The American Express Corporate and Government Cards are examples of these. Still other special-use cards, such as Purchasing Cards, lower the costs and add process efficiency related to business-to-business purchasing (discussed further in Chapter 20).

Because of their flexibility and convenience, new payment card products are certain to appear, filling all niche needs as they arise.

At its onset, SET Version 1.0 is explicitly geared to support these brands of cards:

- Visa
- MasterCard
- American Express
- Diners Club
- JCB
- Novus (Discover Card)

Because SET emulates the work in payment card processing over the Internet, it's instructive to first understand how Point-of-Sale (POS) processing occurs in the non-Internet world.

Although payment cards also include debit cards (those tied to a consumer's checking or savings account), this discussion is limited to credit and charge cards. *SET Version 1.0 does not support debit cards, but in all likelihood will in some future version.*

Steps in a Payment Card Transaction

Without considering where the Internet comes into play for charge processing, let's follow a credit card charge from its origins on a POS terminal to its final resting place—as a debit to the buyer and a credit to the supplier.

Point-of-Sale Processing

Imagine you're shopping at Abe's Corner Store; you've finished making your selections, and have taken your goods to the register for check out. You've elected to use your MasterCard that was issued from Bob's Bank (an Issuer Bank) for payment. (POS terminals are everywhere nowadays!) Abe has signed up for MasterCard *Merchant Processing Services* from Carl's National Bank (an Acquirer Bank) and is happy to accept your card as payment for your purchase. While Carl's National Bank provides Merchant services for any Merchants who sign up, it's too small to operate the systems needed to process charges—rather, Carl's commissions the work to a *third-*

party processor. Let's say David's Card Processing Service handles that work on behalf of Carl's. David's Card Processing Service was also the business to set up the equipment at Abe's, and is geared to service the requests that originate from Abe's, as well as from other customers.

The cashier at Abe's swipes your MasterCard on the POS terminal, keys in the amount of the sale, and hits the SEND button. This kicks off the first step of an *authorization* request. Based upon on the data contained on the card (*account number*, etc.), the POS terminal *knows* where the request needs to be routed. Since they're somewhat intelligent (programmable), POS terminals will typically support a feature known as split-dial to process multiple card brands. With routing information in hand, the terminal initiates a phone call to David's Card Processing Service that finds the records for your account at Bob's Bank via the bank *Interchange Network*. The *open-to-buy* amount on your account is reviewed, and if it's sufficient for the sale amount you're requesting, an *authorization code* is provided to allow the sale's completion. This authorization step creates a temporary debit to your account under the assumption that the charge will be settled at some point in the near future. These debits prevent you from exceeding your credit limit with any subsequent charges. They'll remain on your account until one of two events occurs—either a *settlement* of the charge is sent in or the debit expires, freeing and returning the requested amount to your open-to-buy availability. The POS terminal then prints out a sale receipt as a record of charge (ROC). The cashier tears it off, has you sign it, checks your signature for a match on the back of your card, and hands you the yellow copy, a register receipt, your card, and your goods. While you'll never actually see what happens to place your charges on your bill, rest assured they will get there indeed.

As these charge authorizations occur, the Merchant's terminal collects what are called *capture records* that uniquely identify the transactions. These records comprise what's called a *Batch Settlement File*. This settlement file may contain dozens, hundreds, or thousands of unique capture records, waiting to be processed through the banks that have issued cards on those accounts represented within the batch. When the batch is deemed sufficiently large (in terms of counts or total dollars), the submission, capture, and settlement processes begin.

Differences That Charge Cards Bring into the Picture

The processing steps for charge cards are identical to those for credit cards with the exception of the mechanics in the authorization request and settlement processing. Since charge cards are not based on preset spending limits, the notion of an open-to-buy is irrelevant. Rather, charge card systems use other means to authorize or decline a charge request: risk models, heuristics, patterns of spending, manual review, and so on.

The sophistication in today's systems also permits card companies to detect acts of fraud during POS transactions. Since consumer buying habits can be modeled as patterns, any out-of-pattern spending may be deemed suspicious. Often, Merchants are asked to call an authorizer (a human being) who asks the Merchant some questions or requests to speak to the Cardholder. On the Internet, this becomes far more difficult to do.

In a closed-loop system, the Cardholder and Merchant accounts are typically operated on the same systems. Settlement (discussed in the next section) then becomes a matter of debiting one side of the system and crediting the other side without any need to access the banking network, except to collect charges from any other Acquirers who may process charges from the closed-loop system brand.

Capture and Settlement

In order for a batch to be settled, the card processor must first receive it. The software in Abe's terminal initiates a file transfer that sends it via the private line to David's Card Processing Service. At David's, the batch is sorted down by the *Bank Identification Number* (BIN—a piece of information contained in the account numbers) in preparation for capture processing. Each set of transactions with the same BIN is sent to the bank identified by the code; the bank will then turn those earlier temporary debits into permanent debits. The bank sums up the total charges on its accounts and performs a wire transfer to the account indicated for Abe's Corner Market at Carl's Bank. This work is performed using *Automated Clearing Houses* (ACHs) that enable wire-transfer operations. At this point, your account at Bob's Bank reflects your charge and awaits the cycle cut that prepares your billing statement.

Figure 2.1 illustrates this batch settlement processing as it moves from the Merchant to the Acquiring Bank to the Banker's Interchange.

Once the entire batch is settled, Abe's account at Carl's Bank reflects the total batch's credits (less returns and voided transactions, and less *processing and discount rate fees*). With the next batch, the process begins anew.

Figure 2.1 Batch settlement processing of card and Merchant accounts.

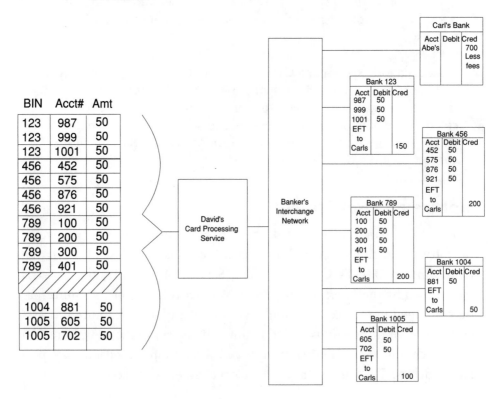

A Note about Networks

The networks involved in the scenario just described consist of dial-up and leased lines between all the parties needing to share information. These private networks are secured through whatever means is deemed required by the payment processor and the banks. Note that nowhere was the Internet mentioned, neither as a transaction medium nor as a communication medium. The Internet poses special problems for charge processing, since it's an insecure and publicly accessible channel. SET's cryptography is used to mitigate these problems, but adds several layers of processing and even new layers of preprocessing. The presence of a Payment Gateway is a requirement to handle the cryptographic preprocessing prior to submitting those transactions for postprocessing on host-based legacy systems. These transactions must be made to look like any other common POS-initiated transaction for the legacy systems at the banks, the payment processors, and the clearing houses.

Those industry standards that cover the processing of financial transactions are defined by ISO Standard 8583—to enable any card processor to work with everyone's card transactions.

Over the course of walking through the process, we've introduced a number of new terms and concepts (shown as italicized text). Let's define them now.

A Charge Processing Glossary

Account Number. A unique number assigned to a Cardholder account that identifies the specific financial institution, type of card, etc. Account Numbers are thought to be *overloaded operators* that are used for several purposes in addition to being unique identifiers.

Acquiring Bank. A bank that does business with Merchants who wish to accept credit cards. Merchants are given an account to deposit the value of a batch's card sales. The bank acquires batches of sales slips and credits their value to the Merchant's account. Banks then submit the charges destined for other banks in the open loop to the interchange network, either directly or through third parties. In the earlier example, Carl's National Bank serves as the Acquiring Bank.

Authorization. A process whereby transactions are approved or declined by the card issuers. Successful authorizations reduce the amount of available credit but do not actually charge the customer, nor move money to the seller. Authorizations can be performed via telephone, POS terminal, or the Internet.

Bank Identification Number. A three- to five-digit code, defined by ISO 8663, that assigns ranges for account number assignments that are explicitly tied to a specific brand or card company.

Batch, Batch Settlement File. An accumulation of card transactions awaiting settlement processing. Batches can be submitted for processing throughout the day or continue to grow until their value is sufficiently large enough and worthwhile to process.

Capture. Converts a previously authorized transaction amount into a billable sale. Transactions cannot be captured unless they were first authorized, and authorizations cannot be captured until the consumer's goods have shipped or the services were performed.

Capture Token. A computerized record that uniquely identifies a captured transaction or captured authorization.

Cardholder. The user (typically a consumer) of a credit or charge card issued by an Issuer Bank.

Charge Processor. Transaction processing company that offers card processing services, billing, MIS reporting, settlement, and other work to banks and card companies. Since operating these systems is rather complex and very expensive, most banks outsource this work to third parties who specialize in such services. In the earlier example, David's Card Processing Service acts as the Charge Processor. Charge Processors are sometimes referred to as Payment Acquirers.

Clearing. The process of exchanging transaction details between the Merchant Bank and the Issuer Bank. Clearing posts charges to Cardholder accounts and reconciles the Merchant's settlement position.

Discount Rate. Merchant fees are determined through the discount rate set by the Merchant Bank as a privilege fee for using their account services. Fees are based on the value of each transaction, and typically range from 1% up to 5%, depending on a number of factors, including charge volumes, risk models, size of the business, methods of submission, bank policies, etc.

Interchange. The banker's interchange exists to exchange information, data, and money between the banks connected to it. The interchange systems are managed by Visa and MasterCard to standardize the network's use across the globe.

Interchange fee. An amount charged to a Merchant Bank by an Issuer Bank to compensate for the time the Issuer Bank needs to wait for payment between settlement time and actual receipt of bill payment from their customer.

Issuer Bank. The bank that extends credit to customers (Cardholders) through bank card accounts. These banks enter into contractual agreements with Visa or MasterCard to issue their respective products. In our earlier example, Bob's Bank serves as the Issuer Bank.

Merchant. Any business operation that accepts payment cards for goods or services. Merchants establish the privilege of accepting payment cards through relationships with Acquiring (Merchant) Banks and card companies.

Merchant Bank. See Acquiring Bank.

Open-to-buy. A piece of information on a credit card account that indicates the difference between the line of credit amount and the balance currently owed by the Cardholder.

Processing fees. Fees that are charged to Acquirer Banks and Merchants for the privileges of using the interchange network or for using Merchant account services. Typically, processing fees are built into the Discount Rates.

Receipt. A hard-copy document that represents the fact that a transaction took place at some point in time.

Record-of-Charge (ROC). See Receipt.

Settlement. A process that occurs when the Acquiring Bank exchanges financial information in return for funds from an Issuer Bank.

Third-party processor. Company that enters into contractual agreements with Issuer and Acquirer Banks to process authorizations and settlement operations on their behalf. See Charge Processor.

Those security problems mentioned earlier arising from using the Internet instead of private leased and dial-up lines are precisely those that SET mitigates. With the high-degree of private and sensitive data flying by, steps to protect those data are essential to maintain the same levels of trust that exist on private networks. The trick then is to make a public network *behave* like a private one.

SET's Role in an On-line Payment Card Transaction

SET is implemented as pairs of request and response messages that serve the same functions as a POS terminal on a private network. These message pairs (described in depth in Chapter 12) are wrapped in cryptography before being placed onto the public Internet to hide their contents to all but those intended to receive and process them.

In person, it's easy to check for a matching signature on a card or to ask a person for ID. On the Internet, it's virtually impossible. Authentication then can only occur through cryptography. SET uses a robust set of digital certificates (see Chapter 4) to accomplish this. Each participant in a SET transaction requires a specific certificate or set of certificates that not only uniquely identifies that participant, but also attests to his privilege as holder of a payment card or hers as holder of a Merchant account. Additional computer processing is then necessary to put these certificates to work in SET message passing.

Cardholder certificates are constructed such that they relate to both the physical piece of plastic and the signature on the back of it. Merchant certificates assure the transaction acquirer and the Cardholders that they're dealing with a legitimate operator who's contractually obligated to the brand to remain honest. Charge Processors and Merchants are assured that they're dealing with Cardholders who have legitimate rights to use a brand product. Both Merchants and Cardholders are assured their transactions are seen and processed only by those Charge Processors who have legitimate rights to see and process them.

SET certificate management and processing is in addition to any other processing that takes place. The sole purpose of such processing is to ensure that certificates are kept current, safe, and always ready for use when needed.

In this section we introduce the notion of a SET Payment Gateway, which is needed to validate SET digital certificates and preprocess authorization, capture, and settlement work. Payment Gateways are operated by whatever company is serving the Charge Processor duties for Merchants and banks. We use the terms Acquirer Payment Gateway and Payment Gateway as synonyms throughout the book.

Since your SET Merchant Server takes the place of POS Terminals, it needs to perform all the work POS Terminals do, and then some. One of the more significant benefits of using the Internet over private networks and dial-up lines is its extremely flexible nature for data communications. With Internet connections, it's possible to avoid some third-party work (with a resultant savings of fees) by connecting directly to acquiring banks or card company Payment Gateways. Your decision to do so or not will depend on your existing card processing arrangements and other factors related to how SET Payment Gateways are marketed to banks and Merchants.

Looking now at only those SET payment system components (ignoring certificate processing for the time being), we find sets of message pairs between Cardholders and Merchant Servers and between Merchant Servers and Payment Gateways.

Steps in a SET Payment Card Transaction over the Internet

Let's revisit Abe's Corner Market, but this time we'll bring SET into the picture to see what's different about the transaction.

Over the months, Abe's business has exploded. Like many other customers, tired of the long lines at the register, you began demanding that Abe offer shop-at-home with same-day delivery services. After careful consideration, Abe decided that this was a terrific idea, and since SET makes payment card shopping perfectly safe, he agreed it was time to accommodate customer needs.

A few months earlier, David's Card Processing Service started offering SET payment acceptance to those banks that it serves. David's built a Payment Gateway to preprocess card authorization requests, and established a partnership with Elliott's Certificate Authority that permits David's banking customers (as well as others) to issue digital certificates to the bank Cardholders and Merchant services customers. The infrastructure they've jointly constructed is a bridge between Cardholders and Merchants, and puts into place all the elements needed to make SET work.

We'll refer back to this processing scenario in several other chapters, so we'll assign phase numbers that relate to processing steps. These are the same phases described in Chapter 1.

Before any transacting can take place, everyone involved needs to own a SET Digital Certificate. Without looking specifically at how they're obtained, let's assume that that process has already occurred and everyone is prepared. Let's call that Phase 0.

Phase 0: All SET Software and Requisite Digital Certificates in Place

Abe's Corner Market Web site at www.abes-store.com is up and running. Abe offers a full line of products for sale through the simple click of a few buttons, and delivery within two hours. His site is a model of customer service. Traffic is on the increase, as are sales. Just last week he took in over $45,000 from Web site sales alone!

Abe's Merchant Server, complete with SET POS software, has the required MasterCard Merchant Digital Certificates from Carl's National Bank, allowing Abe to successfully process any MasterCard charge request.

David's Card Processing Service (which Carl's National Bank uses) also has its MasterCard Payment Gateway certificates in place, allowing David's to process all MasterCard charge requests from any of the Merchants and banks it serves. Carl's National Bank and David's Card Processing Service obtained their MasterCard Digital Certificates from Elliott's Certificate Authority.

You now have a SET Cardholder Digital Certificate; MasterCard customers at Bob's Bank have been able to obtain these certificates as a companion to their plastic MasterCards for a month now. Bob's Bank makes it rather easy to get them too. Through its Web site, Bob's Bank offers loads of information to help consumers like yourself understand how SET makes Internet shopping completely safe. The site also makes it easy for customers to download the Electronic Wallet (E-wallet) that's needed to request, store, and manage all their SET digital certificates. After a short visit to Bob's Bank site, MasterCard customers can walk away with their E-wallets, their digital certificates, and a high degree of confidence that any Internet purchase they make from that point on will be safe, private, and painless.

From a conceptual viewpoint, Figure 2.2 illustrates a transaction-ready processing environment under SET.

Phase 1: The Shopping Experience

Back at Abe's "Corner Store on the Web," customers are also helped out preparing for SET. Abe's has hypertext and content on his home page to attract people into using SET for shopping there. He links in E-wallet information sites, local bank Web sites that offer SET to their credit card customers, and the "Shop Safe" logo from MasterCard that presents visible evidence of Abe's concern for his customers' shopping safety and enjoyment. He's certain that once you are hooked on SET, you'll never turn back!

With a single click on Abe's home page "Shop Now" button, you and other SET-prepared shoppers can browse through the vast catalog of items, examine product details—even nutritional information—and decide what you want to purchase.

Figure 2.2 An example of a SET-ready transaction processing environment.

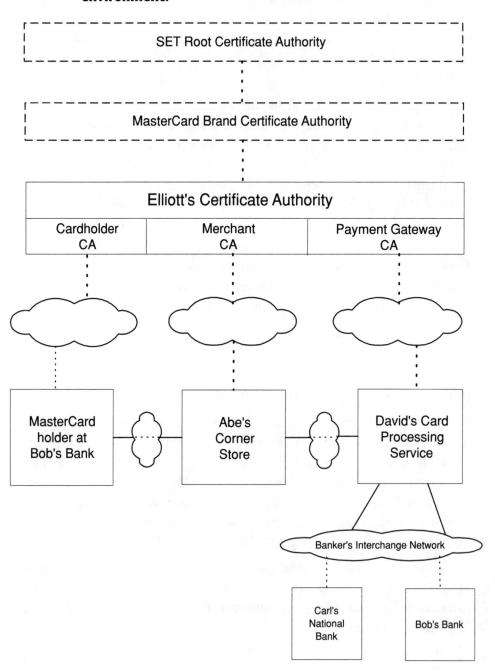

Phase 2: Item Selection

You select goods by choosing a link directly below the product photograph and price. The shopping cart software that Abe's Merchant Server uses dynamically tallies up the sale.

Phase 3: Check Out

Just as a shopper in Abe's Corner Store pushes his shopping cart to the cash register, the on-line consumer at Abe's "Corner Store on the Web" clicks the "Check Out" icon found on every page. The shopping cart software adds up the items in it, adds sales tax, delivery and handling fees, and presents you with a list of the items and the totals. When you're satisfied with your order, you proceed to the payment selection phase.

Phase 4: Form of Payment Selection

With order totals still displayed on your screen, you are given a choice of payment options. You may select from MasterCard, Visa, American Express, and Discover Card. You also have the option of COD or credit card payment by phone prior to order delivery. Let's say you choose MasterCard as the form of payment. **SET is now initiated.**

Phase 5: Payment Initiation Processing

Once you have selected SET-enabled MasterCard payment, Abe's Merchant Server sends a special message to your browser, telling your E-wallet to *wake up*. This wake-up message tells the E-wallet to prompt you to enter your secret password, which opens the wallet. The E-wallet also initiates the first SET payment processing message pair, called the Payment Initialization Request, which is generated and sent back to the Merchant SET POS software (a component of the Merchant Server cash register functions). With a successful Payment Initialization Response, the E-wallet then creates a SET Purchase Request message. This message has two components to it—a Purchase Order piece and a Payment Instructions piece. The Merchant POS software can only read the Purchase Order. The Payment Instructions, containing information about your MasterCard account, can only be deciphered and processed by David's Payment Gateway software.

Phase 6: Payment Authorization Request

Along with the Payment Instructions, Abe's SET POS software prepares a SET Authorization Request message that's intended for David's Payment Gateway. The message contains the details about the amount of the sale, the Merchant account requesting it, and the previously created Payment Instructions component that the Cardholder E-wallet software generated in Phase 5.

With a successful decipherment, David's Payment Gateway creates a standard authorization request and places it on the bank's Interchange Network that locates your account at Bob's Bank. With an approval code from Bob's Bank to proceed with the sale, the Payment Gateway responds with a SET Authorization Response that tells Abe's POS software to complete the sale. It then creates a Purchase Response message intended for your E-wallet that confirms the sale and produces an electronic version of a receipt or record of charge.

Phase 7: Delivery of Goods

An hour and a half goes by, and you hear a knock on your door. As a premier customer, you can be sure Abe will give you his best service. You collect your box of goods and head for the refrigerator and pantry to put them away. With a signature on the delivery form, Abe is assured that you're satisfied and the sale is final.

Phase 8: Capture and Settlement

With the successful authorization code from Phase 6, Abe's SET POS software received a capture record (SET calls these tokens). With the sale completed and the goods delivered, Abe's POS software can initiate a Capture Request to finalize the sale with David's Payment Gateway system. With each Capture Response, the Settlement File builds up, awaiting Abe's decision to deposit these receipts into his Merchant account at Carl's National Bank in exchange for funds transfer. Settlement File or Batch Processing is also carried out via the Internet using SET's Batch Administration message pairs, designed specifically for those purposes.

SET to Integrate into the Internet

While the actual processing work is identical to the work initiated via a POS terminal operating on a private network, SET makes it possible to use the Internet through its cryptography and message passing mechanisms. It turns the *public* Internet into a *private* network that's virtually defined with each new message pair. In fact, it's more secure than the traditional networks upon which POS systems rely.

SET uses two forms of messages that relate to requests and responses to processing between the Cardholder and the Merchant, and between the Merchant and the Acquirer Payment Gateway. There is never a direct link between the Cardholder and the Payment Gateway—the Merchant always serves as the message broker between them.

As we'll see later on, SET messages have very specific purposes. Throughout the book we look at various facets of these messages, including the cryptography that's being used, detailed explanations of SET Digital Certificates, SET message processing flows, and significant detail about the contents of each message pair.

In Chapter 3 we continue by looking at the roles, responsibilities, and interactions between Cardholders, Merchants, Payment Gateways, Payment Card Brand Associations, and Certificate Authorities as defined by SET.

SET's Participants

3

S ET's security features are partially implemented through Public-Private Key (PPK) cryptography in the form of digital certificates. These certificates indicate different kinds of relationships in on-line credit card uses. Each participant in a SET transaction requires one or more related digital certificates. The roles and responsibilities of each participant are specific. To help you gain an understanding of these various roles, responsibilities, and obligations, this chapter offers a comprehensive definition of digital certificates, then a high-level overview of how they affect:

- Cardholders
- Merchants
- Acquirer Payment Gateways
- Credit and Debit Card Brand Associations
- Certificate Authorities

Digital certificates embody each participant's role. Participant obligations become a matter of managing the safe-keeping and currency of their certificate(s).

What Are Digital Certificates?

An authentication certificate (sometimes called a digital certificate or digital ID) is a fairly recent technological development that uses Public-Private Key (PPK) cryptography to identify people, privileges, and relationships. Digital IDs are the electronic counterparts to driver licenses, passports, or membership cards. You can present a digital signature created electronically with a digital

ID and encryption keys to prove your identity or your right to access on-line information or services, such as credit card presentation and processing.

Digital certificates bind a person's identity to a pair of electronic encryption keys that a person uses to encrypt or sign digital information. A digital certificate helps to verify your electronically transmitted claim that you are who you claim to be and that you have the right to use the encryption keys. This prevents people from using phony keys to impersonate other people. Used in conjunction with encryption, digital certificates provide a more complete security mechanism than nonencryption processes. A generic digital certificate typically contains:

- Owner's public key
- Owner's name
- Expiration date of the public key
- Name of the certificate issuer
- Serial number of the certificate
- Digital signature of the certificate issuer

The most widely accepted format for digital certificates is defined by the CCITT X.509 international standard; thus, such certificates can be read or written by any application complying with X.509. SET's version of digital certificates are a special "flavor" designed exclusively for credit cards. SET *extends* the X.509 standard for e-commerce uses to permit its international presence without the concern for export controls on encryption products or services.

How Digital Certificates Are Used

You can perform a variety of electronic transactions including e-mail, electronic commerce (*à la* SET), groupware, and electronic funds transfers more securely when you integrate encryption and digital signatures into the system.

Encryption

Encryption techniques (discussed in further depth in Chapter 4) hide information from all but those intended to receive it. SET uses a form of cryptography based on pairs of public and private keys, also called Public-Private Key (PPK) cryptography. Messages encrypted with a private key may only be decrypted with the public key, and vice versa.

X.509 certificates enable security of e-mail messages or other forms of information transfers (FTP, etc.). Your digital certificate binds you to the private key you use to encrypt your messages. As digital security becomes more transparent through advances in software technology, you'll see encryption techniques used more routinely.

Digital Signature

A digital signature is an on-line substitute for your written signature in the off-line world. Your digital signature is also your authentication that you are who you claim to be. Digital signatures are your legally binding endorsement of the document you transmit. They help to ensure that the information in your messages is not altered in any way. If your message is altered in any way (even just a single byte), the signature of the message becomes invalid and alerts your recipient to the alteration.

Digital signatures may eventually carry greater legal status than handwritten signatures. If a 20-page contract is signed by hand on the last page, one cannot be sure that the first nineteen pages were not altered. However, if the contract was signed using digital signatures, the parties can verify that not one single byte of the contract has been altered. Some courts have found digital certificates to be valid, and there is a movement in state legislatures, led by Utah, to pass statutes specifically legalizing digital signatures.

Transactions

Digital certificates are essential for SET. They are used to "sign" messages prior to their transmission. The resultant "digitally signed" message helps to assure consumers that the Merchants with whom they're transacting are who they claim to be, that they have a good standing relationship with the company that can honor the credit card charge, and that certain safeguards are in place to keep transmitted credit card data a secret. Merchants are assured that the credit card presented is the legitimate account holder's and no one else's. Payment processors are assured that both the Cardholder and

Merchant have legitimate rights to request or settle charges under the service they provide.

Dual Signatures

SET incorporates a new use for digital signatures, called dual signatures. They appear within authorization requests to hide information from the Merchant as it passes through to the Payment Gateway, which can read it. An example of how they're used may be found in Chapter 5.

Certify Me, Please!

Public-key cryptography (discussed in Chapters 4 and 5) requires that all users obtain key-pairs in a secure manner that's impervious to attacks. Since the cracking of keys requires inordinate time and effort, would-be thieves typically will strike at the management and maintenance systems that store keys, rather than attempting cryptanalysis to get at the keys themselves.

Digital certificates can help keep private keys secure while aiding in the dissemination of the related public key (together they form the key-pair). If and when a private key is discovered (either by cryptanalysis or by theft), that fact needs to be shared so that the recipients of messages signed with the stolen key know to reject or disregard them.

SET Digital Certificates attest to the binding of an end-entity's public key to the end-entity itself. American Express, for example, helps Cardholders, Merchants, and Payment Gateway operators obtain AMEX Brand Certificates that attest to their legitimacy as participants where AMEX cards are used as forms of payment. Let's suppose Charles presents his payment instructions using his American Express Gold Card certificate. When a Merchant receives his message and subsequently forwards it for processing, both the Merchant and the Payment Gateway can verify Charles's claim that the message and the certificate is his and no one else's. Since the private key tied to the AMEX Brand Certificate was used to sign Charles's certificate, and Charles's message can only be decrypted using Charles's public key from the certificate, two things must be true: the message *must* have come from Charles, and upon successful traversal of the AMEX Brand Trust Tree, the certificate must have been signed using the private key tied to the American Express Brand Certificate, and no other.

In their basic forms, digital certificates contain the private-key holder's public key (half of the key-pair), his name, the certificate's expiration date, a serial number, the name of the authority that issued the certificate, the policies under which certificate use is permissible, and any other information the issuer deems vital or useful. Most important, it contains the digital signature of the issuer. SET Certificates follow the CCITT's ITU Recommendation X.509 for Version 3 certificates.

Let's review how certificates work in an Internet payment card transaction.

Step 1. With shopping and order-totaling steps completed, a Cardholder selects the payment card she wishes to use by choosing from the options available on the Merchant's SET Payment Module (Phase 4 from Chapter 2).

Step 2. The Merchant SET Payment Module "wakes up" the Cardholder E-wallet, and begins sending it a chain of certificates and/or certificate *thumbprints*. This certificate chain is specific to the Card Brand selected (Phase 5 from Chapter 2). It includes the Merchant Signature and Key-Exchange Certificates (for messages intended for their processing), and the Payment Gateway Signature and Key-Exchange Certificates (for messages intended for processing at the predetermined Payment Gateway).

Step 3. The Cardholder's E-wallet begins to traverse the Tree of Trust for the Brand selected using the certificate chain supplied. Recall that no one is trusted prior to full traversal of the trust tree. Upon a successful traversal, the E-wallet then returns a copy of the Cardholder Signature Certificate to use in signing messages intended for return to the E-wallet. Note that Cardholders normally will not possess Key-Exchange Certificates, since they are not responsible for message processing work. Only Merchants and Payment Gateways require these Key-Exchange Certificates; they are then used by Cardholders to encrypt the contents of messages intended for Merchants or Payment Gateways.

Step 4. With certificate exchange and trust tree traversal steps complete, all parties are now authenticated and processing will begin appropriately. Message protection and confidentiality can be assured, since all parties now "trust" one another.

Once trust is fully established by the fact that all certificates "roll up" to the appropriate Root Key, the mechanics of using private keys and their associated certificates follows:

• Cardholder-initiated messages to Merchants are encrypted using the Merchant's encryption public key and are signed with the Merchant's signing public key. Only the Merchant can open these envelopes and decrypt these messages.

• Cardholder-initiated messages (payment instructions) to the Payment Gateway are encrypted using the Payment Gateway's encryption public key and are signed with the Payment Gateway's signing public key. Only the Payment Gateway can open these envelopes and decrypt these messages.

• Merchant-initiated messages to Cardholders are signed using the Cardholder's signing public key. Only the Cardholder can open these envelopes.

• Merchant-initiated messages (authorization, capture, and settlement) to the Payment Gateway are encrypted using the Payment Gateway's encryption public key and are signed with the Payment Gateway's signing public key. Only the Payment Gateway can open these envelopes and decrypt these messages.

With a basic understanding of what digital certificates are, let's turn our attention to how participants in a SET transaction obtain, manage, and use their digital certificates. We'll also look at how participants interact with other participants through the sharing of certificates and other information.

> **What's a Thumbprint?**
>
> Thumbprints represent the hashed values (digests) of Certificates, Certificate Revocation Lists (CRLs), and CRL Identifiers. Thumbprints are a shortcut way to identify the certificates, CRLs, and CRL Identifiers that end-entities hold. Certificate chains can become rather long (in terms of bytes) very quickly, so thumbprints can help in keeping chain lengths shorter. Thumbprint use reduces both processing times and communication channel use.

Cardholders

Users of credit- and charge-card accounts need digital certificates to transact in the on-line world of SET, in the same way they need a plastic representation in the off-line world. Cardholders interact with two other parties in the SET umbrella: with Certificate Authorities (discussed later in this chapter) to obtain new certificates and renew existing ones, and with Merchants with whom they intend to shop and buy.

Roles and Responsibilities

In using a Web browser to visit and shop, a component called an Electronic Wallet (E-wallet) that *understands* how to carry out the salient SET messages is a fundamental requirement. These wallets embody the SET protocol and provide a means to store and manage the certificates to digitally sign messages, along with the security aspects consumers demand to keep private data private.

Not all browsers work alike, but Netscape Navigator and Communicator as well as Microsoft's Internet Explorer support either E-wallet *plug-ins* or E-wallet programs as *helper* applications. How an E-wallet interfaces with a Web browser is not specified within the SET Standard and is left to the discretion of E-wallet developers.

As a Cardholder, you will visit a Web site that has SET E-wallets available for download and "grab" a copy of one. After installation, the E-wallet is configured for the specific Web-browser(s) you wish to use for shopping. Once the E-wallet is working properly, it's time to obtain a digital certificate for each charge or credit card you want to use in the on-line world. To do this, you'll visit a Certificate Authority (CA) to request a SET Digital Certificate. Once you're at the Brand CA site you'll present certain information presumably only you possess to *prove* your identity and your right to obtain a certificate. This authentication information is not defined under the SET Standard. It is left up to the Card Issuers to decide how to authenticate. Some card companies may insist on *strong authentication* to verify your proof of identity up front, while others may rely on *weak authentication,* relying on back-end system processing during a transaction to catch questionable uses of their cards.

Cardholders *must* ensure that their PC-resident E-wallet is protected at least as well as their real wallet is protected in the off-line world. This means keeping their private key component private (through password protection). It also means that when sending any personal information across the Internet, they make sure they are using a browser that supports Secure Sockets Layer (SSL) encryption. An example of how you can tell that SSL is active is shown in Figure 3.1. When Cardholders visit the CA to obtain a digital certificate, the session should be protected using SSL, or their private and sensitive information may be at risk for theft while in transit.

Once a Cardholder's digital certificate is properly installed and she is ready to shop, she should also be certain that the shopping sites she visits support SET. The SETMark helps Cardholders identify those Merchants who actively support shopping using SET.

Interactions

An example of how Cardholders might interact with a CA to obtain or renew a digital certificate is shown in Figure 3.2. The middle column of the diagram represents the SET message pairs (described in depth in Chapter 12) that are used for requests and issuance of a Cardholder Digital Certificate. The Cardholder's PC-resident E-wallet is the source of all request messages and the destination for all response messages. SET governs the entire

Figure 3.1 The Netscape browser SSL activity indicator.

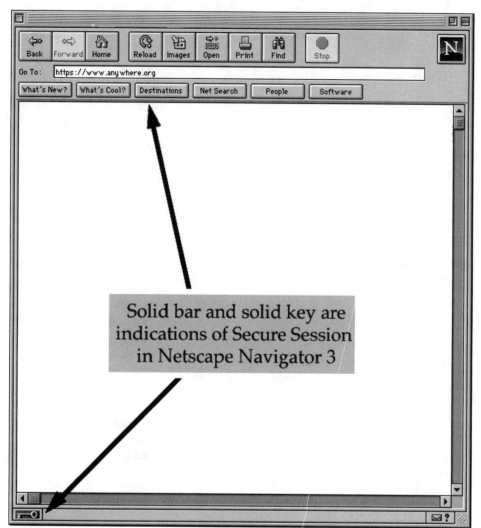

Solid bar and solid key are indications of Secure Session in Netscape Navigator 3

process, using its encryption to protect the information being shared while en route over the Internet. To the end users, this process is transparent—all they need to do is supply the correct information as it's requested, and their certificates will be generated and sent over for storage and use.

Figure 3.2 Cardholder/Certificate Authority interaction.

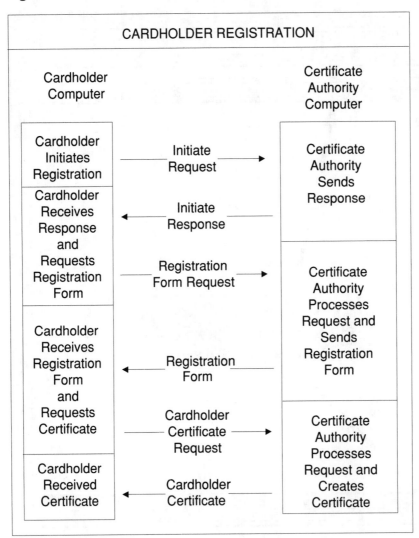

An example of how Cardholders might interact with Merchant Server POS software is shown in Figure 3.3. This illustration (Phase 5 from Chapter 2) only describes the payment processing steps where SET is at play. Unlike SSL, which only encrypts traffic going across the Internet at the

Figure 3.3 Cardholder/Merchant interaction.

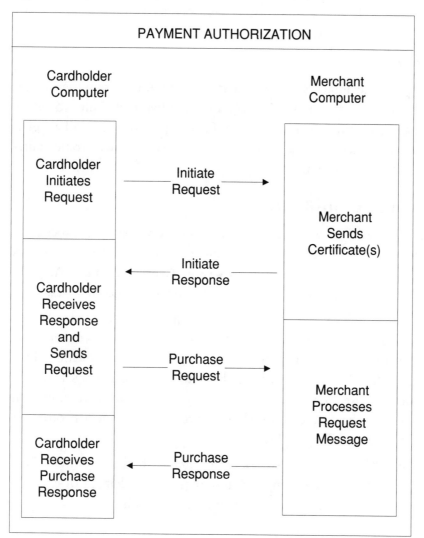

Transport Layer, SET encrypts every message at the Application Layer, rely-ing on SET software to make sense of the encrypted messages.

Again, the middle column of the diagram indicates the SET message pairs used by a Cardholder to initiate the purchase and by the Merchant to complete the purchase. An interim set of message pairs are generated between the Merchant and the Payment Gateway, as described in the following section.

Merchants

Merchants, like Cardholders, communicate with a CA to obtain their requisite Merchant SET certificates. Merchants require two certificates for every brand of payment card they accept: a Key-Exchange Certificate and a Signature Certificate. Together, these two certificates serve as an electronic equivalent to the Brand decal that's displayed in a Merchant's establishment.

Roles and Responsibilities

Merchant Server POS software performs the tasks of cryptographic processing, message preparation, and Merchant certificate management. Merchant Servers communicate with both the Cardholder's Web browser/E-wallet and Acquirer Payment Gateways that serve the bank(s) and payment card companies.

When a Cardholder initiates a purchase request to a Merchant Server, the Merchant Server POS component determines the Brand selected and forwards a copy of the appropriate Brand Payment Gateway certificate (which it stores) and the Merchant Certificate back to the Cardholder's E-wallet. The E-wallet will use these certificates to encrypt payment instructions and order information back to the Merchant Server. This payment protocol is discussed at length in Chapter 11.

Merchant POS software also communicates with the Acquirer's Payment Gateway for authorization of charge requests, settlement of charges, and batch administration work (see Chapter 2 for details).

Interactions

Interaction occurs between the Merchant Server and the Cardholder's E-wallet, and between the Merchant Server and the Payment Gateway. Figure 3.3 illustrates the first of those interactions. Figure 3.4 describes one set of messages between the Merchant and the Payment Gateway for a charge authorization request (Phase 6 from Chapter 2).

Figure 3.4 Merchant/Payment Gateway charge authorization processing.

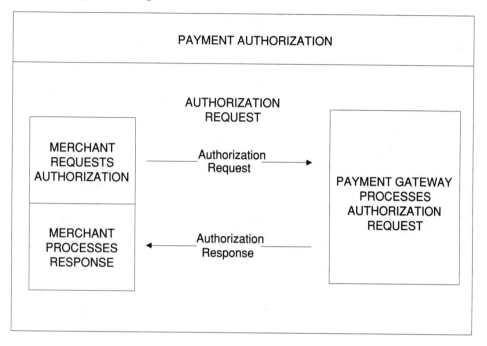

This SET message pair represents the interim processing for Figure 3.3. Between the Cardholder's Purchase Request and the Merchant's Payment Response, the Authorization Request/Response is processed between the Merchant and the Payment Gateway. If approved, the subsequent Purchase Response notifies the Cardholder's E-wallet that the charge was approved. If not, the Purchase Response indicates the reason for denial that only the Cardholder can read. The Merchant is simply told by the Payment Gateway that the charge request was declined without any further details as to why.

Figure 3.5 illustrates the steps the Merchant Server performs to process a payment capture from the Payment Gateway (Phase 8 from Chapter 2).

With the delivery of goods or completion of services, the Merchant can request the completion of the sale by using the Capture Request and

Figure 3.5 Merchant/Payment Gateway capture request.

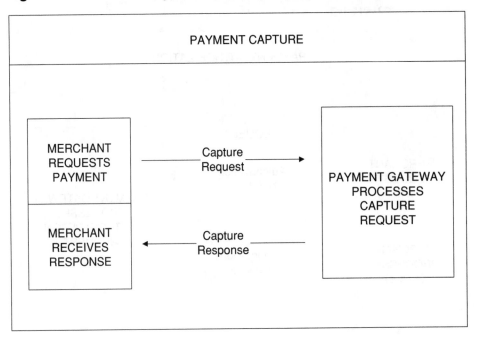

Response message pair (the middle column of the diagram). A charge can only be captured once the goods have shipped, and only if a previously approved authorization response code is contained in the Capture Request. The Capture Response contains all the data the Merchant will need to settle the transaction with its Acquiring Bank.

Acquirer Payment Gateways

Payment Gateways serve as the interface between an Acquiring Bank and the banking network that supports Card Issuer authorization and settlement systems.

Roles and Responsibilities

Payment Gateways are typically operated on the behalf of many financial institutions. Some gateways are operated directly by the banks or card companies, while others are outsourced to third parties, such as First Data Merchant Services (a subsidiary of First Data Corporation in Omaha, Nebraska). The primary purposes of the Payment Gateway include checking the currency and legitimacy of all certificates presented and maintaining an appropriate interface to traditional banking systems that permits the Internet to *behave* as though it's a private leased line connection into the banking networks.

The interfaces between Payment Gateways and Acquirer back-office systems are not defined by SET, and are left to the financial institutions for implementation details.

Interactions

Payment Gateways communicate with the Brand Payment Gateway Certificate Authority for certificate management and, as described above, with Merchant Servers to authorize and settle charges. At no time do Cardholders interact directly with a Payment Gateway, but messages are passed between them through the Merchant, who is, however, unable to read those components (e.g., payment instructions).

Payment Card Brand Associations

Payment Card Brand Associations consist of the financial institutions that offer specific card products to Cardholders and serve as an authority for acceptance of their products by Merchants. The distinct Visa and MasterCard Associations initiated the development of SET Standard, but other card brands (e.g., American Express and JCB) hopped on the bandwagon to ensure SET's viability with non-Visa and non-MasterCard credit or charge cards.

Roles and Responsibilities

Brand Associations themselves do not specifically participate in SET transaction activity. They retain the responsibility for maintaining the SET *root key* (see Chapter 7 for more details) that's used to sign all Brand Certificates and establish Brand Certificate Authority hierarchies. Presently the independently operated SETCo is charged with creating and distributing SET root keys and certifying commercial SET products that meet their rigid standards for compliance with SET specifications.

Interactions

Beyond the initial signing of Brand Certificates, establishing them for legitimate SET uses, there are no direct interactions with any of the entities discussed above. In the unlikely catastrophic event of a compromised Brand private key, the SET Root Authority needs to share that fact with all interested parties. Please see Chapter 8 for a discussion of key compromise and key recovery.

Certificate Authorities

Certificate Authorities (CAs) are commissioned by the Brand Associations or Card Issuers to carry out the work of managing SET digital certificates. CA services may be run directly within Card Issuer facilities or may be outsourced to companies who specialize in such work.

Roles and Responsibilities

CAs perform the following activities to assure the highest degrees of security as outlined under SET:

- Gathering authentication information from Cardholders, Merchants, and Payment Gateway operators who request certificates

- Forwarding the authentication data to the Issuer or Acquirer for verification and subsequent approval or denial of certificate issuance

- Renewal processing of previously issued certificates

- Maintaining the Brand root keys

- Certifying the presence of other Certificate Authorities below them in the Brand Tree of Trust (see Chapter 7 for more details)

- Revoking certificates on canceled accounts as instructed by the Card Issuers

- Maintaining the Certificate Revocation List (CRL) for all compromised private keys that are tied to certificates that they signed (see Chapter 7 for more details)

The two largest independent CA service companies operating SET-compliant facilities today are GTE CyberTrust and VeriSign Corporation. In the future, as the technology and expertise mature, CAs may be found virtually everywhere.

Interactions

A detailed discussion of how CAs interact with other CAs and with SET end-entities (Cardholders, Merchants, and Payment Gateway operators) can be found in Chapter 7, as part of the discussion of the SET Hierarchy of Trust.

You now have an understanding of what digital certificates are, how they operate, and how SET transaction participants interact with one another. We build upon these ideas in the next section of the book, where we look at the cryptography within SET and how it's used with SET Digital Certificates.

AN OVERVIEW OF CRYPTOGRAPHY

4

S ET's features are implemented through applied cryptography—the science of secret writing. Cryptography enables the storage of information in forms that reveal it only to those permitted and hide it from everyone else.

In the 20th century, national governments began to adopt the use of cryptography to protect their private and sensitive information and for communications purposes. Up until the last 20 years or so, governments and military organizations were the exclusive users of cryptography to secure their own private data and to try and crack everyone else's. Today, cryptography is considered a munition and as such, its uses and export are tightly controlled by various U.S. government agencies, including the U.S. National Security Agency (NSA).

Since the 1970s, academic interest in cryptography has grown at a tremendous rate, and with the research, private citizens have gained access to various cryptography techniques permitting personal information protection and enabling the conduct of secure electronic transactions, as under SET.

Although the U.S. government continues its struggle to control forms of strong cryptography for domestic and export purposes, advancements in the field continue. With the aid of supercomputers, massively parallel processors, communities of hackers who work together to try and crack the strongest cryptosystems, and the increasing sophistication of modern computer technology, cryptography stands to evolve into a set of highly reliable and well-established practices.

Since SET uses multiple layers of cryptographic elements, it's worthwhile to gain an understanding of some basic approaches to cryptography. In this chapter, we focus on the following:

- Some basic terminology and concepts
- A survey of several cryptosystems and their relationships to SET
- A high-level overview of SET's applied cryptography

Some Basic Terms and Concepts

A *cryptosystem* disguises messages such that only selected people can see through the disguise. *Cryptography* is the science (or art) of designing, building, and using cryptosystems. *Cryptanalysis* is the science (or art) of breaking a cryptosystem. *Cryptology* is the umbrella study of cryptography and cryptanalysis.

Cryptographers rely on two basic methods of disguising messages: *transposition*, where letters are rearranged into a different order, and *substitution*, where letters are replaced by other letters.

A strong cryptosystem is considered strong only until it's been cracked. While that may sound like common sense, one can never prove that a cryptosystem is strong—one can only ensure that certain properties are present within it. Each defeat of an attempt to crack a cryptosystem serves to strengthen the belief in its ability to be secure. Similar to currency, a cryptosystem has value because its users believe in its worth. Once that belief is proven to be unfounded, the cryptosystem collapses and no one relies on it anymore.

Plaintext is the message that is passed through an *encryption algorithm*, or *cipher*, and becomes *ciphertext*. When ciphertext is passed through a *decryption algorithm*, it becomes plaintext again.

A Perfect Cryptosystem?

There is one cryptosystem in existence that's proven to be mathematically unbreakable. Unfortunately, it's impractical to use. The One Time Pad (OTP) or Vernam Cipher performs exclusive-or (XOR) operations on plaintext using a fresh randomly generated key every time. It's impractical because sharing these keys for every message makes for a nightmare.

All strong cryptosystems have similar characteristics. Their algorithms are made well-known to the public by the developer's posting of them to on-line forums and public-accessible documents. The strength of a cryptosystem's algorithm rests in the keys used to encrypt and decrypt (the longer the key the better). The basic idea is to keep the keys a secret rather than keep the algorithm a secret. Because keys are typically created using strong cryptography algorithms, the likelihood of their discovery or breach, through any method other than theft, is nearly zero. Strong cryptosystems will produce ciphertext that always appears random to standard statistical tests. They also resist all known attacks on cryptosystems and have been brutally tested to ensure their integrity. Those cryptosystems that have not been subjected to brutal testing are considered suspect.

> **Random Number Requirements**
>
> Perfectly random numbers, while thought to exist in nature, are impossible to achieve using deterministic devices, like computers. The best a computer can do is generate pseudo-random numbers. Cryptography demands far more from pseudo-randomness than most other applications, such as computer games. For a string of bits to be considered cryptographically random, it must be computationally infeasible to predict what the nth random bit will be, given full knowledge of the algorithm and the values of the bits already generated. Since computers are deterministic, at some point a random number generator becomes periodic, i.e, it begins to repeat. The challenge then is to build random number generators that won't repeat sequences of bits predicably often. Some of the pseudo-random number generators available today show randomness through 2^{256} bits, making them more suitable for use in cryptography than the kinds of random number generators built into programming language compilers.

When the same key is used to both encrypt and decrypt messages, it's called *symmetric key cryptography*. When different keys are used, it's called *asymmetric key cryptography*. The Data Encryption Standard (DES) uses the former technique, while RSA (named after its inventors—Rivest, Shamir, and

Adelman) uses the latter technique. Pretty Good Privacy (PGP), a public-domain cryptosystem invented by Phil Zimmerman, also uses asymmetric key cryptography. SET uses a combination of DES and RSA cryptography to implement privacy, security, and authentication services.

A Simple Example

Although the actual mechanics of cryptosystems are not directly required to implement SET from the Webmaster's viewpoint, understanding the complexities involved helps one to appreciate what's going on within your SET-compliant system.

Using the transposition technique with a symmetric key (shared secret), let's take a look at how encryption and decryption might operate manually.

Assume the plaintext message we want to encrypt is:

ATTACK AT SUNSET

We'll use the word SECTION as our key and send the keyword to our intended recipient using a secure channel that ensures the recipient has it when the ciphertext arrives.

Encrypt the message through the following steps:

1. Write the key horizontally as the heading for columns:

S	E	C	T	I	O	N

2. Assign numerical values to each letter based on the letter's appearance in the alphabet.

S	E	C	T	I	O	N
6	2	1	7	3	5	4

3. Align the letters of the plaintext message with the key/value column headings, starting a new line when the last column of the matrix is reached.

S	E	C	T	I	O	N
6	2	1	7	3	5	4
A	T	T	A	C	K	A
T	S	U	N	S	E	T

4. Read down each column according to its ordinal value to produce
    the ciphertext (C-1 is the first column, E-2 the second, and so forth):

    TU   TS   CS   AT   KE   AT   AN

5. Send the ciphertext to the recipient using any channel desired. The
    recipient already possesses the shared secret (i.e., the keyword), we
    don't need to worry about keeping the ciphertext itself secure.

    Upon receipt of the ciphertext, the recipient will decrypt it through the
following steps:

1. Write the key horizontally as the heading for columns:

    S   E   C   T   I   O   N

2. Assign numerical values to each letter based on the letter's appear-
    ance in the alphabet.

S	E	C	T	I	O	N
6	2	1	7	3	5	4

3. Transpose the ciphertext, two letters at a time, using the ordinal
    value of each column to determine its placement. Since C is Column
    Value 1, the first group of letters, TU, is written vertically under C-
    1. Group two belongs under E-2, and so forth:

S	E	C	T	I	O	N
6	2	1	7	3	5	4
A	T	T	A	C	K	A
T	S	U	N	S	E	T

4. Read the message horizontally to reveal the plaintext message:

    ATTACK AT SUNSET

Had the message been longer, for example:

    ATTACK AT SUNSET TUESDAY

the ciphertext groups would have contained another row of letters and
would have grown longer with the length of the message.

    This example does not include the use of numbers or special characters;
if it did, we'd have to treat them separately and agree on their positional val-

ues in the alphabet we're using, otherwise our algorithm goes out the window. Even with a simple example like this, you can begin to see the protocol developed to make it work. Steps must be performed in order, cannot be skipped, and cannot be altered in any way. Computer-based cryptography, while far more robust than anything that could be accomplished by hand, uses the same approaches, if not the same algorithms themselves.

Cryptography itself becomes extremely complicated extremely quickly, but it need not be totally intimidating to the casual observer. To those with a keener interest in the application of strong cryptography, you're encouraged to read *Applied Cryptography* by Bruce Schneier, considered by many to be the bible of modern cryptographers and cryptanalysts.

Cryptosystems—Yesterday and Today

Before looking at specific implementations of data encryption and secure electronic transmissions, it's important to understand that different situations call for different levels of security. A college student sending an e-mail home to his parents for money is mainly concerned that the note reach its intended destination and that no one tamper with the contents of the note. An internal corporate memo to all employees, on the other hand, might contain sensitive information that should not go beyond the company's intranet. The president assumes that when she sends the note, only the intended audience will read the note. Likewise, the employees assume that the note did indeed come from the president and no one else. No real authentication is performed because the company's e-mail system relies on the notion of trust. Each employee must have an ID and password to access the e-mail system, but beyond that, any guarantees of authenticity require implicit trust in the users of the system.

Ensuring that electronic commerce is secure, however, requires an implicit *distrust* in users of the Internet. Most users are law-abiding citizens who use their payment cards for legitimate purchases. They are who they say they are, and they enjoy the convenience that Internet shopping affords. Unfortunately, given the decentralized design of the Internet and the potential for an unscrupulous few to wreck havoc, electronic card payments can never be made *too* secure. A little bad press goes a long way.

SET, consequently, is built using many instances of data encryption and authentication techniques to convince users that the party or parties they are dealing with can prove their identity. SET in some sense has taken the best of earlier designs, incorporating them into a system of checks and balances the likes of which have never been seen before. For example, SET uses digital signatures, a combination of public/private key-pairs as part of the authentication process (described further in Chapter 5). Private keys, used for years by financial institutions to assign PIN (Personal Identification Number) numbers to ATM Cardholders, by themselves are too cumbersome and unwieldy for a global electronic commerce implementation. However, when combined with public keys which the user makes freely available to the world, private keys provide the kind of authentication that users demand and expect when buying and selling goods.

SET is being implemented across the country today because businesses saw deficiencies in earlier solutions for conducting electronic commerce safely and securely on insecure channels such as the Internet. As the number of credit card purchases that consumers and businesses conduct over the Internet increases, and as Merchants continue to create new and more sophisticated on-line ordering systems, the software industry has recognized that other security systems such as SSL and PGP do not address the concerns of consumers and Merchants for a completely safe shopping environment. These other "tools" were not designed with today's explosive electronic commerce growth in mind. SET owes its existence largely to past efforts in the field of data encryption and secure data transmission—efforts that did not take into account the blitzkrieg of electronic commerce on the Internet.

One approach to history tells us that we know where we are going based on where we have been. A brief review of previous labors of mathematicians, cryptographers, cryptologists, and software developers gives us a greater appreciation of the stature and significance of implementing the SET protocol. Here we'll take a look at a few cryptosystems that have become popular over the years. Some of them form the building blocks of SET, while others represent attempts at solving those types of problems that SET ultimately solves. Those cryptographic systems or techniques include:

- Hash signatures

- Secure Sockets Layer (SSL)

- Pretty Good Privacy (PGP)

- Secure/Multipurpose Internet Mail Extensions (S/MIME)

- Data Encryption Standard (DES)

- Rivest, Shamir, Adelman (RSA) Cryptosystem

Hash Signatures

A hash signature is created through a scrambling technique that encrypts data blocks one block at a time and modifies the bits. Hashing is a technique that produces a unique value for a given message or file contents. You can think of a hash value as a fingerprint of the data. The signature uses a secure hash function to produce a hash value from a file, then concatenates the user's secret key to the file, then hashes the union of file and key. The result, called the hash file, is sent to the receiver, who then decrypts the file with his copy of the secret key.

A common example for a one-way hashing algorithm is the UNIX password protection system. The passwords stored in the /etc/password file have been run through this one-way hash prior to their storage to prevent unauthorized access. When you log-in to a UNIX server, the password you type is run through the same one-way hash and compared to the stored result. Access is provided when and only when they match. For more information about how SET uses hashing, see Chapter 5.

Hash signatures suffer from the same problems as private key or symmetric encryption. By themselves, hash functions are simply too difficult to implement because the receiver of a hash-based signature must have a copy of the sender's private key to read the digital signature and decrypt the message.

In terms of benefits, hash signatures require fewer computations than public key cryptography, and for that reason this method appeals to those using payment systems where processing costs are critical. On the other hand, the problems with maintaining and administering systems based on secret-key cryptography make hash signatures impractical for large electronic commerce applications.

The SSL Protocol

At the lowest layer, sitting on top of a reliable transport protocol such as TCP, the SSL Record Protocol is used to encapsulate other higher level protocols. One such protocol, the SSL Handshake Protocol, authenticates the client and server to each other and enables them to decide upon an encryption algorithm and cryptographic keys before this higher level protocol sends or receives data.

SSL addresses some of the same concerns as SET. Its goals are to ensure the privacy of the connection, to authenticate a peer's identity, and to establish a reliable transport mechanism for the message using integrity checks and hashing functions. However, it does not go far enough in the eyes of most security analysts.

The Secure Sockets Layer (SSL) protocol was designed for client/server applications, preventing the unwanted tampering of data transmission, whether it be eavesdropping, data alteration, or message forgery. Its goal is to ensure the privacy and reliability of communication between two applications. To do this, SSL consists of two layers.

A benefit of SSL is that it allows higher level protocols to sit on top of it and communicates with them without dictating a specific application protocol. SSL uses private key or symmetric cryptography (e.g., DES) for data encryption, and authenticates a peer's identity using public key or asymmetric cryptography techniques. See Figure 4.1 for an illustration of the "handshake" between the various layers of protocol in SSL.

One problem with SSL resides in the concept of "hierarchies of trust" involving the use of digital certificates. In a nutshell, a digital certificate is a stream of data, possibly several thousand bytes long, that encapsulates the user's public key and endorsement by a Certificate Authority (CA). The certificate moves the burden of verification off the user's shoulders and puts it squarely on the CA, promoting the level of trust up to a higher rung on the security ladder (hierarchy).

As Peter Wayner pointed out in a recent *Byte* magazine article, most users' computers that are SSL-enabled stop at this first level in the certificate hierarchy. For example, if a user's Web browser connects to a server that uses SSL, the server establishes its identity by sending a copy of its public key wrapped in a certificate. The browser then sanctions the certificate by checking the signature. Unfortunately, the browser has no real way of knowing if the signature is valid. No further verification is performed up the hierarchy because most certificates used by SSL are known as "root" certificates.

Figure 4.1 The SSL "handshake."

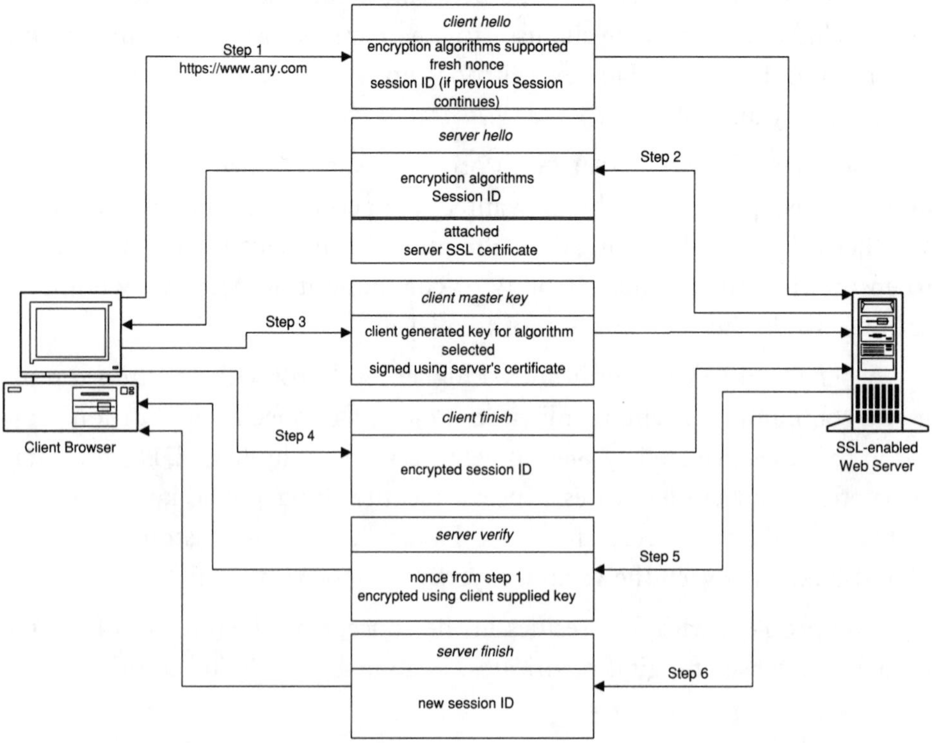

In an article entitled "Encryption Goes Mainstream," *Computerworld Emmerce Webzine* cites the "Top 10" problems of SSL according to Cryptography Research:

1. SSL does not work well with proxies and filters.

2. SSL adds computational overhead both at the client and the server.

3. SSL adds extra network roundtrips to implement its handshake.

4. Migrating from nonpublic key infrastructures requires significant effort.

5. SSL does not work well with existing cryptography tokens.

6. SSL key management tends to be expensive.

7. SSL requires a Certificate Authority with appropriate policies for its use.

8. Encrypted SSL communications do not compress, resulting in slow transmission through devices such as modems.

9. International export restrictions complicate everything about SSL.

10. Few companies possess the expertise required to build, maintain, and operate secure systems.

Until it's matured and these problems are worked out, SSL won't provide the level of security found in the SET protocol. What's important to note is that the method of private and public key encryption used by SSL is also used by SET, with the major difference that SET goes well beyond the ability of SSL to authenticate all parties in an on-line card payment transaction.

Pretty Good Privacy (PGP)

PGP is a distributed key management approach that does not rely on Certificate Authorities. Users can sign one another's public keys, adding degrees of confidence to a key's validity. Someone who signs someone else's public key acts as an introducer for that person, with the idea that if the recipient trusts the introducer, he should also trust the person who's being introduced. SET uses a different approach to key management than PGP, thereby excluding its use.

PGP was written by Phil Zimmerman in the mid-1980s. It remains popular because of its ability to encrypt e-mail. Zimmerman distributed his first version of PGP over the Internet as freeware, then ran into legal problems because he didn't realize he had given away the rights to public key cryptography patents (most notably the RSA patent). Legal matters were eventually straightened out in 1993 when ViaCrypt, a company with a valid license for the patent, worked out a deal with Zimmerman to distribute a commercial version of PGP.

PGP followed in the footsteps of other systems used for encrypting e-mail. Charlie Merritt had previously developed a system called SECURE/32 which uses public key cryptography. Shortly thereafter, RSA Data Security developed a system called MailSafe, a more robust e-mail encryption system. This application uses encryption and decryption, digital signatures, and cryptographic keys to secure e-mail. PGP, many experts claim, borrowed from MailSafe without acknowledgment. Others claim that both systems owe a heavy debt to SECURE/32.

One of the main criticisms of PGP is its reliance on what is known as an informal "Web of Trust" rather than the more structured hierarchy ("Tree of Trust") that's found in SET (see Chapter 7 for details). Figure 4.2 compares the Tree of Trust with the Web of Trust.

A hierarchy (tree) of trust defines the path a certificate's endorsement follows. In this design, the U.S. Government serves as the Root Authority, endorsing certificates for member states, which in turn endorse certificates for local municipalities (counties, cities, boroughs, etc.), which in turn endorse the certificates for its citizens.

The Web of Trust, shown in the bottom portion of the diagram, permits multiple people to certify the authenticity of a person's public key. At times, entities may authenticate one another's public key (shown using bidirectional arrows). Other times, authentication of the public key is one-way only.

Critics claim that you can't, for example, get a user's public PGP key from the Internet and feel secure that the public key really belongs to whom you think it does. Limitations on the Web of Trust at the current time make

Figure 4.2 Two ways to trust.

Tree of Trust

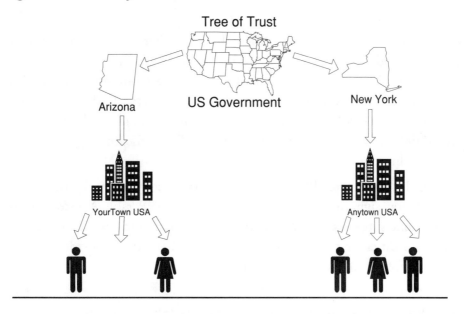

US Government

Arizona

New York

YourTown USA

Anytown USA

Web of Trust

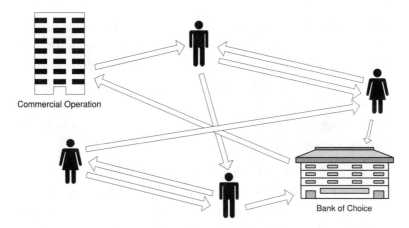

Commercial Operation

Bank of Choice

PGP's uses too impractical for conducting electronic commerce on the Internet. Instead, banks and credit card companies use their own hierarchical networks because of highly sophisticated risk models that the Web of Trust simply does not satisfy.

S/MIME

Based on technology from RSA Data Security, the Secure/Multipurpose Internet Mail Extensions (S/MIME) offers another standard for e-mail encryption and digital signatures. Both S/MIME and a version of PGP called "Open PGP" are implemented in Netscape Communications Web browsers. Unfortunately, the dual e-mail encryption standards are creating problems for users while vendors clash over whose standard should dominate. Mainly intended for e-mail uses, S/MIME's applicability to SET renders it too limiting.

S/MIME and Open PGP use proprietary encryption techniques and handle digital signatures differently. Simply put, if Person A uses a Web browser that supports S/MIME and tries to communicate with Person B who uses a different browser supported by PGP, the two individuals most likely will not be able to communicate successfully.

Another problem with S/MIME, like PGP, stems from the fact that it works well on closed networks but charts new territory when running on open networks such as the Internet because of interoperability issues.

Furthermore, Bruce Schneier sees problems with the fact that S/MIME uses a 40-bit encryption, which he finds woefully inadequate in today's marketplace—so inadequate, in fact, that Schneier claims he has written software that can use networked computers to decode S/MIME-encoded messages using the "brute force" technique. "If you have a big office, you can do it in an hour," Schneier claimed during his interview with Sharon Machlis in an online news story.

In its defense, supporters of S/MIME state that their product does support 168-bit key encryption, but again the question of interoperability rises. PGP doesn't claim rights to its technology and has made it available to the public as freeware, while S/MIME uses the public key algorithm that is still patented and must be licensed for use. Meanwhile, while the IETF tries to decide upon an open standard for e-mail delivery, the global electronic commerce community won't wait.

SET's Cryptosystems

Today, SET moves cryptography to a new level. It incorporates the best of the designs described above and mitigates some of the problems through careful design of its own. SET is defined using two of the most common, popular, and nonproprietary cryptosystems to carry out its work and ensure its openness. Those two are Data Encryption Standard (DES) and the Rivest, Shamir, and Adelman, or RSA cryptosystem.

Data Encryption Standard (DES)

DES was developed by the IBM Corporation at the request of the U.S. Government. It was adopted as the Federal Information Processing Standard (FIPS) in 1976 for use on unclassified government communications, and uses 64-bit blocks of data with a 56-bit private key. DES is the same as the ANSI Data Encryption Algorithm (DEA) Standard defined in ANSI X3.92.1981. DES is commonly used by financial institutions to encrypt Personal Identification Numbers (PINs), where your ATM and your bank share the same secret. Since you can't perform the DES encryption of your PIN, the ATM does it for you. Access is granted only when the ciphertext of your PIN that the ATM generates matches the ciphertext of your PIN that your bank stores.

RSA

RSA uses Public-Private Key (PPK) cryptography, whereby two mathematically related keys are used. Messages encrypted with one key can only be decrypted with the other, and vice versa. One of the keys is called the public key and the other is called the private key or secret key. Whoever can decrypt a message using a public key can be assured that the message *must* have come from the private key holder, provided they have not shared their secret with anyone else. Conversely, those messages encrypted with their public key can only be decrypted by the private key, thus ensuring that only the intended recipient can read the message as plaintext. PPK cryptography relies on the notion that private keys will remain private and are never shared with anyone else. It also presupposes that the private key holder's public key is freely available to anyone who wishes private communications with them.

Without the use of directory services, it's impractical to use symmetric or secret-key cryptography over open channels with large groups of people who have no ongoing relationships and don't share the secret. A better approach uses PPK where all parties involved in a transaction share their public keys at the time they're needed, thus allowing everyone to send and receive secure messages.

SET's Applied Cryptography

Chapter 5 looks at some specific ways that SET makes use of certain cryptosystems. For now, let's take a high-level point of view and look at how SET combines the DES and RSA cryptosystems to carry out its work.

By combining DES and RSA cryptography, SET provides:

- Confidentiality through message encryption

- Message integrity and participant authentication through digital signatures

- Additional participant authentication through digital certificates

In general, the first step of a SET transaction involves the distribution of public keys. For example, once you've made all your shopping selections and decide to "check out," if you opt to use your American Express Card as the form of payment, the Merchant software will transmit to your E-wallet a copy of its AMEX Merchant encryption public key (see "Digital Certificates" section below) and a copy of the AMEX Payment Gateway encryption public key to use for communications. Your E-wallet will first validate that all the certificates it receives are checked. All credentials under SET are always checked through the Tree of Trust that's in place at the time (see Chapter 7). No one is trusted before the trust tree is successfully traversed. After your E-wallet completes its checking process, it will in turn send a copy of your encryption public key (digital certificate) for messages intended to be returned back to you.

Message Encryption

Under SET, message data is encrypted using a randomly generated DES encryption key. When a message is sent, it's encrypted using the DES key, and the key itself is encrypted using the recipient's public key to produce a *digital envelope* for the message, which is sent along with the encrypted message itself. When the digital envelope is received, the recipient uses a private key to decrypt it, revealing the DES key, which is then used to decrypt the ciphertext.

Digital Signatures

Using PPK cryptography and *message digests*, encryption allows transaction participants to *digitally sign* messages.

A message digest is a value that's unique to a particular message. SET uses an algorithm that generates 160-bit message digests. It works such that changing a single bit in the message changes roughly half the bits in the message digest. The odds of two messages computing the same message digest are 1 in 10^{48}. Message digests are created by passing the message through a one-way cryptographic or hashing algorithm that cannot be reversed. You can think of a message digest as the *fingerprint* of a message, but the message itself cannot be recovered from the digest.

When the message digest is encrypted using the sender's private key, and is appended to the message itself (encrypted as above), the result is called the digital signature of the message. When the message is received, the receiver can be assured that the message *must* have come from the legitimate holder of the private key and that the message itself was not altered in any way while in transit. To see how this is accomplished, let's follow the digital signature process through its steps:

1. SENDER: Compute the message digest for the message to be sent.

2. SENDER: Encrypt the message digest with your private key.

3. SENDER: Append the message digest to the message, creating the digital signature.

4. SENDER: Encrypt the digital signature using the RECEIVER's public key and transmit the message to the RECEIVER.

5. RECEIVER: Decrypt the message using your private key, revealing the message and digital signature.

6. RECEIVER: Decrypt the digital signature using the SENDER's public key, revealing the message digest.

7. RECEIVER: Compute the message digest for the message and compare the two digests for a match.

8. RECEIVER: If the two digests are the same, message integrity and SENDER authentication are assured.

9. RECEIVER: If the digest values fail to match, disregard the message, since the message must have been corrupted en route.

By using this approach, both message integrity and user authentication are performed via a single set of steps.

In reality, SET uses two key pairs in the creation of digital signatures. Each participant (aside from the Cardholder) possesses a key-exchange pair to encrypt and decrypt messages and a signature pair to create and verify digital signatures.

Digital Certificates

In using PPK cryptography and signature pairs, it's necessary to trust that the sender's public key truly belongs to the sender and not to someone else masquerading as the sender. Since it's impractical to always transmit these signature keys to recipients over private channels, the use of a trusted party, called a *Certificate Authority* (CA), is desirable. The CA, working on behalf of those who issue credit cards or operated by the card companies themselves, attests to the sender's identity once it's proven to the CA in ways that satisfy the card issuer. CAs create a message that contains a copy of the sender's public key along with the sender's identifying information for the issuer's purposes. This message, called a digital certificate, is signed using the CA's private key, thus creating a hierarchy of trust that permits the trusting of a single set of keys (the CA's keys) for all related participants. All Cardholder, Merchant, and Acquirer Payment Gateway digital certificates from the same Brand will be signed by a single Certificate Authority that serves on the Brand's behalf.

The two companies offering SET CA services are GTE CyberTrust (cybertrust.gte.com) and VeriSign (www.verisign.com). Visa has selected VeriSign for its CA services, while American Express and MasterCard have selected GTE CyberTrust.

SET digital certificates are governed by the X.509 Standard for Digital Certificates, discussed at length in Chapter 5.

Dual Signatures

SET introduces a new use for digital signatures, namely dual signatures. They're used under special circumstances, like authorization requests, to hide information between two sending parties but reveal the information to the processing party. An example of their use better illustrates their purpose.

Carol operates an on-line auction house for antique furniture and accepts fund transfers from winning bidders. Donald places a bid for a Victorian rolltop desk that turns out to be the highest. When he sent his bid, he also sent an authorization to his bank to transfer funds if his bid is the highest, but he doesn't want his bank to see the details of the purpose of his transfer, nor does he want Carol to see his account information. In addition, he wants to link his bid to the transfer of funds if and only if he wins. He can do this by signing both messages with a single signature operation, thus creating a dual signature.

To produce a dual signature, a message digest for both messages is computed and concatenated together. A message digest for the result of the concatenation is then encrypted using the signer's private key. Recipients of either message can compute the message digest for the message they receive, concatenate it with the message digest from the other message, and compute the message digest for the result. If the newly computed message digest matches the decrypted dual signature, the recipients can trust that the message is authentic and could have only come from the holder of the private key used to create the dually signed message.

With a combination of cryptosystem uses, SET ensures the highest degree of security, privacy, and user authentication for all transactions. In Chapter 5 we look at how SET applies cryptographic principles, algorithms, and processing to messages. We also introduce the notational standards for SET messaging, along with a high level overview of Abstract Syntax Notation One (ASN.1), which is used to codify the SET protocol.

SET's Application of Cryptography

5

Building on the rudimentary knowledge established in Chapter 4, we can turn our attention to the specific uses of cryptography that are found within the SET Protocol.

This chapter looks at the ways cryptographic algorithms are combined and nested to provide SET's services of:

- Confidentiality

- Authentication

- Message integrity

- Linkage between two or more messages

This chapter also introduces the notation for the SET Specification to help you understand the specific SET message pairs, as outlined in Chapter 12. Fundamental to this discussion is a high-level understanding of the Abstract Syntax Notation One (ASN.1) that's used in defining the formal SET Protocol contained in Book 3 of the SET Specifications. This chapter offers an introduction to ASN.1 with Distinguished Encoding Rules (DER) as well.

SET Is Designed for Independence

Because no single company can offer a single solution to all those wishing to support SET in the marketplace, the designers went out of their way to ensure a global architecture that enables anyone willing to develop software to implement it. In doing so, they relied upon a diverse set of existing industry standards and notations that help ensure the highest possible degree of interoperability and readability without ambiguities. All crypto-graphic processing under SET is rooted in publicly available, vendor- and platform-neutral industry-wide standards for cryptography, most notably the Public Key Cryptography Standards (PKCS). PKCS is used to represent the required parameters for all message encapsulation constructs under SET.

SET is formally defined using the ISO/IEC and ITU-T Abstract Syntax Notation One (ASN.1) using the Distinguished Encoding Rules (DER). When implemented according to these rules, messages can be passed through a variety of both real-time (HTTP, FTP, etc.) and non-real-time (e-mail) mechanisms between any other compliant implementations.

Ensuring its neutrality, SET is designed using the following public standards.

DES

Data Encryption Standard (DES) is SET's default symmetric key encryption algorithm, defined by the Federal Information Processing Standard (FIPS) 46-2 and published by the National Institute of Standards and Technology (NIST). SET uses the Cipher-Block Chaining mode of DES, yielding an effective key length of 56 bytes.

CDMF

The Commercial Data Masking Facility (CDMF) is used as a data scrambling technique that relies upon DES to mask, rather than encrypt, data. Its use is primarily for passing messages between the Acquirer Payment Gateway and the Cardholder as the messages move through the Merchant Server. It might, for example, be used for a dunning notice on a past-due card account balance or for a message giving the reason for denial of a charge request.

SHA-1

The Secure Hash Algorithm (SHA-1) is used for hashing all data under SET. It is defined by FIPS 180-1. The Keyed Hashing Mechanism (HMAC) also uses SHA-1 as its basis.

Digital Envelopes

Digital envelopes under SET are created using a symmetric-key algorithm, like DES, with further encryption of the key using an asymmetric-key algorithm, like RSA. The results of the processing from the two algorithms are then combined into one construct.

OEAP

Optimal Asymmetric Encryption Padding (OAEP), as developed by Bellare-Rogaway, is used in conjunction with SET's encapsulation operators, discussed later in this chapter.

Message Freshness Challenges

Nonces, salts, or freshness challenges are techniques used within SET to defeat what are called "playback attacks." Along with other techniques such as transaction IDs, freshness challenges aid in implementing SET's feature of *idempotency*. An example might be where multiple copies of the same request message are received, but should only be processed once. If a recipient receives duplicate copies of a message (same transaction ID, same nonce), they can ascertain that the message had already been processed. Essentially a nonce (think short for nonsense) is a random number that's generated for the purpose of being copied into a return message, helping to ensure it came back from the original message recipient and not from anyone else. Each message that requires nonces will use unique values, thus ensuring higher levels of message and processing integrity than what's possible in their absence.

Public-Key Cryptography Standards

The Public-Key Cryptography Standards (PKCS) family of public-key cryptography standards used by SET include:

- RSA encryption for the construction of SET digital signatures and digital envelopes

- Diffie-Hellman key agreements that define how two people, with no prior arrangements, can agree on a shared secret key that's known only between them and used for future encrypted communications

- Password-based encryption to hide private keys when transferring them between computer systems, sometimes required under Public-Private Key cryptography

- Extended certificate syntax to permit the addition of SET extensions (adding information such as certificate usage policies or further identifying information) to standard X.509 digital certificates

- Cryptographic message syntax describing how to apply cryptography to SET-related data, including digital signatures and digital envelopes

- Private-key information syntax describing how to include a private key along with algorithm information and a set of attributes to offer a simple way of establishing trust in the information provided

- Certification request syntax describing the rules and sets of attributes needed for a SET certificate request from a SET Certificate Authority

What Is Idempotency?

When processing can be repeated a number of times with no harm being done, it's said to be idempotent. In SET, idempotency is a property of how recipients respond to messages. SET requires that any unresponded messages be re-sent, since it's impossible for the sender to determine if the original message was lost or the response was lost. Retransmitted messages must be identical to the original message, since duplicate messages are not considered to be error conditions under SET. If the processor of a message determines that the request was already processed, it should retrieve the response outcome and resend it without any additional processing. SET implementations guarantee idempotency by examining transaction (XID) or request-response pair (RRPID) unique identifiers. Certain messages require the idempotency feature, while others do not. For example, a Payment Gateway will not reprocess authorization requests which were already processed, but Merchant systems may respond over and over to a purchase inquiry request—where no harm occurs. SET idempotent messages are identified in Chapter 12.

The PKCS Family of Standards

The following standards define how to use the algorithms and techniques listed above. Some of them describe syntax rules, while others describe protocols to use.

- PKCS #1 describes the syntax for the construction of RSA public and private keys.

- PKCS #3 describes the protocols used to establish secure connections for use with key-agreements.

- PKCS #5 describes how to derive a secret key from a password using DES. It's used to implement password-based encryption techniques.

- PKCS #6 describes the syntax to extend the uses of X.509 standard digital certificates.

- PKCS #7 describes the syntax for data that's later encrypted to form digital signatures or digital envelopes.

- PKCS #8 defines an alternative to using digital signatures in establishing trust of information through the uses of encrypted private key information. It works in conjunction with PKCS #5.

- PKCS #9 defines the signing of messages, certification requests, extended certificates, and encrypted private key information.

- PKCS #10 defines certification requests in support of using these certificates to create PKCS #7 digital signatures and digital envelopes.

PKCS #2 and #4 have been incorporated into PKCS #1, and are no longer active. PKCS provides the basis for interoperability and significant compatibility with existing industry standards such as Open Systems Interconnect (OSI). One of the design goals for PKCS was the eventual incorporation into OSI for worldwide use.

PKCS #7, in particular, is used as the basis for message encapsulation for all SET messages. As such, the ASN.1 encoding rules are preserved, leading to a single format for the definition of all SET message pairs throughout the specification.

Those readers with a further interest in PKCS are encouraged to visit the RSA Laboratories FTP site at ftp://ftp.rsa.com/pub/pkcs for complete information on all the salient standards.

SET Message Pair Notation Standards

Rather than try to decompose a SET message into its components, it's far easier to look at the fundamental building blocks for messages first, then combine them to form complete messages later. With the various layers of cryptographic processing in place, it's instructive to see how messages are built up from primitives.

Shown below is an example of one-half of the Inquiry Request/Response Processing message pair (InqReq/InqRes)—the Inquiry Request. It's used to inquire about the status of an order between the Cardholder and the Merchant end-entities. Under SET's notation, the InqReq appears as:

```
S(C, InqReqData)
```

where S indicates that the message is Signed by Entity C (Cardholder) using InqReqData, a component that's fully defined in ASN.1 code.

SET uses several other cryptographic treatments besides signing. As you'll see in Chapter 12, a robust set of notations and conventions are used to describe SET message pairs. These notations include:

- Elementary notations for data and certain operations on that data

- Notation for cryptographic treatments and operations that describe how to apply which algorithms to which data elements

- Message wrapper notation that describes how to construct a top-level SET message

Elementary Notations

Tuples are groups of zero or more data elements that represent documents or message components. Tuples are defined using alphanumeric symbols or identifiers. The notation for tuples is:

{A,B,C}

Components of a tuple are defined when a tuple is given a name. The notation for components is:

T={A,B,C}

An ordered concatenation of components means that an explicit order of variables is requested and is denoted as:

A | B | C

Optional items are shown in brackets and may be found in conjunction with selection (A or B or C) and may be nested in any order. Optional components are notated as [A]; selection of components is notated as <A,B,C>; and optional selection of components is notated as:

[<A,B,C>]

Multiple instances of components are indicated through the following notations:

One or more instances of A: {A +}

Zero or more instances of A: {A *}

One or more instances of A in an ordered array where any instance of A is optional (could be NULL): {[A] +}

Bitwise Exclusive-OR (XOR) operations are indicated by the symbol $\oplus$.

Cryptographic Notation and Conventions under SET

Operations within SET employ a variety of cryptography treatments of the components of a message, including *hashing, signatures, dual signatures, encryption,* and *encapsulation.*

Hashing Treatments

Hashing transforms a data element into a unique value or fingerprint for that data element. SET uses algorithms such that the chances of two messages computing to the same hash value are 1 in 10^{48}—the odds of drowning while surfing in the Sahara Desert are far better. Hashing is used by

SET to create message digests that permit the checking of data integrity upon its receipt.

Using a 160-bit SHA-1 hash of tuple t, the *hash* notation appears as H(t).

Using a 160-bit HMAC-SHA-1 hash on tuple t using key k, the *keyed-hash* notation appears as HMAC(t,k).

DigestedData (DD) operations on tuple t corresponds to a 160-bit SHA-1 hash embedded into a PKCS-defined DigestedData format. Its notation appears as DD(t).

Linkage between two messages is indicated via a reference or a pointer between the elements. It appears as L($t1,t2$).

Signature Treatments

Signing a message involves computing a message digest for the data portion and appending it to the data. Once received, the hash value for the data portion is recomputed and compared to the hash value received. If they match, the data must have arrived unaltered.

Figure 5.1 illustrates the concept of a signed message.

Signed messages, like the InqReq message shown earlier, use the signature of entity s on the tuple t through the RSA algorithm with an SHA-1 hash, indicated as S(s,t).

Signature-Only (SO) operators use the signature of entity s on tuple t without the plaintext portion of tuple t. Signature-Only corresponds to PKCS #7 extended signatures for enveloped data. They are indicated as SO(s,t).

Encryption Operators

Encryption is used to hide information by transforming it into a jumbled string of bits. See Chapter 4 for a high-level overview of SET-related encryption techniques.

Asymmetric Encryption or digital envelopes are created by encrypting tuple t using a fresh DES key which is subsequently inserted into a PKCS #7

Figure 5.1 Components of a signed message.

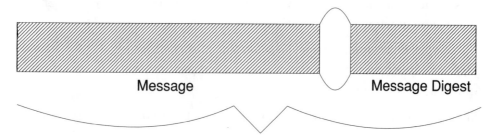

Digitally-Signed Message

envelope intended for recipient *r* using their public key taken from their certificate. Asymmetric encryption corresponds to PKCS #7 EnvelopedData of tuple *t* encrypted for entity *r*. It is indicated as E(*r,t*).

Integrity Encryption, similar to E above, provides an extra degree of integrity by including a hash of tuple *t* with the encrypted tuple *t*. Its notation is EH(*r,t*).

Extra Encryption is also similar to E above, except that *t* and *p* are the parts of a two-part message. Tuple *t* is encrypted using ordinary symmetric encryption, and *p* is a parameter, or the portion that's subjected to the extra processing. Under OAEP, the *t* portion is placed in the ordinary slot and the *p* portion is placed in the extra slot. Extra encryption serves as a linkage mechanism between two messages. Its notation is EX(*r,t,p*).

Extra Encryption with Integrity is similar to EX above, but also includes a hash of tuple *t*. Its notation is EXH(*r,t,p*).

Symmetric Encryption with Provided Key is an instance of PKCS #7 EncryptedData and indicates the operation to encrypt the plaintext in tuple *t* with provided key *k* using either DES or CDMF. Its notation is EK(*k,t*).

Encapsulation Operators

Encapsulation combines the uses of encryption and signatures to ensure the highest degree of message integrity and end-entity authentication. Encapsulation is performed on almost all SET messages. Since encapsulation processing adds further complexity, the steps that are performed to implement it are shown below each operation.

Simple Encapsulation with Signature is an instance of PKCS #7 SignedData in EnvelopedData: a signed, then encrypted message. Its notation is Enc(s,r,t) and it is created as follows:

Step 1. Using the Signature Operator (S), sign the contents of tuple t using the private key for entity s.

Step 2. Append the result of Step 1 to tuple t.

Step 3. Using the Asymmetric Encryption Operator (E), encrypt the results of Step 2 using the public key for recipient r.

Step 4. Return the result.

Simple Encapsulation with Signature and Provided Key creates signed messages that are encrypted with a shared secret key that was provided by the sender in a previous message. Its notation is EncK(k,s,t) and it is created as follows:

Step 1. Using the Signature Operator (S), sign the contents of tuple t using the private key for entity s.

Step 2. Append the result of Step 1 to tuple t.

Step 3. Using the Symmetric Encryption Operator (EK), encrypt the results from Step 2 using secret key k.

Step 4. Return the result.

Extra Encapsulation with Signature creates two-part message encryption with the first part of the message in the ordinary slot of OAEP and the second part of the message in the OAEP extra slot. Its notation is EncX(s,r,t,p) and it is created as follows:

Step 1. Append the contents of parameter p to the contents of tuple t.

Step 2. Use the Signature Operator (S) to sign the results of Step 1 using the private key for entity s.

Step 3. Append the results of Step 2 to tuple t.

Step 4. Using the Extra Asymmetric Encryption Operator (EX), store parameter p in the extra slot and encrypt the results of Step 3 using the public key for recipient r.

Step 5. Return the result.

Simple Encapsulation with Signature and Baggage creates messages that contain extra "baggage" with their return. Examples of extra baggage include tokens that are returned for later processing with a successful response to a charge authorization request, or other sensitive information (e.g., card account numbers) that is returned to the Merchant for record-keeping or dispute processing. It's desirable to *superencrypt* such data to add additional levels of security and protection. The notation for the operator is EncB(s,r,t,b) and it is created as follows:

Step 1. Compute the SHA-1 hash of extra baggage b.

Step 2. Link tuple t with baggage b by appending the results of Step 1 to tuple t.

Step 3. Using the Signature Operator (S), sign the results of Step 2 with the private key from entity s.

Step 4. Append the results of Step 3 to the results of Step 2.

Step 5. Using the Asymmetric Encryption Operator (E), encrypt the results of Step 4 using the public key for recipient r.

Step 6. Append the baggage b to the results from Step 5.

Step 7. Return the result.

Extra Encapsulation with Signature and Baggage is used for two-part messages with external baggage. Its notation is EncBX(s,r,t,b,p) and it is created as follows:

Step 1. Compute the SHA-1 hash of extra baggage b.

Step 2. Link tuple t with baggage b by appending the results of Step 1 to tuple t.

Step 3. Append the contents of parameter p to the results from Step 2.

Step 4. Using the Signature Operator (S), sign the results of Step 3 with the private key from entity s.

Step 5. Append the results of Step 4 to the results of Step 2.

Step 6. Using the Extra Asymmetric Encryption Operator (EX), store parameter p in the extra slot of OAEP and encrypt the results from Step 5 using the public key for recipient r.

Step 7. Append the baggage b to the results from Step 6.

Step 8. Return the result.

Message Wrappers

All SET-related processing begins with the MessageWrapper, a top-level ASN.1/DER encoded data structure that presents information to the receivers of messages upon receipt. MessageWrapper structures do not involve any cryptography but do identify both the type of message being received and its unique ID that aids in the detection of duplicate messages.

When a MessageWrapper is received and decoded, the Message component within it cannot be processed, but its type may be determined from the message type field within it. Processing decisions may be made upon the discovery of the message type and ID fields.

A MessageWrapper is encoded as follows:

```
{ MessageHeader, Message, [MWExtensions] }
```

And MessageHeader is encoded as follows:

```
{Version, Revision, Date, [MessageIDs], [RRPID], SWIdent}
```

where Version is the version of SET, Revision is the revision of SET, Date is the date and time the message was generated, optional MessageIDs may contain local and transaction IDs for convenience reasons, RRPID is the Request-Response Pair Identification for this cycle of processing, and SWIdent is the identification of the software (vendor and version) that initiated the request. The Message Identifier itself (e.g., InqReq, AuthReq, AuthRes, Error, etc.) is the next element in the MessageWrapper definition. Following it are optional

MessageWapper extensions, which may be used where desirable. Details about the actual messages, their uses, and their contents are fully defined in Chapter 12.

A Better Example

With the conventions and notation in hand, we can now dissect a more complex SET message through example.

Let's take a look at the Authorization Request and Response (AuthReq) message pair. This particular message is used between the Merchant and the Payment Gateway to process an authorization for a charge, as first initiated by the Cardholder via a Purchase Request/Response (PReq/PRes) message pair between the Cardholder and the Merchant.

This message pair contains both the Purchase Order and Payment Instructions components.

The format of AuthReq is:

```
EncB(M, P, AuthReqData, PI)
```

AuthReqData is defined as:

```
{ AuthReqItem, [Mthumbs], CaptureNow, [SaleDetail] }
```

The format of AuthRes is:

```
AuthRes < EncB(P, M, AuthResData, AuthResBaggage),
EncBX(P, M, AuthResData, AuthResBaggage, PANToken >
```

AuthResData is defined as:

```
{ AuthTags, [BrandCRLIdentifier], [PEThumb], AuthResPayload }
```

The EncB operator tells us that the AuthReq message is encoded using Simple Encapsulation with Signature and Baggage, and contains four components as described earlier in this chapter. The M indicates the message is from the Merchant and P that the recipient is the Payment Gateway. The message contains two data components: Authorization Request Data and Payment Instructions (PI). AuthResData is a tuple consisting of AuthReqItem, an optional Mthumbs, a CaptureNow component, and an optional SaleDetail component.

The authorization response (AuthRes) message is a selection of one of two forms: Encapsulated with Baggage (EncB) or Encapsulated with Extra Baggage (EncBX), where the extra baggage is indicated by the Payment Account Number (PAN) Token component. Both forms contain AuthRes-Data and AuthResBaggage. It is sent from the Payment Gateway entity (P) to the Merchant entity (E).

AuthResData uses AuthTags, an optional BrandCRLIdentifier, optional PEThumbs, and AuthResPayload. Message components may be further defined as collections of other components, and further operations may be performed on them. As an example, within the AuthReqItem a component called CheckDigests is defined as {HOIData, HOD2}. HOIData is defined as DD(OIData), and HOD2 is defined as DD(HODInput), both requiring the DigestedData operation that places a digest of Order Information (OIData) and Order Description and Purchase Amount data in a PKCS-defined DigestedData sequence.

In Chapter 12, each SET message pair is decomposed to its elementary contents, and their meaning and the operations required on them are described. There you'll find the full array of treatments and operators described earlier. You'll need sufficient familiarity with SET's notation to understand how to interpret SET message pairs and the components within them.

SET datatypes and operations are explicitly defined through Abstract Syntax Notation One (ASN.1). SET Book 3 (Formal Protocol Definition) is encoded and published as ASN.1 with Distinguished Encoding Rules (DER) source code.

A Brief Introduction to ASN.1/DER

According to the Federal Standard 1037C—A Glossary of Telecommunication Terms, published by the General Services Administration, Abstract Syntax Notation One is defined as:

> *A standard, flexible method that (a) describes data structures for representing, encoding, transmitting, and decoding*

data, (b) provides a set of formal rules for describing the structure of objects independent of machine-specific encoding techniques, (c) a formal network-management Transmission Control Protocol/Internet Protocol (TCP/IP) language that uses human-readable notation and a compact, encoded representation of the same information used in communications protocols, and (d) is a precise, formal notation that removes ambiguities.

Even though ASN.1 appears to be obscure, its uses can be found in common, everyday occurrences. Every time you place a cellular phone call in North America, Europe, or Japan, your call results in TCAP Protocol messages that are defined using ASN.1. When you place a 1-800 number call, ASN.1 messages are exchanged between switching computers and network databases to route your call to the common carrier and local phone number that maps to the 800 number. The ground-to-ground and ground-to-air message exchange protocols used by the FAA and International Civil Aviation Organization are described through ASN.1 and encoded using ASN.1's Basic Encoding Rules. Federal Express uses ASN.1 to track package movements from station to station, too. Wherever you find some form of a communication protocol, you'll likely find ASN.1 there as well.

ASN.1 is based on the concept of data typing, the same concept used in many programming languages. Its abstract syntax frees it from any machine-oriented restrictions or constraints. ASN.1 refers to four classes of datatypes:

Universal datatypes. Application-independent types and constructs.

Application-wide. Relevant datatypes defined by other standards.

Context-specific. Relevant datatypes applied in a limited context.

Private. Datatypes defined by users and covered in any standard.

ASN.1 is used to define datatypes and data values. A type definition takes on the form of:

```
<type name>::=<type definition>
```

An example of ASN.1 encoding of a person's name might be accomplished this way:

Informal name: Joe R. Smith

ASN.1 Type Definition (IA5String is equivalent to an ASCII character string):

```
Name::=[APPLICATION 1] IMPLICIT SEQUENCE {
firstName IA5String,
midInitial IA5String,
familyName IA5String}
```

A formal definition of the name under this structure is:

```
[firstName "Joe", midInitial "R", familyName "Smith"}
```

In ASN.1, a type is a domain of values, some with a finite number of possible values and some with an infinite number of possible values. ASN.1 uses four kinds of types, simple types (those that are atomic), structured types that contain components, tagged types that are derived from other types, and the CHOICE and ANY types for selection purposes. An example of the ASN.1 code for the sample SET message AuthReq described in the previous section is:

```
665 AuthReq ::= EncB { M,  P,  AuthReqData,  PI }
```

(just like before)

```
1061 AuthReqData ::= SEQUENCE {
1062     authTags      AuthTags,
1063     checkDigests    [0] CheckDigests OPTIONAL,
1064     mThumbs         [1] Thumbs OPTIONAL,
1065     authReqPayload AuthReqPayload
1066 }
628 PI ::= CHOICE {
629     piUnsigned      [0] PIUnsigned,
630     piDualSigned    [1] PIDualSigned,
631     authToken       [2] AuthToken
632 }
```

(Bracketed numbers serve as tags for choices or sequencing within a set of values.)

The source-code line numbers shown indicate the row number of the source code defined by the protocol, outlined in SET Book 3, and are similar to line numbers used by other programming languages. Like other programming languages, ASN.1 compilers compile ASN.1 code, but their output is language-specific source code that the programming language compiler will compile into executable code. Typically, datatype definitions compile into C-structures or C++ and Java classes.

Distinguished Encoding Rules (DER)

ASN.1 encoding rules are used in transforming data specified by the language into standard format that can be decoded by any other system based on the same decoder rules. Encoding rules represent ASN.1 abstract objects as strings of 0s and 1s. Basic Encoding Rules (BER) offer one or more ways to represent any ASN.1 value as an octet string and is the default for encoding under Open Systems Interconnect (OSI). Distinguished Encoding Rules (DER), on the other hand, provide *exactly one* way to represent ASN.1 values as an octet string. DER is intended for use in applications where unique, unambiguous values are required, as with security-conscious applications such as SET.

In Chapter 12, you'll find complete applications for the information found in this chapter. Because this information fits in with an overall discussion of cryptography, it appears in this section of the book, but its actual uses are seen later.

In Chapter 6 we look at ways that cryptographic processing is implemented via software, toolkits, hardware, and combinations of the three. Depending on your predictions for your SET Merchant Server's popularity, you may find yourself needing more robust hardware-assisted cryptography. Chapter 6 guides you through some choices.

Hardware or Software Cryptography?

6

S ET requires tremendous processing power to handle the complexity of its cryptographic nature. While 10 SSL transactions per second can be processed on a 100 to 200 MHz Pentium server, that number drops to one or two per second for SET. Security-related calculations often absorb up to 95 percent of a server's processing capability, leaving little room for other work. These bottlenecks are responsible for server overloads, refused connections, and losses of business. Clearly, people won't wait forever for their charges to process, and they certainly won't return to an on-line store if they're expected to wait.

SET is highly dependent on robust encryption, and the challenge is to provide the power necessary to match demand. Depending on your site, your budget, your historical and predicted numbers of sales transactions, and your current Web server technology, you're going to need the appropriate processing power to handle the traffic or risk losing business.

As we discussed in Chapter 4, SET uses encryption for a variety of features, including:

- Authentication
- Privacy
- Message integrity

SET requires continuous access to cryptographic processing to implement these features. As an example, SET uses signing, hashing, and certificate verification a minimum of 15 times during a single purchase request message pair process.

The cryptography for SET can be implemented through software routines (processor intensive) or hardware operations (processor assisting). Software toolkits offer these routines, invoked as calculations are needed by programs. Hardware "crypto-boxes" appear as either add-on boards or separate computers that operate as servers for off-loading the work in client-server fashion. Either approach yields complete transparency to the programs affected and to the users affected. A Merchant server that's based on software encryption communicates equally well with a Payment Gateway as one that's based on hardware encryption, regardless of how the Payment Gateway implements its cryptography.

Some major factors in helping you decide whether hardware or software-only cryptography is appropriate include:

- Costs of products and availability of investment capital for your site
- Performance requirements to serve your customers in a reasonable time
- Number of purchases per unit of time that require cryptographic processing

This chapter leads you through some cryptography hardware and software that's currently available and offers some ideas to help you decide what's best for your SET POS system implementation.

Encryption Is an Abstract Process

SET requires cryptographic calculations for every message pair it uses to process charge requests, capture requests, and for administrative purposes. Within the "shopping experience" itself, the payment presentation portion relies on cryptographic processing at the consumer's E-wallet, the Merchant's POS system, and the Acquirer's Payment Gateway. Typically, the higher the volume of transactions, the higher the need for robust cryptographic processing, and the higher the cost of delivering that processing.

Merchant SET POS systems might rely upon software developer toolkits that integrate encryption libraries with existing Merchant commerce servers. An example of this is the GlobeSet POS, which uses the RSA S/PAY toolkit.

[97]

H A R D W A R E   O R   S O F T W A R E   C R Y P T O G R A P H Y ?

Programmers typically use off-the-shelf software in the form of Application Program Interfaces (APIs) that may be invoked as required. End products ship the requisite toolkits to *bolt on* to compatible commerce servers.

E-wallets already containing those components of the toolkits needed for local processing may be downloaded and installed into compatible Web browsers with the click of a few buttons. For most consumers, software routines within the E-wallet will be sufficient for personal use, since the demands are relatively light. For Merchants, far higher levels of processing may be required as determined by the success of the shopping site.

SET's cryptographic work may also be implemented via hardware through specially designed encryption components (crypto-boxes and crypto-cards). Merchants can add security/encryption cards into the same servers that provide Web shopping access. The current array of encryption boards support most major computer operating systems. These add-on boards operate in a fashion similar to the math coprocessor boards that are present where high computational power is required.

As we also discussed in Chapter 4, cryptography becomes rather complicated rather quickly. Here it's worthwhile viewing how SET's cryptography processing is conducted by treating it as a series of abstract layers:

- Primitive cryptographic processing (computing a hash, generating random numbers, etc.)

- SET message-level cryptographic processing (SHA-1 hashes, DES encrypt, PKCS envelope creation, etc.)

- SET application software invocation of SET message-level cryptography

Each of these "layers" is delivered in forms of software that we call *toolkits*. These toolkits provide access to their services via APIs that are called by a higher layer program (as viewed by moving up from primitive processing through application layer processing).

The Microsoft CryptoAPI is a general-purpose cryptography toolkit that developers may use instead of developing their own cryptography programs from scratch. RSA's S/PAY enables the cryptographic processing that's specific to SET by combining primitive cryptographic steps into those standard algorithms that SET uses (SHA-1, PKCS envelopes, DES encrypt, etc.). Finally, the POS application layer software uses S/PAY (or a similar toolkit) in the actual preparation and processing of SET message pairs.

Furthermore, the operations performed by the lowest (primitive) layer may be implemented via software only or a combination of software and firmware. This firmware consists of cryptographic algorithms in Programmable Read-Only Memory (PROM) that operates at the speed of electricity.

Because they're abstract layers, it makes no difference (from the system's point of view) whether you use software cryptography, hardware cryptography, or a combination of the two. Where it does indeed make a difference is in the way your actual implementation behaves once it's operating.

Primitive Cryptography APIs

The lowest layer of cryptographic processing instructs hardware to perform some work (compute a hash, generate a random number, etc.). Developers of cryptography APIs include Microsoft (CryptoAPI), RSA, and others. These libraries are required by the developers of SET application software. They are typically part of any SET system you'll purchase, and you'll probably never know they're there.

An example of a cryptography software routine contained as an API is shown in Figure 6.1. The Merchant POS software relies on the Key Management Administration service to interface with the security AIR, which in turn interfaces with the cryptography API as computations are requested.

SET Cryptography Toolkits

SET toolkits like RSA's S/PAY are the next higher layer of software that use the primitive cryptography APIs as needed to perform security work. S/PAY *knows* how to carry out the work that SET messages need without requiring the developer to specify each step. For example, with its API, a developer can simply supply the content and call a DES ENCRYPT operation. The result can be placed directly within a message while it's being constructed. These toolkits not only spare the developer from considerable

Figure 6.1 A cryptography Application Program Interface (API) example.

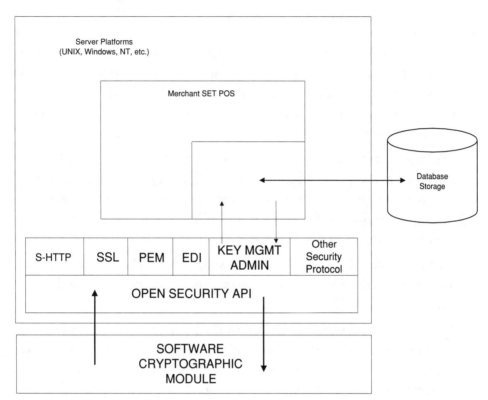

effort, they also help ensure that cryptographic processing is consistent, removing any concerns of proprietary implementations. RSA, as one of the architects of SET, has removed one of the most formidable barriers to SET application-level software development with S/PAY, and most commercial SET products rely upon it. Once again, these SET toolkits will typically be a component of any SET system you purchase, and you'll probably never know they're there either.

SET Application-Layer Toolkits

SET Merchant application (POS) software is what you'll actually purchase and install. Such applications rely on the two lower-level toolkits, adding SET-specific business and processing rules. They also offer a series of APIs that you'll use to customize the installation for your business. These APIs provide flexibility to enable relatively simple programming to link in legacy system data sources, request in-process information from the system, and so on. As we discuss in the chapters on implementation, you'll find prebuilt class libraries that you can use in your programs. These toolkit library functions may be modified or expanded to meet any of your specific needs. Additional functions can be added through programming languages such as C, C++, or Java. Table 6.1 lists some different SET POS systems. Further details can be found in Chapter 10.

It's important to realize that what you're buying is *not* an off-the-shelf, install, and run solution—it's a programmer's library that *knows* how SET works. Your task is to make it work specifically for your environment by adapting your existing software to it, or bolting it onto your existing Web operations.

The intent here is not to discourage you, but to help you best prepare for what lies ahead. As we mention several times throughout the book, there are *no shortcuts* to SET!

Once you're past selection, customization, implementation, and testing, you still may wonder if software-only cryptography suits your needs. Your purchased SET POS system (software) will likely ship with a software-only implementation of cryptographic processing. Over time, you may find certain processing too slow, creating bottlenecks, or worse—bringing your server to a grinding halt. If that occurs, you might consider hardware-assisted cryptography.

Table 6.1 Some SET POS Toolkits

	GlobeSet	**IBM**	**VeriFone**
Product Name	GlobeSet POS	CommercePOINT eTill	vPOS
Support for Hardware-assisted Crytography?			
	YES	YES	YES
Web URL	www.globeset.com	www.ibm.com	www.verifone.com

Hardware-assisted Cryptography

Like any other investment decisions, decisions about cryptographic hardware should be made using a cost-benefit analysis mindset. Several factors play into the analysis, but the primary items that should be considered are the processor utilization and the number of payment processes that are going to be performed at peak performance times (heaviest uses).

Performing a cost-benefit analysis is tricky enough when all the parameters are known and measurable, but it is made trickier when you try to determine the costs of lost business due to increased processing times on your Web servers.

When SET encryption work is added to a server, processing times can slow from several hundred transactions a second to as little as a few transactions per second. Hardware specifically designed for encryption comes to the rescue when system processing begins grinding to a halt.

Encryption hardware prices are dropping from several thousands of dollars to a few hundred dollars, with even lower prices expected as more and newer products appear on the market. Encryption hardware is supplied as either stand-alone servers (security servers) or as add-on boards that are installed into open slots on the POS system server hardware.

Hardware encryption devices can also monitor the security of the data they process and alert system administrators when problems occur. They can also monitor the activity of private keys. If a security breach is detected, the data at risk may be "zeroed-out," rendering the breach ineffective. Encryption hardware reduces or eliminates the risk of private key theft by placing private keys inside the encryption hardware itself. One drawback of storing private keys in hardware is that it makes changing them relatively difficult or, in some cases, impossible. If hardware has been "stamped" by the manufacturer with a preassigned private key, you may need to exchange the board to obtain a different key. This may require that you keep a spare board on hand.

Add-on Boards

Cryptography add-on boards and servers function using the same layered approach that's used by software-only cryptography. Some board manufacturers provide toolkits that interface the S/PAY toolkit to the APIs used to control the device's operation. Hardware providers may supply their own libraries but often use the same toolkits that software cryptography uses. If you start out with software-based cryptography and later move to hardware-assisted processing, it's best to look for the same SET toolkit support to minimize or eliminate the need to rewrite functions.

Cryptography APIs are stored in the memory (PROM) of add-on boards and servers, along with any private keys that must be stored. They typically contain their own RAM storage to speed up processing. By placing keys and certificates directly into hardware, you're assured that SET-sensitive data is not vulnerable to outside attacks, thus meeting several of the environmental security assumptions for SET, as discussed in Chapter 8.

Security Servers

Security servers follow a client-server architecture model, with the SET POS system as the client. Since these security servers contain their own processors, they provide an operator's console interface to control connectivity, key management, and certificate management services.

Hardware implementations are special-purpose devices that offer both physical and logical security. Hardware Cryptography Modules (HCMs) are connected to other server platforms through a physical I/O connection (direct or via the network). They use their own databases to store the keys that are not within the hardware itself. An API similar to software APIs permits multiple applications to access the device's services.

Some advantages in using an HCM include:

- Increased security, since you are offloading the processing to hardware that you can protect in ways you deem best. Hardware storage of key information discourages even the most tenacious thieves.

- Improved performance through the off-loading of processing, removing any requirement to share processing cycles from other servers on the network.

- Reduction of development costs, since multiple applications can share the same device. Furthermore, a single API can be used to switch from software-only processing to hardware-assisted process-ing, eliminating the need to modify existing programs that require it.

Based on your specific circumstances, an add-on board or a dedicated cryptography server could eliminate any SET-related processing problems you may experience.

Some Hardware Cryptography Choices

Table 6.2 lists some attributes for a few hardware-assisted add-on boards and security server products commonly found on the market today.

Your decision for any purchase will be guided by budgets, processing requirements, cryptography APIs already in use, type of server platform(s) supported, and operating system(s) supported.

Table 6.2 Some Hardware-assisted Cryptography Choices

	Atalla	**Spyrus**	**Rainbow Technologies**	**IBM**
Hardware type	Boards or servers	Boards	Boards	Boards or servers
Supported APIs	Microsoft CyptoAPI	Board-specific and Microsoft CryptoAPI	Cryptoki, CDSA, Microsoft CryptoAPI, NSAPI	Board-specific Microsoft CyptoAPI compatible
Supported Operating Systems	Windows NT, Unix	DOS 3.0, Windows 3.x, Win95, Windows NT, SunOS, AIX, other Unix systems	Windows NT Linus, BSDI FreeBSD, Soaris, MacOS, other Unix systems	AIX, OS/2 Windows NT
Full SET Protocol supported Web URL	Yes www.atalla .com	Yes www.spyrus .com	Yes isg.rnbo.com	Yes www.ibm .com/security/ cryptocard .html

SET's implementation of cryptography may require you to consider a more robust processing environment than what is available through software cryptography alone. As problems begin to surface in your environment, you may be able to easily remove the trouble-causing software and replace it with problem-solving hardware. Since SET software developers can't possibly anticipate all environments within which their products will operate, they've developed their systems to permit this type of growth with reasonable amounts of effort on your part.

In the next section we shift the discussion from cryptography itself to how SET uses these cryptographic principles. In Chapter 7 we take a look at how SET Digital Certificates form the core of the protocol's features of trust.

SET's Hierarchy of Trust

With a basic understanding of cryptography, its use with digital certificates, and how message signing operates, we can take a look at how SET management principles and techniques apply to SET digital certificates.

Recall that a digital certificate binds a previously authenticated private key holder (a person) to the public key that accompanies it. This attestation, performed by a trusted party commissioned by the card companies and banks, creates a message containing the person's identification information, her public key, certificate usage rules, and other information. This message is then signed using the CA's private key, and returned to the private-key holder. SET's Hierarchy of Trust uses this concept to manage the public keys for all SET certificate holders.

A great deal of thought was put into designing the structure under which these certificates are governed. In this chapter, we'll cover the following topics as they relate to:

- The SET Certificate Management architecture
- The various Certificate Authorities and their responsibilities
- End-entity certificate issuance, renewal, and revocation

Trusted parties like Certificate Authorities require a consistent and predictable structure under which they operate to ensure their constant availability as needed for transaction processing.

SET's Certificate Management Architecture

SET relies upon a hierarchical (tree structure) arrangement of nine components for the management of digital certificates. The Tree of Trust, as shown in Figure 7.1, graphically represents how various Certificate Authorities have authority over aspects of other Certificate Authorities in the branches below.

CAs appear in different forms. Some CAs are operated directly by the Brand or card-issuer internal systems, but more often than not, CAs are

Figure 7.1 The SET Certificate Management Hierarchy of Trust.

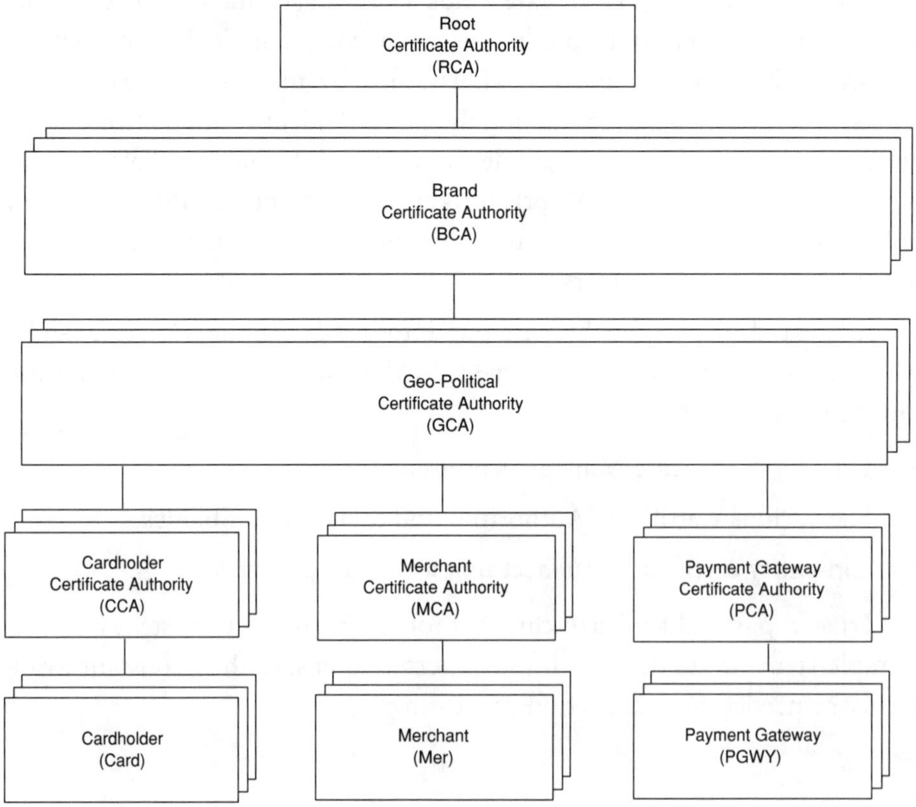

operated by third parties who are commissioned to perform the work on behalf of the Brand or the Issuer. GTE's CyberTrust (www.cybertrust .gte.com) and VeriSign (www.verisign.com) are the two largest commercial providers of SET CA services.

Work Performed by Certificate Authorities

Key and certificate management are not tasks to be taken lightly. Nor are they for the faint of heart. Extremely tight security is an imperative to maintain the trust that SET requires (see Chapter 8 for more details). At their essence, CAs provide three basic services to the entities (other CAs or end-entities) directly below them in the tree:

- Certificate issuance

- Certificate renewal

- Certificate revocation

Each end-entity is provided these services in differing ways. A discussion of each may be found under the respective types of certificates.

SET's Hierarchy for Certificate Authorities

In the section below, we'll examine the structure and responsibilities for each component in the Hierarchy of Trust under SET.

Root Certificate Authority (RCA)

The highest level, or root, of the Hierarchy of Trust is the Root Certificate Authority (RCA). It is maintained off-line and only accessed when needed for signing purposes. Root CA responsibilities also include the generation and distribution of the Certificate Revocation List (CRL) in cases of any Brand Certificate private key compromise.

The SET Root Certificate is self-signed and linked to the next active SET Root public key (if it exists at the time). Its presence is required for validating the SET certificate chain. SET-compliant software that you purchase will normally supply a copy of the SET Root Certificate including consumer E-wallets. SET Root Certificates sign Brand CA (BCA) Certificates, Brand CA CRLs, and Brand CRL Identifiers.

Management of the SET Version 1.0 Root CA rests with the newly formed SETCo, sponsored by Visa, MasterCard, American Express, and JCB. It's SETCo's responsibility to manage and distribute SET Root keys in accordance with its by-laws.

> **What's a Certificate Revocation List (CRL)?**
>
> The idea behind a CRL is to stop the use of any certificates that are tied to private keys which were compromised (stolen). If thieves gain a copy of a private key and possess its accompanying certificate, they've essentially stolen the identity of the private key holder. If the theft is not detected, the thieves could use the key-pair (certificate and private key) to masquerade as the legitimate key holder without any suspicion; or, they could use the private key to sign forged certificates (if it's a CA key that was stolen). Once a theft or compromise is detected or suspected, it's critical that the CA which signed the key-pair be informed about it by notifying them. The CA will then place the certificate's serial number on the CRL immediately and republish the list.
>
> CRLs are defined by the X.509 Standard for publication and distribution of the identity of revoked, unexpired certificates. The Brand CRL Identifier (BCI) field is defined by SET and is included in all downstream messages. With the possession of the BCI and the list it identifies, Merchants and Payment Gateways can be assured that they're screening certificates against the latest revocation data. CRLs are composed of the serial numbers for all revoked certificates, with the CA that signed those certificates responsible for its near-real-time maintenance to prevent any fraud or abuse using compromised private keys.

Brand Certificate Authority (BCA)

As you might have guessed, CA key management is a recursive activity. When a Brand obtains a SET Root-signed Certificate, the ramification process begins. Management of the Brand Root from that node forward is the responsibility of the Brand. Management of all SET branches is at least as important as management of the SET Root key.

Each Brand is, however, given certain autonomy in setting the policies for use of its SET Root-signed Brand CA key. Certificate Practice Statements (CPS) often dictate the practices whereby keys and certificates are maintained (see Chapter 8 for more information about CPS).

Geo-Political Certificate Authority (GCA)

When signed using a Brand CA key, each card Brand can distribute the management of certificates to various geographic or political regions. Geo-Political CAs, while similar to other CAs, offer degrees of flexibility that Issuers may find desirable. While Geo-Political CAs are optional under SET, certain foreign governments may require that American companies conducting business abroad operate the CA for certificates held by their citizens within the borders of their country. Card issuers might establish Geo-Political CAs by continent, by country, or by whatever subdivisions serve their interests best.

Cardholder Certificate Authority (CCA)

The CCA generates and distributes Cardholder Certificates to authorized Cardholders as defined by the Issuers policies and practices. CCAs may accept certificate requests via e-mail or via the World Wide Web. The other CA responsibilities hold true for CCAs, with the exception that they do not distribute a Cardholder CRL (not used in SET Version 1.0). They must, however, distribute the CRLs for the Root, Brand, Geo-Political, and Payment Gateway CAs.

Merchant Certificate Authority (MCA)

The MCA generates and distributes Merchant Certificates to authorized Merchants as defined by the Acquirers policies and practices. All CA responsibilities hold true for MCAs, with the exception that they do not distribute a Merchant CRL (not used in SET Version 1.0). They must, however, distribute the CRLs for the Root, Brand, Geo-Political, and Payment Gateway CAs.

Even without CRLs at the Cardholder and Merchant levels, revoked certificates by either entity still could not be used in a transaction. When a transaction authorization request using a revoked Cardholder or Merchant certificate reaches an authorized Payment Gateway, the back-end systems with which it communicates will detect that something is amiss and stop a successful authorization from occurring.

Payment Gateway Certificate Authority (PCA)

The PCA manages certificates for SET Payment Gateways. They may be operated by the Brand, the Acquirer, or by a third party as determined by the Brand. In addition to their other duties, PCAs are responsible for generating, maintaining, and distributing CRLs for any compromised Payment Gateway certificates that it issued.

Certificate Authority Compromise Recovery

Although the chances of a successful attack on a CA are rather low, if one were to occur, the old certificate would need to be revoked and a new one issued. Additionally, all those certificates that the CA signed would also need to be revoked and reissued. In effect, this occurrence would be considered a catastrophe. Until all-new certificates are reissued, no transacting would be possible.

Note that up to this point, the discussion has centered around managing the distribution of certificates, and which certificates are used to sign other certificates. None of these CA certificates are actually used for transacting. Only those certificates found at the "leaf" level of the tree are used in transactions. Ultimately, CA Certificates attest to the legitimacy of the "leaves" and all those in the chain leading to the SET Root.

Cardholder Certificates (Card)

Recall that Cardholder SET Certificates serve as stand-ins for plastic. They act as both the front of the card's embossed information and the authorized signature. Cardholders obtain their certificates from the CCA. The certificate issuance protocol is as follows:

Step 1. The Cardholder initiates a request for a certificate.

Step 2. The CCA responds to the Cardholder request by sending its encryption certificate for the Cardholder to use in protecting the transmission of account number information back to the CCA.

Step 3. The Cardholder's E-wallet encrypts the account number using the CCA-supplied encryption certificate. The message is then returned to the CCA.

Step 4. The CCA responds with a payment-card-specific registration form (template) for the Cardholder to complete.

Step 5. The Cardholder completes the form with information that presumably only he possesses. His E-wallet then encrypts it and returns it along with a new public key from a freshly generated key-pair.

Step 6. The CCA validates the information on the form in accordance with the Card Issuer requirements. If the validation is successful, the CCA generates a Cardholder certificate using the Cardholder-supplied public key, signs it, and returns it to the Cardholder's E-wallet for storage and maintenance.

The successful completion of these steps corresponds to a Cardholder's preparedness for Phase 0 of a SET transaction, as described in Chapter 2.

Cardholder Certificate Renewal

Cardholder Certificates are renewed under steps similar to those used for original certificate issuance. Certificates will require renewal processing when either (1) the underlying payment card reaches its expiration date, or (2) the certificate expiration date has passed.

Renewal requirements are determined by the Card Issuer based on its CPS and its policies.

Cardholder Certificate Revocation

Although no CRLs exist (under SET Version 1.0) for Cardholder Certificates, the certificates require revocation under the following conditions:

- If the Cardholder's private key is compromised or is suspected of compromise, the Cardholder Certificate should be revoked. In the event that a Cardholder's computer or laptop that stores an E-wallet is stolen, or if the password that's used to protect the E-wallet is discovered, the Cardholder should notify the Issuer to request a revocation of the certificate from the CCA.

- When an underlying payment card is canceled by the Card Issuer, the related certificate should be revoked. In most cases, the Issuer's authorization system stops a transaction from occurring on a canceled card, but the accompanying certificate should also be revoked.

- When the identification information in the certificate changes (e.g., name change through marriage), a new certificate should be issued.

Merchant Certificates (Mer)

Merchant SET Certificates serve as stand-ins for the payment card decals that appear on storefront windows and cash registers. In the on-line world, they're proof that the Merchant has established a relationship with an Acquirer of those payment cards represented on the Merchant Server. Merchants obtain their certificates from the MCA. Certificate issuance takes place under the following protocol:

Step 1. The Merchant initiates a request for a certificate.

Step 2. The MCA responds with a payment-card-specific registration form (template) for the Merchant to complete.

Step 3. The Merchant completes the form and returns it along with two sets of public keys from two freshly generated key-pairs.

Step 4. The MCA performs validation of the information on the form in accordance with the Acquirer requirements. If the validation is successful, the MCA generates a Merchant Key-Exchange Certificate and a Merchant Signing Certificate. The MCA then signs and returns them to the Merchant Server for storage and maintenance.

The successful completion of these steps corresponds to a Merchant's preparedness for Phase 0 of a SET transaction, as described in Chapter 2.

Merchant Certificate Renewal

Merchant Certificates are renewed under steps similar to those used for original certificate issuance. Certificates will require renewal processing when the certificate expiration date has passed.

Renewal requirements are determined by the Acquirer based on its CPS and its policies.

Merchant Certificate Revocation

Although no CRLs exist (under SET Version 1.0) for Merchant Certificates, the certificates require revocation under the following conditions:

- If the Merchant's private key is compromised or is suspected of being compromised

- If the underlying Merchant relationship with the Acquirer is terminated or suspended for any reason

- When the identification information in the certificates changes (e.g., change of business name or ownership), new certificates should then be issued

Payment Gateway Certificates (PGWY)

Payment Gateway operators obtain their certificates from the PCA. Certificate issuance takes place under the following protocol:

Step 1. The Payment Gateway initiates a request for certificate.

Step 2. The PCA responds with a payment-card-specific registration form (template) for the Payment Gateway operator to complete.

Step 3. The operator completes the form and returns it along with two sets of public keys from two freshly generated key-pairs.

Step 4. The PCA performs validation of the information on the form in accordance with the Acquirer requirements. If the validation is successful, the PCA generates a Payment Gateway Key-Exchange Certificate and a Payment Gateway Signing Certificate. The PCA then signs and returns them to the Payment Gateway for storage and maintenance.

The successful completion of these steps corresponds to a Payment Gateway's preparedness for Phase 0 of a SET transaction, as described in Chapter 2.

Payment Gateway Certificate Renewal

Payment Gateway Certificates are renewed under steps similar to those for original certificate issuance. Certificates will require renewal processing when the certificate expiration date has passed. These certificates will normally expire often, based on the notion that the more messages a certificate signs, the greater the chances of private key discovery.

Renewal requirements are determined by the Acquirer based on its CPS and its policies.

Payment Gateway Certificate Revocation

Payment Gateway Certificates will normally require revocation if the associated private key is discovered. The revoked certificate's identity must be made known via the CRL and shared with Cardholders and Merchants in all downstream messages.

Summary of Certificate Types

Table 7.1 summarizes all certificate types and uses defined by SET.

Shown in Figure 7.2 is an example of a Cardholder's Digital Certificate from the SET Specification Book 2 (Programmer's Guide). The data structure is 693 bytes long. Preceding dots (.) indicate nesting depths. Certain field values are specified by the Brand and enforced by the CCA. Other SET certificates follow a similar format but contain information relevant to the certificate type.

We've seen how SET relies on a robust set of highly trusted and secured Certificate Authority layers that require the highest forms of private key protection. Chapter 8 looks at some of the ways CAs protect these private keys through management practices, cryptoperiods, and physical devices.

Table 7.1 Certificate Types Summary

Certificate Type	Digital Signature	Key Encryption	Certificate and CRL Signing
Cardholder	X		
Merchant	X	X	
Payment Gateway	X	X	
Cardholder Certificate Authority	X	X	X
Merchant Certificate Authority	X	X	X
Payment Gateway Certificate Authority	X	X	X
Brand Geo-Political Certificate Authority	X		X
Brand Certificate Authority			X
Root Certificate Authority			X

Figure 7.2 A Sample Cardholder SET Certificate structure.

```
    This example is for illustration purposes only.

UnsignedCertificate
.version
.serialNumber
.signature
..algorithm
```

continued

```
..parameters
.issuer
..countryName
...type
...value
..organizationName
...type
...value
..organizationUnitName
...type
...value
.validity
..notBefore
..notAfter
.subject
..countryName
....type
....value
..organizationName
...type
...value
..organizationUnitName
...type
...value
..commonName
...type
...value
.subjectPublicKeyInfo
..algorithm
...algorithm
...parameters
..subjectPublicKey
.extensions
..keyUsage
...externID
```

continued

```
...critical
...extnValue
..privateKeyUsagePeriod
...extrnID
...extnValue
....notBefore
....notAfter
..certificatePolicies
...extrnID
...critical
...extnValue
....policyIdentifier
..certificateType
...extrnID
...critical
...extnValue
..basicConstraints
...extrnID
...critical
...extnValue
..authorityKeyIdentifier
...extrnID
...extnValue
....authorityCertIssuer
.....directoryName
.....countryName
.....type
.....value
.....organizationName
......type
......value
.....organizationUnitName
......type
......value
....authorityCertSerialNumber
```

SET KEY MANAGEMENT PRINCIPLES

8

Protecting the private keys that are tied to a digital certificate's public key, *especially* those keys that are used to sign lower-level digital certificates, is essential to SET.

Stolen (copied) private keys from any end-entity could be used to transact without any cause for suspicion. It's the same as a stolen identity, where a thief masquerades as the legitimate key-holder without giving anyone any reason to suspect wrongdoing.

Similarly, if the keys for a Certificate Authority were compromised, the repercussions could be severe. With a stolen (copied) CA key in hand, a thief could issue bogus certificates without any way to detect the forgery. Protection of all CA keys is absolutely critical to maintain SET's level of trust.

The more a private key is used to sign messages, the more instances a would-be attacker can obtain for cryptanalysis. If these keys are changed often and regularly, stored under NORAD-like conditions, and managed well, they'll remain safe from all forms of attack.

SET's cryptographic uses are extremely sophisticated, to deter would-be cryptosystem attackers. Because of its robustness, it's not really worth the effort to try breaking the cryptography. Even with all the computers on the planet working in tandem, an attacker would still find a tough time in reverse-engineering or attempting brute-force methods (trying all possible combinations of a key) to determine the key. CAs will normally guard against such attacks anyway by using extremely long keys. They'll also change their keys regularly and reissue new certificates whenever they do. Rather than try to discover the key, thieves are better off trying to steal the actual key from where it's stored, so extra precautions must be taken to ensure this can't happen. Because CAs clearly understand the value of the keys in their possession, they go out of their way to keep them safe from all possible attacks, physical and logical.

On the other hand, certificates cost money. The processing involved in generating a certificate is significant, and SET will place millions, if not hundreds of millions of key-pairs into the hands of millions of people. Clearly, a balance must exist between key safety and ongoing key usage. As such, validity periods for SET's key-pairs are preestablished by SET's governing body (SETCo), by the Brand Associations, by the Issuers, and by the CAs themselves—all SET end-entities (Cardholders, Merchants, and Payment Gateway operators) are obligated to replace their digital certificates whenever their key-pair expires or when a known compromise occurs.

In this chapter, we look at some levels of system security required by SET and security of private keys. Operating a Merchant POS system obligates you to establish the highest forms of private key security. With reasonable steps, you should be able to offer such protection, but it's important to understand why this security is needed. To help in that effort, here we cover these key management topics:

- Assumptions about the environments under which SET applications operate

- Key and Brand Certificate validity periods

- Private key storage required by all SET end-entities

- Certificate Practice Statements (CPS) used by the Card Issuers

- Payment Gateway and CA private key compromise recovery

Environment Security Assumptions

The SET Specification outlines several assumptions about the environments under which SET application software operates. These assumptions primarily apply to Merchant Servers, Payment Gateways, and CA Key Management systems, but include some aspects about Cardholder systems too:

- The operating system will remain in its original state without modifications beyond configurable parameters. Security-related configuration settings must remain active to prevent server security breaches.

- SET application software will remain in its original state and will not be modified.

- The processing space and internal memory of the systems cannot be examined or altered by any external sources during the execution of a SET process.

- System clocks must not be changeable by external sources and will remain sufficiently accurate to support SET's requirements.

- Monitoring software will block all external attempts to modify the operating system and the SET application software.

- The environment will include virus detection and prevention software.

- All interfaces with external devices (e.g., security hardware) will be implemented using secure communication lines and secure device connections.

If the environment offers these hardware- and software-level security measures up-front, then SET can build upon them with its series of application-layer security features. You can think of these as the *baseline requirements* for the safest possible uses of SET. All Merchant POS systems, Payment Gateway systems, and CA systems should be built with these requirements in mind.

Beyond the technical environment, policies and practices in certificate management help to maintain SET's security where human factors are concerned. Since it's ultimately people who use and maintain the environments, some nontechnical concerns are addressed through SET as well.

SET establishes cryptoperiods (lifetimes) for its private keys and certificates. A rule of thumb states that the private key tied to a certificate should expire before the certificate itself expires, allowing it to still be used to obtain a new certificate. The expiration of the certificate is determined at issue time and follows SET policies. Brands are, however, permitted to establish custom expiration periods if those times are shorter than what SETCo's policies require.

Key and Certificate Validity Periods

There's a direct relationship between the validity period of a key-pair and the certificate in which the public key is stored. Private keys will normally expire before the certificate, to allow the certificate's use for renewal. CAs should accept a renewal request using an unexpired certificate that's tied to an expired private key (at least for a short period of time—e.g., 30 days or less).

There is also a direct relationship between the expiration date of a certificate and the CA Signing Certificate's expiration date. Each level of certificate up the certificate chain must remain active slightly longer than the certificates it signs.

In the way of example, the following two tables show some possible maximum validity periods for private keys and certificates. Table 8.1 lists maximum private key lifetimes. Each Brand will establish its own validity periods. All end-entities using specific Brand certificates are responsible for renewing them as established by the Brand's policies.

Table 8.1 Examples of Maximum Private Key Lifetimes

Entity	Signature	Key Encipherment	Certificate Signature	CRL Signature
Cardholder	3 years	N/A	N/A	N/A
Merchant	1 year	N/A	N/A	N/A
Payment Gateway	1 year	1 year	N/A	N/A
Cardholder CA	1 year	1 year	N/A	N/A
Merchant CA	1 year	1 year	1 year	N/A

Entity	Signature	Key Encipherment	Certificate Signature	CRL Signature
Payment Gateway CA	1 year	1 year	1 year	1 year
Geopolitical CA	1 year	1 year	1 year	1 year
Brand CA	1 year	1 year	1 year	1 year
Root CA	1 year	1 year	1 year	1 year

Table 8.2 lists maximum certificate lifetimes, illustrating the practice of giving some of them longer lives than the corresponding private keys in Table 8.1.

CA certificates will typically expire far later than the private keys that they're tied to. This permits a full-term use of certificates that were signed

Table 8.2 Examples of Maximum Certificate Lifetimes

Entity	Signature	Key Encipherment	Certificate Signature	CRL Signature
Cardholder	3 years	N/A	N/A	N/A
Merchant	1 year	1 year	N/A	N/A
Payment Gateway	1 year	1 year	N/A	N/A
Cardholder CA	1 year	1 year	4 years	N/A
Merchant CA	1 year	1 year	2 years	N/A
Payment Gateway CA	1 year	1 year	2 years	2 years
Geopolitical	N/A	N/A	5 years	2 years
Brand CA	N/A	N/A	6 years	2 years
Root CA	N/A	N/A	7 years	2 years

with the private CA key. By using a relatively short private-key validity period, CAs can reduce the threat of stolen keys, while still allowing certificates signed by older keys to remain active for transacting.

The requirement of key-pair and certificate replacement at regular intervals offers a degree of protection; beyond this, how people actually store their private keys determines their vulnerability to attacks. Obviously, the more valuable the key, the more that's needed to protect it.

Private Key Storage

Every end-entity under SET is responsible for the safety of its own keys and certificates. This is a central theme of SET. Assurances of authentication, message integrity, privacy, and security cannot be realized once keys get into the wrong hands. Private keys are valuable. Although some are considered more valuable than others, that doesn't lessen the degree of care required for all keys at all times.

Private key holders should never treat the storage of their keys casually. Private keys *must* remain private.

Cardholder Private Key Storage

Cardholder private keys are typically stored on hard drives or diskettes, depending on where their E-wallets are kept. Security of the E-wallet is essential to keep private keys private. When a Cardholder accesses his E-wallet, he'll be asked for a password to open it. This single password protects all private keys for all the certificates within the E-wallet (see Chapter 10 for more details).

A Cardholder private key theft could occur if the Cardholder's PC was stolen or was used by someone other than the Cardholder. A home PC user's E-wallet might manage the Digital Certificates for the entire household. A husband's password will only open his portion of the E-wallet, while his wife's password will open her portion. A single E-wallet may then use several passwords, making it more vulnerable, since the chances of guessing one correctly increases. If a correct guess does open the E-wallet, the thief instantly assumes the identity of the authorized key-holder. She can then shop and spend to her heart's delight or at least until the credit lines are maxxed out. If the theft is not reported, the Issuer is left with no other choice than to believe that those transactions were performed in earnest, regardless of where the goods were shipped. At certificate-issuance time, Cardholders are made aware of these consequences when they agree to the Use Policies before accepting their certificates.

In the event the Cardholder's PC or disk is stolen, the password will continue to protect the E-wallet, unless it's easily guessed. Clearly, Cardholders need to keep their E-wallets at least as safe as their real wallets. Common password setting guidelines (combinations of letters and numbers, seven characters or longer, etc.) should offer sufficient security to prevent password attacks on the E-wallet.

In future releases of SET, Smart Cards protected by a PIN may replace disk storage of certificates entirely and behave more like ATM-type cards that require entry of the PIN each time they are used. At this time, how these will be implemented (multipurpose cards, single card for each Brand, etc.) is anyone's guess.

Merchant Private Key Storage

Since Merchant private keys sign far more messages than Cardholder private keys, they need extra security in how they're stored. Like E-wallets, Merchant SET payment software typically relies on password protection for private keys associated with Signing Certificates and Encryption Certificates. Only authorized personnel can create and use these passwords, since a theft of a Merchant's private key and certificate would constitute a theft of their identity. The same password-setting rules as above apply, but also require strict policies wrapped around them that hold employees accountable for any damage they cause. High-volume and high-profile Merchants may consider using hardware encryption devices that provide both key storage facilities and hardware-assisted cryptography processing. See Chapter 6 for more details on hardware-based cryptography. Hardware-based devices (discussed below) can offer Merchants, Payment Gateway operators, and CA system operators the degrees of security that they seek.

Figure 8.1 illustrates one possible configuration for a SET-compliant environment for Merchants using cryptographic storage of keys on a separate hardware device.

Figure 8.1 Separated hardware-based storage and management of Merchant private keys.

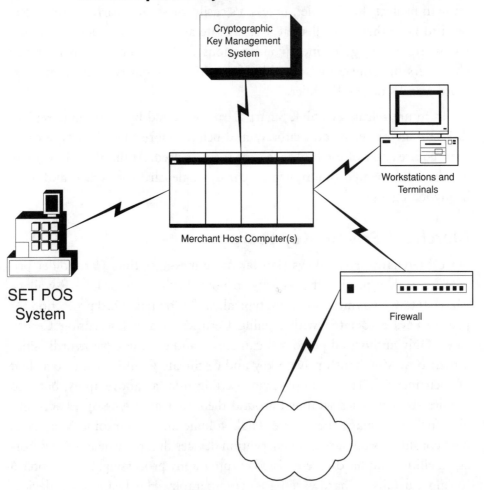

Theft of a Merchant private key could allow the thief to set up a shopping site on the Internet and masquerade as the real Merchant. Suddenly, with a similar-enough domain name, high-rankings in consumer Internet search engines, and a glitzy shopping site, the thief could divert sufficient traffic to his fraudulent site to wreak havoc. Although it doesn't seem likely that someone will go to the effort of setting up a bogus SET-compliant shopping site, stranger things have happened. At first, this option won't be very attractive, but as SET goes to the mainstream, the numbers of those who might try is likely to increase. When Merchant certificates are issued, these consequences are outlined. Merchants must agree to certain safety requirements outlined in the Use Policy before they accept their certificates.

There's another important safeguard that Merchant System operators must implement, but it's outside of the scope of SET. SET's designed to keep card payment account numbers out of the hands of Merchants while transacting, identifying a transaction only by its ID. Unfortunately, most of today's back-office systems require account numbers to identify transactions to resolve disputes and issue credits when necessary. In most practices, during Capture and Settlement processing, these account numbers are sent back to Merchant Servers for storage and back-office processing. It's essential that those account numbers NEVER fall into the wrong hands. Once decrypted, storage of all related financial information MUST be moved to systems behind firewalls to keep it away from Internet predators.

Payment Gateway Key Storage

Payment Gateway private keys sign messages in support of thousands or millions of transactions. The levels of physical storage security that they require approaches that needed for CA keys. Typically, Payment Gateway systems will use hardware-assisted cryptography, so storing keys in hardware (PROM) seems natural.

Theft of a Payment Gateway private key permits a thief to try and set up a bogus Payment Gateway and somehow divert traffic to his site. Beyond the difficulty he'll face in trying to steal the key, the effort involved in "fooling" Acquirers that he's operating a legitimate system on their behalf seems extreme. With the levels of security offered via hardware storage and temptations of better success for thieves elsewhere, SET Payment Gateways will likely remain safe.

One hardware-based key storage device from BBNPlanet (www.bbn.com) is its SafeKeyper Certificate Management System. The SafeKeyper Signer component generates and stores key-pairs and aids in key recovery efforts. The private key portion of the key-pair never leaves the unit, protecting it from ever being seen "in the clear." If the unit fails or is damaged, another SafeKeyper Signer can recover the embedded key to ensure continuing operations without reissuing all-new certificates with a new key-pair. Some other components of the SafeKeyper Certificate Management System (CMS) include:

- **SafeKeyper Registrar.** A registry-like interface to the CMS.

- **SafeKeyper Sentry.** E-mail and Web-based services.

- **SafeKeyper Server.** Provides database services, certificate-chain validation processing, and CRL generation functions.

- **SafeKeyper Adjuster.** Automated rule-based engine that evaluates certificate request messages.

The Trustmaster Cryptography Service Provider (CSP) from Atalla Corporation is another choice for hardware-assisted cryptography, key storage, and compromise recovery. It's both a Microsoft CryptoAPI-based processor and private key management system, delivered as an add-on board. Similar products may also be obtained from IBM, Rainbow Technologies, and other vendors.

Private keys at every level are considered targets for attack. CA systems are the most vulnerable, since their private keys are used to sign potentially millions of Brand-specific CA and end-entity digital certificates. Clearly, CAs require the highest forms of private-key security, since they hold the most valuable keys of all within SET.

Attacks on CA Systems

CA systems may be the subject of attacks through several different ways. Besides hacker attacks from the outside, CA operations are vulnerable to collusion, sabotage, disgruntlement, or outright theft by employees from within.

External Attacks on the CA

External attacks attempt to steal private keys using computers located outside the physical CA system environment. The attacks may arrive via the Internet, break-ins to private lines, or back-door methods through a Local Area Network within the CA. The break-ins might attempt to foil Web page security, to exploit known operating system flaws, or to gain control of the server. As mentioned earlier, monitoring software and tight isolation of the CA system from all other domains will offer the highest protection against outside attempts to gain unauthorized access.

Internal Attacks on the CA

At least as great a threat to private keys lies with those employees responsible for operating and maintaining the CA system. CA private keys are an attractive target to those who work with them.

CAs can help lessen their attractiveness to internal theft by limiting their access and ensuring that *no one person* has full knowledge of a complete key. Beyond storing keys across several devices like SafeKeyper, the CAs can make the environment in which the hardware itself resides ultrasecure. Strict access control, electronic monitoring, and intruder detection on each device should deter even the most tenacious would-be thieves.

Theft of a CA private key is considered a catastrophe. With the proper systems, a CA key thief could establish himself as a CA, ready to issue certificates for a brand. These forged certificates would be undetectable as forgeries and could be used without question. If the fake CA could divert traffic from the real CA, thieves would be in a position to glean account numbers directly from Cardholders as they request new and renewal certificates. There'd be no guessing or extra efforts required, only the SET encryption that protects the number on the RegFormRes Message (see Chapter 12).

To ensure the levels of protection required for SET keys, each Brand will decide how to implement the security it deems necessary. These policies will be clearly outlined and published to all related parties. You can obtain copies of a Brand Certificate Practice Statement (or subset) from your Acquiring Bank.

Certificate Practice Statements

Beyond the limits of physical and logical protection of keys used to sign certificates, CA policies and procedures are clearly spelled out in Certificate Practice Statements (CPS). These cover those human factors mentioned earlier in this chapter. CPSs consist of detailed descriptions of certificate policies and how they're implemented by a particular CA. The American Bar Association defines them this way: "A CPS is a statement of the practices which a certification authority employs in issuing certificates."

When CAs negotiate cross-certification services, they'll examine and compare each other's CPSs. The liability that certificate issuers and end-entities assume plays a role in the degrees of trust.

SET's X.509 certificates contain certificate policies, as extension data, that allows certificate holders to decide how much trust to place in their certificates. According to X.509 Version 3, a CPS is "A named set of rules that indicates the applicability of a certificate to a particular community and/or class of application with common security requirements."

A sample of a CPS from the University of Colorado may be found at www.cu.edu/~security/pki/ph2/Cpsdrft2.htm.

The Internet Engineering Task Force's (IETF) "Certificate Policy and Certification Practice Statement Framework" working draft by the PKIX Working Group may be found at www.ietf.org/html.charters/pkix-charter.html.

CPSs primarily apply to Card Issuers, CA service companies, and CA software developers, where certificate issuance and maintenance concerns are chief. Merchants should be aware of their existence and should understand their responsibilities clearly when dealing with each Acquirer's CA.

Again, each end-entity is responsible for reporting theft or suspected theft of a private key that's tied to an active certificate. Cardholders should call their Card Issuer to report the theft and make certain no further charges can be made on their accounts. Theft of a certificate should be considered and treated the same as an actual theft of the plastic card.

Merchants should also notify their Acquirer that a breach has occurred to prevent illegal uses of their stolen storefront decal. With Payment Gateway or CA key theft, additional efforts are required to keep it from illegal uses.

Payment Gateway and CA Key Compromise Recovery

As mentioned in Chapter 7, Certificate Revocation Lists (CRLs) are maintained for all levels of the trust tree, with the exception of Merchant and Cardholder certificates. The certificate chains that the Payment Gateway distributes and are used to drive every transaction also contain a list of Brand CRL Identifiers (BCIs). These chains may be refreshed with each transaction, but they will be refreshed *at least* once per day.

When a Payment Gateway private key is compromised, the CA that signed its certificate is notified and the serial number of the certificate is placed on the CRL and redistributed with the next message. CRLs are checked with each and every transaction to ascertain the validity of all the certificates being used.

A CRL's Contents and Distribution Process

CRLs contain a CRL number, a list of revoked certificate serial numbers, their date of revocation, the date the CRL was generated, its expiration date, issuer name, and the serial number of the CA certificate used to sign the CRL.

Figure 8.2 illustrates the repeating groups of revoked certificates contained in a CRL.

CRLs are distributed to Merchants and Cardholders with every initialization message response. Along with the CRL, the Brand CRL Identifier (BCI) is distributed too. It lists all the CRLs that are current for the Brand. BCIs are

Figure 8.2 A CRL's contents.

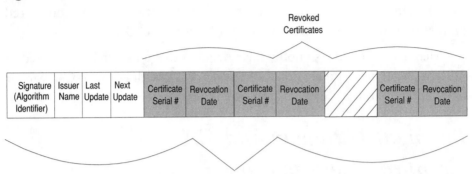

used by all end-entities to verify that they hold all the up-to-date CRLs for the Brand. A BCI is returned in every downstream SET message response.

BCI Contents

Brand CAs update the BCI whenever any sublevel CA within the Brand's tree updates its CRL. BCIs contain an identifying number, the Brand name, a validity period, lists of all the CRL numbers it identifies, lists of the *Distinguished Names* of the CAs that issued CRLs, the Issuer name, and the serial number for the Brand CA certificate that was used to sign the BCI. BCI generation follows the distribution schedule that's determined by Brand policy.

With the safety of private keys assured, those other aspects of security provided by SET will maintain the safest possible environment for payment card uses on the Internet. Next we turn our attention to some SET software that's used for storage of private keys and digital certificates, as well as conducting transactions. In the next couple of chapters we look at specific implementations of Cardholder E-wallets and Merchant SET POS systems. In Chapter 9 we begin with Cardholders systems.

ELECTRONIC WALLETS AND CONSUMER DIGITAL CERTIFICATES

9

In Chapter 2 we looked at the eight phases of an on-line payment card transaction, introducing the notion of electronic wallets (E-wallets) and Cardholder Digital Certificates for SET. Recall that these certificates serve as an Internet stand-in for the plastic cards that millions of people carry in their leather wallets every day.

SET mirrors the physical world of payment card acceptance and processing within the digital world of electronic commerce. Experts believe that if the activities of electronic payment resemble what consumers and Merchants already understand today, they will quickly embrace the digital counterpart.

In this chapter, we focus on the consumer elements required for transacting under SET. (While it's important for Merchant operators and business owners to understand how consumers interface to their Merchant Servers, it's not the direct Merchant responsibility to ensure that consumers are ready for charging. That's the job for the Card Issuer banks and credit card companies to conquer.)

Here you'll find information concerning E-wallets, Cardholder Digital Certificates, and how both interface to Merchant POS software (explained in further detail in Chapter 10).

To prepare for buying, consumers must possess at least two components required for a SET transaction:

- An E-wallet—Web-browser companion software that stores and manages credit card accounts

- A Digital Certificate (or Digital ID)—identification that serves as a stand-in for both a physical piece of plastic and the signature on the back

Why Wallets?

E-wallets allow the consumer to store private information—credit cards, debit cards, name and address information—on his PC and retrieve that information quickly and securely. Once an E-wallet is available to his Web browser, a Cardholder can begin the process of obtaining his SET Digital Certificate. In simplest form, for each card account a Web user holds and wishes to use in the on-line world, the following steps must be performed:

1. The user visits the appropriate Card Issuer's certificate issuance site.

2. An application form (authentication form) is completed for each specific credit or charge card.

3. A security check for authenticity is performed by the Issuer on the data presented.

4. An approved response from the Issuer begins the process of certificate generation. Once ready, the certificate is transmitted back to the Cardholder for storage and management by the E-wallet.

E-wallets address two important issues related to SET: they offer both security and convenience. The consumer can open his password-protected

---

So What Is the Next Big Thing?

So asks Nicholas Negroponte, author of *Being Digital*. If you believe Negroponte, the change that jingles in our pockets, the bills tucked away in our leather wallets, will soon become bits on magnetic disks—not just credit or debit cards, but stored value, bits hiding in the workstation or intangibly residing in the E-wallet. As Negroponte puts it, "Anonymity, universality, and the capacity for small payments are just a few benefits."

SET could easily precipitate a new world economy where currency coined by governments is replaced with "unique, serialized, digital coins" which the consumer can spend anywhere and anyway. Banks as we know them may outlive their usefulness as the consumer turns to the open global marketplace. Counterfeiters may soon be out of business as consumers reach for their E-wallets.

wallet only when the password matches, and once he makes a purchase, his identity is validated through the use of the Digital Certificate.

Consumers no longer have to fumble for credit cards and type the same information into electronic forms time and time again. Rather, they'll enter payment and address information once into the wallet and point and click their way through purchases on-line. Without this ease-of-use, consumers would simply return to more traditional payment methods such as mail order and telephone order (MOTO) purchasing.

Characteristics of E-wallets

A number of vendors are beginning to offer E-wallets via the Internet. Any SET-compliant E-wallet must feature these bare minimum characteristics if it's to be considered useful:

- It should support a graphical user interface that the consumer finds easy to use.

- It must be able to manage multiple certificates for various cards and card types (credit cards, debit cards, etc.).

- It must offer access (password) protection, much like the PIN protection of bank ATM cards.

- It should create a "friendly" environment in which consumers can easily manage their certificates. Without this ease-of-use, consumers will be reluctant to transact.

- It must be able to communicate with SET-compliant Merchant Servers. The importance of this point cannot be lost, and will be addressed later in this chapter.

Physical Wallets, Virtual Wallets

In the physical world, the Card Issuer verifies the identity of a customer before issuing a physical credit card. The customer then uses a conventional wallet to store the credit cards which she has received from one or more issuing banks. When the customer makes a purchase at the local department store, she chooses from her physical wallet a credit card and hands it to the

Merchant. The Merchant swipes the customer's card in a POS device, waits for payment authorization, and hands the customer the electronic slip, which she then signs. The Merchant compares the signature with that on the back of the physical card and, if they match, hands the customer her purchase, her card, and her receipt.

Virtual wallets, however, reside inside the customer's PC. Rather than make a trip to the local mall to do her Christmas shopping, the customer goes shopping over the Internet. Traversing her favorite Web site, which greets her with personalized gift suggestions based on past purchase history, she selects the goods she wishes to purchase and places them in her *shopping cart*. To complete the payment portion of her transaction, the customer opens her E-wallet and selects the already stored certificate to complete her purchase. Never leaving her chair and unbeknownst to her, the user *signs* her transaction with her Digital Certificate and off the SET transaction goes. The Merchant's SET-enabled server then receives the transaction, decrypts the message, performs authentication, and sends an acknowledgment to the customer that her order has been received and is undergoing processing.

Some E-wallet Concerns

E-wallets must be easy to use—easier than the traditional forms of buying. If customers find E-wallets too cumbersome to use, SET will be left wanting.

For this reason, major vendors of E-wallets, such as IBM, Microsoft, and GlobeSet, have addressed several issues that experts in the field of electronic commerce have raised.

How Easy Is It to Obtain an E-wallet?

Some Web browsers already enable the customer to download an E-wallet from the Internet. A major concern is how long it will take to obtain the wallet. The issue here is not just the size of the file but how long it takes to perform the download. The actual production release of E-wallets, such as IBM's CommercePOINT Wallet, will be smaller than the beta versions (which often contain debugging utilities). The licensees of the various E-wallets will decide how they want to distribute them.

Other frequently asked questions about E-wallets include these:

- Will the E-wallet Support Multiple Root Hierarchies? SET does not support multiple root keys. When SET moves versions beyond the 1.0 hierarchy, wallets will support the migration and should not need to be replaced.

- Do E-wallets currently support SET 1.0? Since SET has become the standard for processing electronic card payment transactions, E-wallets must be interoperable and work with any SET-enabled Merchant Server. Major vendors of E-wallets have committed to supporting the open architecture of the SET protocol.

- Will multiple users be able to share the same wallet? This is a tricky questions on multiple dimensions. Is it wise to share the secret password that opens access to the wallet? What if several consumers at the same household want to shop with their own credit cards on the same PC using the same E-wallet? What happens if passwords are lost or forgotten? What if a consumer wants to use the same account on both his desktop and laptop PC? How are digital certificates copied between computers?

Which E-wallet Should I Use?

A number of companies have committed to providing SET services and products including Merchant Servers, Payment Gateways, CA products, and SET software libraries (toolkits)—so many, in fact, that deciding how to differentiate between various offerings can lead to confusion and frustration. E-wallets are no exception. IBM, Microsoft, and GlobeSet all offer E-wallets, as do other vendors like BankGate and Maithean. This section describes several of these E-wallets, including their functions and their features.

GlobeSet Wallet

The GlobeSet Wallet was used by American Express and Wal-Mart in June 1997 to complete the first U.S. Internet transaction in which actual goods were purchased using the SET protocol. GlobeSet Wallet is an electronic wallet "plug-in" for Web browsers and other applications. Among its functions are the generation of purchase requests, receipt of purchase responses, and the displaying of purchase transaction detail and history. GlobeSet describes its Wallet as "fully extensible," meaning that it can support "multiple types of financial instruments and transactions" through plug-in modules. GlobeSet's Wallet works with other GlobeSet products such as GlobeSet POS and Merchant Server, but more importantly it *interoperates* with payment systems from other SET software vendors.

The GlobeSet E-wallet also supports branding by credit card issuing institutions, allowing them to extend their brand identity across the Internet. GlobeSet cites the following as features of the GlobeSet Wallet:

- An "intuitive" user interface for making purchases on the Internet

- A fully configured Cardholder profile, including Cardholder billing address, shipping address and instructions, account information for multiple credit cards, the binding of specific credit card accounts to specific purchases, and the assignment of Personal Identification Numbers (PINs) as an additional level of security

- A concise display of purchase transaction information, including Merchant contact and address information and 800 support numbers, sales quotes including quantities, pricing, taxes, and shipping costs, "real-time" display and tracking of the parties conducting the transaction, and detailed purchase receipts

- A history log of "in-progress" quotes as well as pending, paid, and failed purchases

- Support for certificate management, transaction inquiry, reversal, and credit

- Support for the archiving of transaction records for Cardholder review, audit, and reports

The wallet acts as both a stand-alone application and a browser plug-in. To administer the features of the wallet, the Cardholder launches it from the desktop as an application. To use the wallet within a transaction, the

Figure 9.1 The GlobeSet Wallet Accounts interface form.

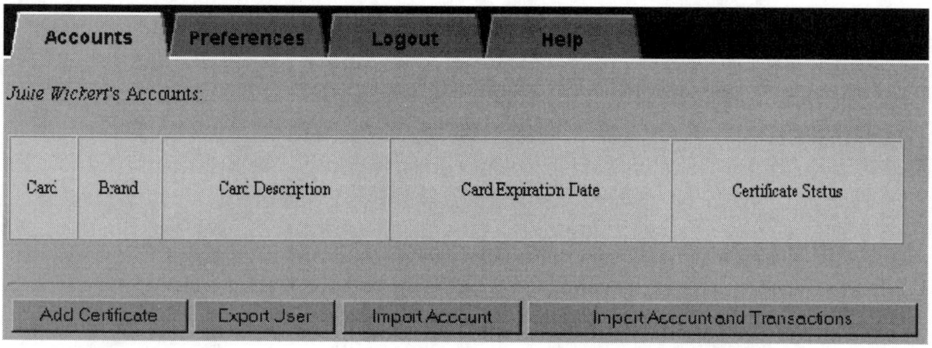

Web browser activates it from within the "shopping experience." Some GlobeSet Wallet interfaces are shown in Figures 9.1 through 9.3. Figure 9.1 shows the Accounts screen when the GlobeSet Wallet application is activated and logged into by the user. In Figure 9.2, the Create User configuration form for the GlobeSet Wallet is shown. This form is used to add multiple people to the same wallet to support shared uses. Each user has her own unique password to protect her own certificates.

Once a payment card is selected, an E-wallet "wake-up" message is sent from the Merchant SET POS system to the Web browser to activate it. Shown in Figure 9.3 is an example of the Payment form that appears to unlock the certificate for the payment card selected.

Figure 9.2 GlobeSet Wallet Create User administration form.

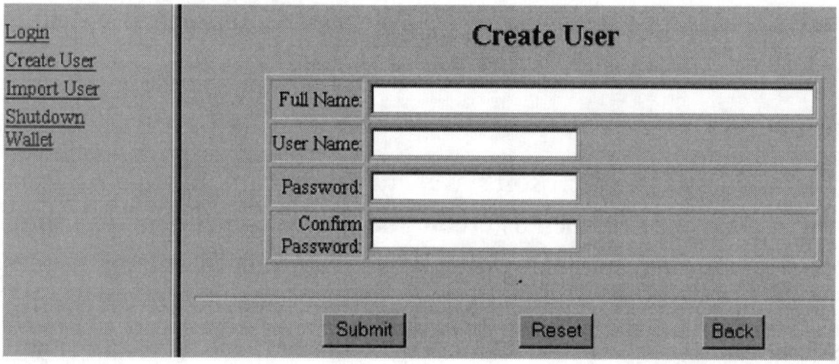

Figure 9.3 A sample GlobeSet Wallet Payment information form.

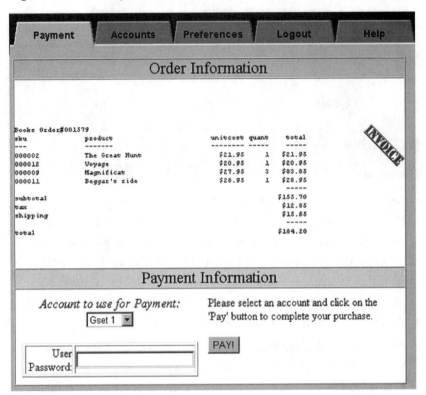

GlobeSet Wallet Version 1.0 was released to the public in December 1997. It operates under Windows NT Server or NT Workstation, Windows 95, and Sun Solaris operating systems. It also requires one of the following Web browsers: Netscape Navigator 3.0X, Netscape Communicator 4.0 or higher, or Microsoft Internet Explorer 4.0 or higher.

Microsoft Wallet

Like the GlobeSet Wallet, Microsoft's Wallet is a software payment system to store private information such as credit and debit cards along with shipping and billing information. Microsoft's Wallet additionally supports other payment methods, including on-line cash and micropayments (generally, payments less than $10). According to Jeff Bell, Microsoft program manager, "We didn't just create a payment solution. The wallet provides a user interface that makes it easy for consumers to store information privately and to use it on a Web site."

Originally developed as a complement to the 1996 edition of Microsoft's Internet Information Server (IIS), the MS Wallet was a response to growing Internet commerce and the accompanying concerns for security on the Internet. According to Richard Martin in his article "Safety in Numbers: The Microsoft Wallet," Microsoft developers working on the Wallet decided to support a number of different encryption methods.

If, for example, the user's PC includes the "Protected Store," a cryptographic storage feature of the Internet Explorer browser, the credit card information is stored there. Otherwise, the Wallet stores the card number on the user's machine registry. Regardless of the storage method, the user must enter a password to access the encrypted information.

The Wallet encrypts the user's credit card number using a hashing key. A digital hash, sometimes called a "tag" or "summary," is a one-way technique that combines the user's password, some of the credit card information, and machine-specific information. A small change in a document creates a big change in the hash.

Unlike the GlobeSet Wallet, Microsoft's Wallet uses the SSL encryption protocol that most browsers and Web servers support. The Microsoft developers decided that, given the lack of an industry standard at the time they were designing their wallet, it was safer to incorporate SSL into their design. Support for SET may be added through third parties developing *wallet plugins* for MS Wallet.

Microsoft's Wallet uses a programmatic interface to third-party development of "private label" credit card support and additional encryption protocols including SET. It has an extensible open Component Object Model (COM) architecture that supports other protocols and payment methods. An example of the MS Wallet interface is shown in Figure 9.4.

IBM's CommercePOINT Wallet

IBM's CommercePOINT Wallet is a browser "plug-in" that provides enhanced security using the SET protocol. It, too, stores electronic payment

Figure 9.4 The Microsoft Wallet interface.

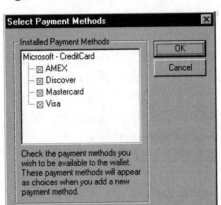

cards and related information and manages electronic payment card activities. The user can easily add and delete payment cards from his wallet and modify billing and shipping information.

To use the CommercePOINT application, the user launches the wallet through his Web browser. Before making a purchase, however, he must first enter a password or PIN, another security feature that is standard with all E-wallets.

Once the user selects the item he wishes to purchase, the transaction (purchase order) data is encrypted separately from the card account data and both *digital envelopes* are transmitted via the Internet. The Merchant Server software can only decrypt the purchase order data, and the account data can only be decrypted by the Payment Gateway. Once the gateway processes the user's card purchase request, it notifies the Merchant that the charge has been approved. Finally, the user sees a Receipt of Order window, which notifies him that his purchase is complete.

To summarize the functions and features of the CommercePOINT wallet, it:

- Supports a graphical user interface
- Allows the user to manage multiple credit cards and certificates
- Uses PIN protection, adding another layer of security

- Provides a straightforward environment for managing credit cards and certificates

- Stores purchase records for personal account management

- Communicates with SET-enabled Merchant Servers

An example of the IBM CommercePOINT Wallet interface is shown in Figure 9.5.

Trintech's PayPurse

PayPurse is another SET-enabled wallet. Whenever the user purchases a product at a SET-enabled Merchant Web site, PayPurse is automatically activated and uses the stored information about the user's credit cards. Trintech provides PayPurse to issuing banks for distribution to their Cardholders. The bank customer can then download the PayPurse installation software from her issuing bank's Web site. The installation software walks

Figure 9.5 IBM CommercePOINT Wallet interface.

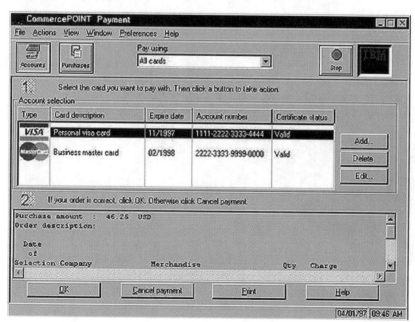

her through the steps needed to load the application on her PC, creating an icon on its desktop for *Trintech PayPurse*. Figure 9.6 shows this initial installation screen.

Figure 9.7 shows the opening screen for Trintech PayPurse. The Pay-Purse main screen offers four primary options:

- Adding a credit card or changing details about the card
- Adding or changing address details
- Reviewing previous purchase transactions
- Downloading a Digital Certificate for a card

VeriFone's vWallet

VeriFone has collaborated with the Brand Associations in the development of SET, using its experience in the physical world of secure payment systems to help develop the SET protocol for the virtual world. Among its SET-enabled software products is its vWallet, which allows the consumer to

Figure 9.6 Trintech PayPurse installation screen.

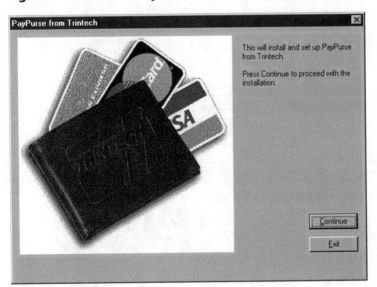

Figure 9.7 Trintech PayPurse Wallet interface.

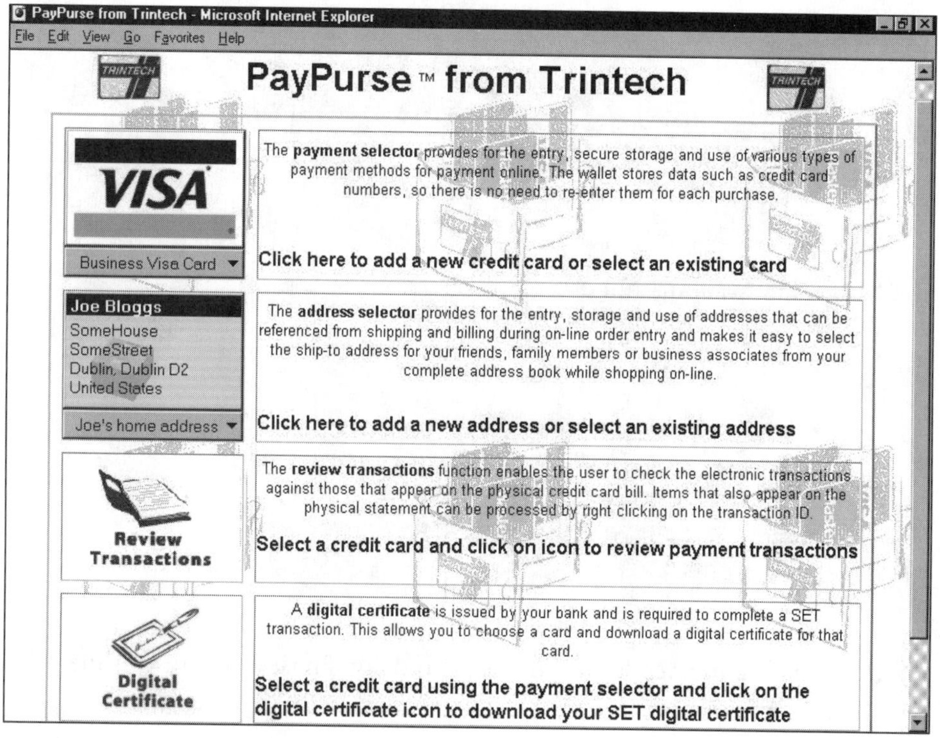

make and track purchases using SET certificates. An example of the Veri-Fone vWallet is shown in Figure 9.8.

Just as a visit to your local department store offers you a variety of payment methods, there are lots of choices for E-wallets. Your specific choice may be limited by a variety of factors, including how compatible a specific brand of wallet is with SET Merchant POS systems, custom branding of wallets by the card companies themselves, and the type of hardware and system software you're operating (e.g., if you're using a Macintosh, you may find fewer choices).

Regardless of the specific wallet you select, its value is in question if it remains empty for long. As discussed in Chapter 8, Cardholder Digital Certificates are essential to SET. Once tucked safely away in your E-wallet, your

Figure 9.8 VeriFone's vWallet interface.

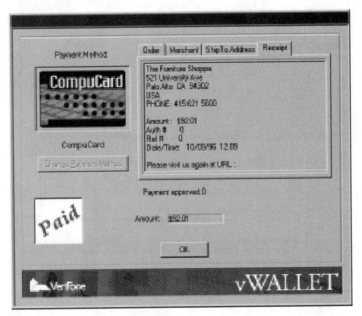

Cardholder Certificates leave you prepared for Phase 0 of an on-line SET payment transaction.

Show Me Your ID, Please

As a consumer, you'll need a unique Digital Certificate for each card you want to use on-line. These Digital Certificates prove to everyone else that you are who you claim to be and that you have a legitimate right to use a payment card on-line.

In Chapter 3 we illustrated the interaction between Cardholder and Merchant systems through the Cardholder Digital Certificates stored in an E-wallet, and the interaction between the Merchant system and the E-wallet itself.

In Chapter 7, we looked at Cardholder Digital Certificate issuance, renewal, revocation, and Cardholder obligations in keeping certificates secure. We also looked at a sample SET Cardholder Digital Certificate to see how SET might use certificates appropriately.

As SET rolls out and as you demand that your bank(s) offer them, SET Digital Certificates for your plastic payment cards will become more commonplace.

In Chapter 10, we look at Merchant counterpart SET components for operation: Merchant POS system software and Merchant Digital Certificates.

MERCHANT **SET POS** SOFTWARE AND MERCHANT DIGITAL CERTIFICATES

10

In Chapter 9 we looked at E-wallet software for certificate storage and payment selection and Cardholder Digital Certificates. In Chapter 10 we shift the focus to Merchant Digital Certificates and SET-compliant Point-of-Sale (POS) software that works within Merchant Server software. Because these digital certificates stand in for the storefront payment card brand decals and are needed to carry out the work otherwise performed by traditional POS terminals, an understanding of how these components interact is essential. Topics we'll cover in this chapter include:

- Distinctions between Merchant certificate types

- Certificate issuance and maintenance processing

- Merchant Server POS software for SET

Merchant Digital Certificates

For each payment card brand that Merchants accept, they'll also need distinct pairs of digital certificates for processing by both the Cardholder E-wallet and Acquirer's Payment Gateway.

The Merchant can be thought of as the central figure in a payment card transaction, since she serves as the bridge between the Cardholder and Payment Gateway.

Key-Exchange or Encryption Certificates are used for encrypting messages intended for return to the Merchant that only she may read. Signing Certificates are used for signing messages from the Merchant, unquestionably identifying the Merchant as the source of those messages.

These pairs of certificates are generated by the Merchant Certificate Authority (MCA) concurrently using the protocol described in the next chapter. Merchants may need additional sets (copies) of these certificates because of physical system requirements, concern for security, or Acquirer policies. The total number of certificates required is a function of the number of key-pairs a Merchant needs, the number of Acquirer Payment Gateways with which the Merchant interfaces, and the number of different payment card brands the Merchant accepts. For practical purposes, it may be necessary to split Internet traffic across several Merchant Web Servers, and each one of those will require a copy of all certificates. In addition, when the private keys tied to these certificates or the certificates themselves expire (most likely at different times), they'll require renewal processing and redistribution to wherever they're used. The same is true in the event of a private key compromise.

Chapter 6 discusses some ways to store the keys using hardware-assisted cryptographic devices that also aid in keeping their maintenance processing requirements low. Chapter 8 discusses the risks of private key compromises and offers Merchants some tips on maintaining a safe operating environment.

Merchant Certificate Issuance Conditions

Before any Brand-specific Merchant Certificates can be issued, certain conditions must be met:

- The Merchant must have already established a relationship with an Acquirer and been assigned a unique Merchant ID.

- Merchant software must be able to generate public-private key-pairs and be able to store them safely.

- The Merchant must have already agreed to Acquirer policies for certificate uses and payment acceptance.

- The Merchant must possess the URL to the Merchant Certificate Authority for the Acquirer.

- Merchant servers must be operating SET-compliant software that can generate certificate processing requests.

Because your Merchant Server takes over the work that your POS terminal would otherwise perform, a special component is added to the *cash register* functions built into your commerce server software.

SET-compliant POS Software for Merchant Servers

Suites of new SET-compliant systems have begun to appear on the scene since late 1997. More often than not, these solutions show up as suites of products that provide end-to-end processing. They include Cardholder E-wallets, Merchant POS software, Certification Authority (CA) Systems, and Payment Gateway application software for Acquirers. Interoperability between these programs is guaranteed, since they're developed with one common understanding of the SET Specification. The trick is to ensure that systems from different providers work together *as though* they were developed by the same people with the same interpretation and understanding of the SET Specification. Unfortunately, this isn't always the case. When SET becomes the rousing success that many believe it will, interoperability between all related components will be a foregone conclusion. In time and with sufficient field and pilot testing, these problems should disappear.

CommercePOINT eTill

IBM offers a component called CommercePOINT eTill that works under their Net.Commerce and Lotus Domino Merchant servers. It can also be integrated into other merchant commerce servers. eTill provides a utility to manage your certificates as well as all the SET-related message formatting, encryption, and decryption services required. A browser-based configuration and administration system is provided with eTill for merchant webmaster uses. A diagram illustrating how eTill is used in a payment transaction is shown in Figure 10.1.

GlobeSet POS

GlobeSet Inc.'s solution is called GlobeSet POS, and is a component of the GlobeSet Payment System, released in December 1997. The payment system

Figure 10.1 eTill in the payment process.

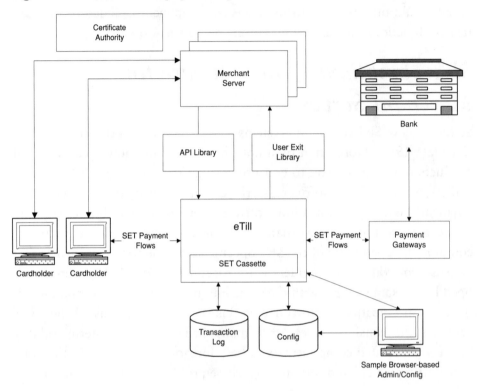

is typically sold through third parties and Value Added Resellers (VARs) who integrate it into turnkey systems. According to GlobeSet, their POS system provides:

- Proven interoperability

- Usage with multiple payment gateways

- An SDK to facilitate storefront application integration

- Support for cryptographic hardware, such as Atalla's PayMaster ISP (see Chapter 6)

- Support for multiple merchant (shopping mall) capabilities and authorization-only capabilities

GlobeSet POS is available for Windows NT 4.0, Solaris 2.5 or greater, HP-UX 10.x, and IBM AIX 4.2. Database systems that are supported include Oracle, Microsoft SQL Server, Sybase, and Informix. GlobeSet offers a software development kit (SDK) to simplify the integration of a Merchant's shopping experience application with the POS software. Its Administration Manager provides a browser interface for its administration functions, including:

- Starting, stopping, resetting, and monitoring the status of the POS server

- Examining the certificates that are available for use

- Configuring the server's logs, URLs, ports, and databases

- Configuring and monitoring current merchants

- Manually processing batch and transaction activity

VeriFone

VeriFone is one of the leading suppliers of POS terminals in retail industries, so it's natural that they support POS operations on the Internet, too. The VeriFone Internet Commerce system provides a SET-compliant Merchant component, called vPOS. Other components in the suite include vGate for Payment Gateways and vWallet for Cardholders. Like the other software developers, VeriFone offers an end-to-end solution for SET transaction processing. vPOS operates under the Microsoft Internet Information Server (IIS), Netscape Enterprise Server, and Oracle Web Server. It also provides a Web browser interface for management and administration of the system.

Systems like CommercePOINT eTill, GlobeSet POS, and VeriFone vPOS all use the RSA S/PAY Toolkit to handle the cryptographic processing needs of SET via APIs. Other APIs that these POS software components add permit you to access its features without requiring you to be intimate with the details of its implementation or to deal with cryptographic-level processing. If you were so inclined, you could write your own implementation of SET POS software using toolkits like RSA's S/PAY and the SET Programmer's

Guide, but with implementations already commercially available, it hardly seems worth the expense and the effort required.

CyberCash

Still another option for SET implementation is available. Currently, Cyber-Cash offers a SET-compliant system, but it differs from traditional card processing systems. The CyberCash solution features payment options such as credit card, cash, and electronic check. CyberCash's global payment protocol builds upon the levels of security already associated with the CyberCash Payment System. According to Jeff Irby, vice president of sales and marketing for CyberCash:

> *The release of SET 1.0 will stimulate the global acceleration of electronic commerce on the Internet. . . . CyberCash is actively developing and piloting SET services that address the security needs of consumers, merchants and the financial community while ensuring SET compatibility across all platforms.*

The use of the CyberCash Payment System mitigates the need to install SET-compliant POS software on your own Merchant Servers, but CyberCash does charge a fee for system use, usually some percentage of the transaction.

What Does the POS Software Do?

We'll use IBM's eTill as one example of how POS systems operate within a Merchant Server. Figure 10.1 illustrates message flows and component interaction. eTill itself consists of the following components:

- A Java application receives messages from both Cardholders and Payment Gateways and sends messages to Payment Gateways.

- The C API Library permits access by any Merchant Server software that's written in C or C++.

- The C Modifiable User Exit Shared Library enables the implementation of optional user exits or callback functions to dynamically retrieve information while a transaction is in process.

- Configuration databases are used to customize the system for flexible access to Payment Gateways and other applications.

- Transaction databases maintain information about orders and SET transactions.

- Sample browser-based forms enable further customization of configuration, administration, reporting, and message generation user interfaces.

- Certificate Registration Utility is used to obtain Merchant Certificates.

eTill uses Configuration Profiles for the installation itself, the SET components, the Payment System configuration, the Acquirer(s) configuration, the Brand(s) configuration, and Acquirer Off-days configurations.

Specific installation and testing procedures can be found in Chapter 16, but it's important to realize that there may be significant programming efforts required to interface with Merchant Servers and back-office accounting systems before you're ready to accept payment cards via the Internet. Unless you're starting from scratch with a complete turnkey solution, count on significant development work by your staff or someone you hire to perform it.

Securing Your Payment Processing Environment

While SET reduces the risk of theft of payment card information while en route between end-entities, it does nothing to ensure the security of the environments in which it's installed. It's the Merchant's responsibility to define a security policy for any hardware or software they install. Here are some things you should consider when developing such a policy:

- Dedicate a server and a firewall to your Merchant Server and POS software, insulating them both from the Internet and from other domains within your organization. Remove all unnecessary server software that's not specifically for operational purposes. This may include language compilers, Perl libraries, administrative utilities, and factory-supplied log-ins and passwords.

- Only open SET-defined protocol ports to computers outside your firewall.

- The firewall should not allow FTP or telnet or remain open on other ports.

- Don't operate software such as FTP, telnet, or e-mail systems on the Merchant Server and POS hardware.

- Whenever remote operations (telnet, xterm, etc.) are needed, make sure the Secured Socket Handler (SSH) and Secure Copy (SCP) are used.

- HTTPD and/or Merchant Server software connections should never be made directly into the POS software (use the APIs instead).

- HTTPD and/or Merchant Server software should be protected against hostile browsers.

In addition to the security of the POS software and the Merchant Server software, webmasters or security administrators should also ensure that all transaction-related information is not vulnerable to outside attacks.

In many purchase transactions, Payment Gateways can be instructed to return the Cardholder's account number for payment reconciliation, auditing, and dispute processing. It is critical that these data be securely stored. Databases should be password-protected, and the system should be configured to guarantee that unauthorized access is not possible.

Once the SET POS software and requisite Merchant Digital Certificates are successfully installed, your Merchant Server is prepared for Phase 0 of the on-line payment card transaction, as discussed in Chapter 2.

In Chapter 11, we begin to connect the pieces of SET into a series of processing steps to perform useful work. There you'll find specific protocols to obtain all types of digital certificates, normal and optional payment processing flows, and a discussion of how batch administration work is conducted.

SET MESSAGE FLOW PROTOCOLS

11

From Chapter 7 to this point, we've looked at SET's uses and the management of Digital Certificates that implement its services of security, privacy, and message authentication. We've also looked at the various responsibilities of all entities within the SET Tree of Trust.

In this chapter we begin to connect the pieces together by examining SET message-passing protocols that implement certificate management and payment system processing. SET provides a wide array of message pairs corresponding to the messaging that occurs between POS terminals and Acquirer payment systems. SET also adds Cardholder-initiated messages since it's operating under a card-not-present environment where swiping the magnetic stripe of a plastic card is not possible.

Here we'll look at messages that span all phases of an on-line SET payment card transaction, as described in Chapter 2. Messages pertinent to the discussion include:

- Inquiry messages
- Payment processing messages
- Authorization reversal messages
- Capture reversal messages
- Credit issuance messages
- Payment Gateway Certificate request messages
- Batch Administration messages
- Certificate issuance messages

- Certificate inquiry messages
- Error messages

Many of these messages are used more than once across protocols, and some may be used more than once within a particular protocol. Some message pairs are optional—used for status inquiries and exception-type processing, like reversals and returned goods credits.

With a technique called *process mapping,* we illustrate these protocols, showing entities involved, messages involved, and message origination/destination points. To understand the process maps, use the following legend:

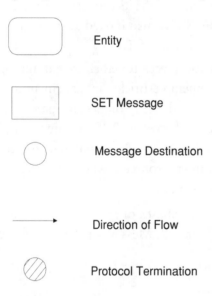

Entity

SET Message

Message Destination

Direction of Flow

Protocol Termination

Details about the contents of each of these message pairs can be found in Chapter 12.

Certificate Issuance Protocols

The three process maps discussed in this section define SET's protocol to request and issue certificates for Cardholders, Merchants, and Payment Gateways. Variations on these flows are possible, based on Issuer and Acquirer implementations of SET. Any variations will be outlined in your Acquirer agreement for SET.

Cardholder Certificate Request Protocol

Figure 11.1 illustrates the protocol that Cardholders and Cardholder Certificate Authorities follow for the issuing of new certificates. Renewal processing may follow a similar flow, but might also vary from Issuer to Issuer.

This diagram corresponds to establishing the Cardholder's preparedness for Phase 0 of the transaction—Cardholder Digital Certificate acquisition message pair processing. The flow is as follows.

Upon a wake-up message (not defined by SET) from the Cardholder Certificate Authority (CCA), the Cardholder's E-wallet prepares a Cardholder Certificate Initiation Request (CardCInitReq) containing a list of the certificates, CRLs, and CRL Identifiers the E-wallet currently holds, using the thumbprints for those items. The request is then returned to the CCA. The CCA responds with a Cardholder Certificate Initiation Response (CardCInitRes) message containing any certificates, CRLs, and CRL Identifiers that the Cardholder will need to verify signatures and encrypt certificate information later in the flow.

Figure 11.1 Cardholder Certificate Request protocol.

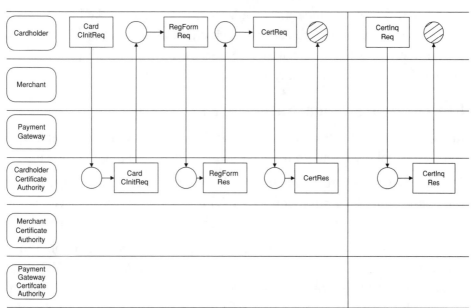

A successful receipt of the CardCInitRes by the E-wallet creates a Registration Form Request (RegFormReq) message that's sent to the CCA. The CCA responds with a Registration Form Response (RegFormRes) that contains a template of information for the Cardholder to complete in accordance with the Card Issuer's rules for Cardholder authentication. The Cardholder completes the form, and the E-wallet encrypts it (along with other information) into a Certificate Request (CertReq) message indicating the Cardholder's readiness to receive his digital certificate. If successfully validated using Issuer guidelines for validation, the CCA prepares a Certificate Response (CertRes) message, containing the prepared Cardholder Digital Certificate, ready for storage by the E-wallet.

In the cases where the digital certificate is not returned in the CertRes, the Cardholder's E-wallet may request the status of the request by using the Certificate Inquiry Request (CertInqReq) message. With the response message from the CCA, the Certificate Inquiry Response (Cert-InqRes) will either contain the prepared certificate or provide information that tells the Cardholder when it will be ready. This message pair is optional under SET.

Once this transaction is successful, the Cardholder will be in possession of the required digital certificate for each credit or charge card he's able to use on-line, and is ready for Phase 0 of a SET transaction. This protocol will be used for every card a consumer decides to register.

Merchant Certificate Request Protocol

In Figure 11.2, the protocol that Merchants and Merchant Certificate Authorities follow is shown for the issuing of new Merchant certificates.

This diagram corresponds to establishing the Merchant's preparedness for Phase 0 of the transaction—Merchant Digital Certificate acquisition message pair processing. The flow is as follows.

The Merchant Certificate Initiation beings the process of obtaining Merchant Digital Certificates for SET. The Merchant Server's SET POS component will begin the process (upon activation by the systems administrator) by preparing a Merchant-Acquirer Certificate Initiation Request

Figure 11.2 Merchant Certificate Request protocol.

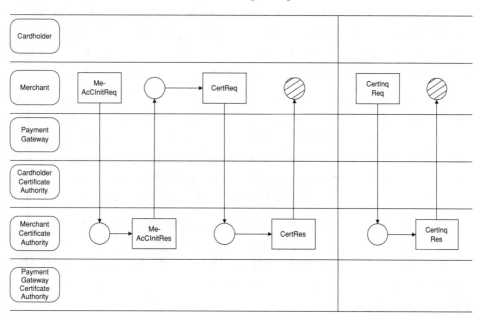

(Me-AqCInitReq) message containing a list of the certificates, CRLs, and CRL Identifiers the POS system currently holds. It also contains bank information, the types of certificates being requested, and a registration form for the indicated bank or card company. If the Merchant requires the registration form, the response message will contain it. The request is then returned to the MCA. The MCA responds with a Merchant-Acquirer Certificate Initiation Response (Me-AqCInitRes) message. The message contains:

- A registration form (template) for the Merchant to complete (if needed)

- Any certificates, CRLs, and CRL Identifiers that the Merchant will use to verify signatures and encrypt certificate information later

- A policy statement for the Merchant to read and agree to

- URLs for brand and card logos

If the request is unsuccessful, the response will return the reason and/or a URL or e-mail address that leads the Merchant to additional information.

A successful receipt of the Me-AqCInitRes by the Merchant SET POS software creates a Certificate Request (CertReq) message that's sent to the MCA. If successfully validated using Acquirer guidelines for validation, the MCA prepares a Certificate Response (CertRes) message, containing the prepared Merchant Digital Certificate, ready for storage by the POS software.

In cases where the digital certificate is not returned in the CertRes, the Merchant POS software may request the status of the request by using the Certificate Inquiry Request (CertInqReq) message. With the response message from the MCA, the Certificate Inquiry Response (CertInqRes) will either contain the prepared certificate or provide information that tells the Merchant when it will be ready. This message pair is optional under SET.

Once this transaction is successful, the Merchant will be in possession of the required certificates that represent the storefront decals for all payment cards she accepts, and is ready for Phase 0 of a SET transaction. This protocol will be repeated for every card Brand the Merchant accepts for payment.

Payment Gateway Certificate Request Protocol

Figure 11.3 illustrates the protocol that Payment Gateways and Payment Gateway Certificate Authorities follow for the issuing of new Payment Gateway Certificates.

This diagram corresponds to establishing the Acquirer Payment Gateway's preparedness for Phase 0 of the transaction—Acquirer Certificate issuance message pair processing. This protocol follows the same flow as the Merchant's Certificate Request protocol, with the only differences being the origination and destination for messages. This protocol flow is between the Payment Gateway and the Payment Gateway Authority (PCA), with all message pairs operating as described for the equivalent Merchant-MCA transaction.

Once this transaction is successful, the Payment Gateway system will be in possession of the required certificates that represent its legitimacy to Cardholders and Merchants in charge processing for a given Brand. This

Figure 11.3 Payment Gateway Certificate Request protocol.

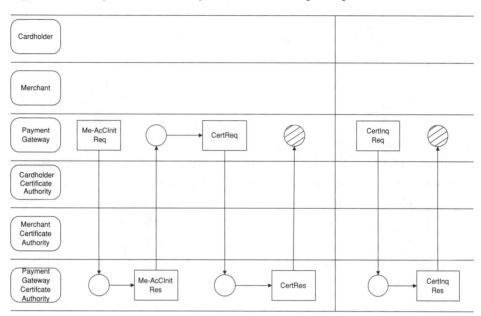

prepares the Payment Gateway system for Phase 0 of a SET transaction. This protocol will be repeated for every card Brand it supports for the Acquiring Bank(s) Payment Gateway services.

Payment System Flows

The next three process models illustrate the messaging that takes place in payment card processing between Cardholders, Merchants, and Payment Gateways.

Normal Purchase Protocol

Figure 11.4 defines the normal flow of processing from the point of Cardholder selection of payment card to the Merchant's completion of the process and the corresponding capture of the charge by the Merchant from the Acquirer Payment Gateway. This protocol corresponds to Phases 4, 5, 6, and

8 of an on-line SET payment card transaction, described in Chapter 2. Recall that SET is outside the scope of transaction processing phases 1, 2, 3, and 7.

The flow for normal payment processing follows.

Upon the completion of the Shopping Experience (Phase 1), the Item Selection Process (Phase 2), and the Check-out Process (Phase 3), the Cardholder will select a form of payment. If he selects a SET-enabled payment card (Phase 4), SET is initiated via the Purchase Initialization Request (PInitReq) message, prepared by the Cardholder's E-wallet (signaling the beginning of Phase 5). This message indicates to the Merchant the identifier of the payment card brand, a local Cardholder-created ID for the transaction, a challenge (nonce) to check the freshness of the response, and the thumbprints for the certificates, CRLs, and CRL Identifiers for the brand that the E-wallet holds in its cache. The Purchase Initialization Response (PInitRes) message from the Merchant contains the original request data, the certificates, CRLs, and CRL Identifiers that the Cardholder will need for further processing, a date, a Transaction ID (XID) created by the Merchant POS software, a reply to the Cardholder freshness challenge, and a freshness challenge of its own.

SET allows for the omission of these messages when used in noninteractive environments (such as CD-ROM catalog shopping), provided the certificates, CRLs, and CRL Identifiers are obtainable by some off-line mechanism (e.g., copies stored on the CD). For our purposes, let's assume the transaction is being conducted via the Internet in an on-line processing environment.

With a successful receipt of the PInitRes by the Cardholder's E-wallet, the Purchase Order Request (PReq) message is prepared. PReq consists of two parts: Order Instructions (OI) intended for the Merchant, and Payment Instructions (PI) intended for the Payment Gateway. This is an example of a dually signed message as described in Chapters 4 and 5.

When the Merchant Server POS software receives the PReq, it possesses all the data needed to initiate an Authorization Request (AuthRes) with the Payment Gateway. The Payment Instructions (PI) portion of the PReq is copied into the AuthReq, but is indecipherable by the Merchant POS System.

Rather, the system tunnels it through from the Cardholder to the Payment Gateway. The AuthReq contains signed and encrypted data about the purchase, along with the PI. This initiates Phase 6 of a SET on-line transaction.

After the authorization processing through the financial network is complete, the Payment Gateway prepares the Authorization Response (AuthRes) message containing the outcome. Details of the contents of this message may be found in the next chapter.

The outcome may indicate one of three possible results: approved, declined, or conditionally declined. A conditionally declined response corresponds to a callIssuer indicator in the AuthCode field. When a Merchant receives such a reply, using out-of-band processing, she may call the Acquirer Bank to arrange to speak with the Issuer Bank. If the Issuer Bank approves the request, it may provide the Merchant with an ApprovalCode while they're on the phone. SET POS software permits the entry of this code prior to the creation of the Purchase Response (PRes) message that's returned to the Cardholder. There may be some delay between the Cardholder's PReq message and the subsequent Merchant PRes reply message, depending on the AuthReq outcome. A successful completion of these steps finalizes Phase 6.

With a successful completion of PReq through PRes, the Merchant, for all intents and purposes, possesses a legitimate customer order that she'll need to fill. Phase 7 covers the delivery of goods process. Once shipment or performance of services is complete, the Merchant can request a capture of the sale from the Acquirer Payment Gateway (Phase 8).

Using information from AuthRes, the Merchant POS System prepares a Capture Request (CapReq) message that may contain one or several previously authorized transactions. Capture requests include information from the Merchant that the Payment Gateway needs to produce bank clearing request messages that the Acquiring Bank processes or sends off to the financial network for processing (not defined by SET). The Capture Response (CapRes) message from the Payment Gateway will indicate the results for each transaction represented within the CapReq, thus concluding Phase 8 of the on-line SET payment card transaction.

When complete, this protocol corresponds to a Cardholder's signing of a charge record produced by the POS terminal in the non-Internet world. In the event of authorization decline, the sale is canceled, or the Cardholder may be asked to select another card, starting over from the beginning.

Other Purchase Systems Message Flows

While the normal payment processing steps are represented in Figure 11.4, other processing may be required at times. Conditions that require credit issuance, reversals of successful authorizations or captures, and inquiry messages are illustrated in Figure 11.5 and Figure 11.6. All messages within these process maps are considered optional under SET.

The Authorization Reversal Request (AuthRevReq) and Authorization Reversal Response (AuthRevRes) message pair may be used between the Merchant and the Payment Gateway to adjust an order because of an inability to ship it all at once. It may break down a previously authorized order

Figure 11.4 Normal purchase flow.

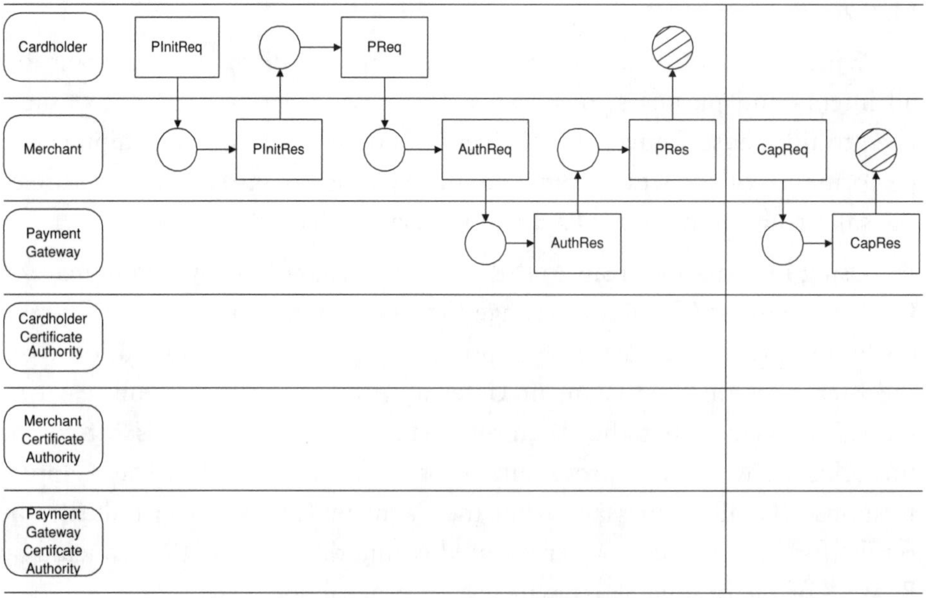

Figure 11.5 Other payment system messages flows, Part One.

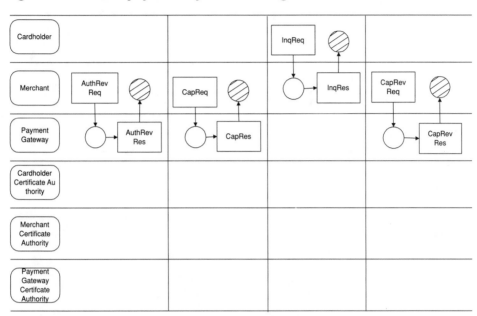

into partial shipments, or remove items from the order. This message is not directly performed within any formal phase of a SET transaction, rather it's used to correct information from Phase 6.

Capture Request (CapReq) and Capture Response (CapReq) are shown as an optional message pair between Merchants and Payment Gateways because SET permits out-of-band processing to accomplish the same work. It's considered a normal payment flow process message pair as described earlier, but is not absolutely essential to SET itself. As we'll discuss in Chapter 18, you may want to your SET Merchant POS software in an Authorizations-only environment, permitting you to collect charge authorizations from any of your sales channels into a single capture and settlement process.

The Inquiry Request (InqReq) and Inquiry Response (InqRes) message pair between the Cardholder and Merchant is optionally used to inquire about the status of an order. This is one of the idempotent SET messages, described in Chapter 5. One or multiple copies of the InqReq message may

Figure 11.6 Other payment system messages flows, Part Two.

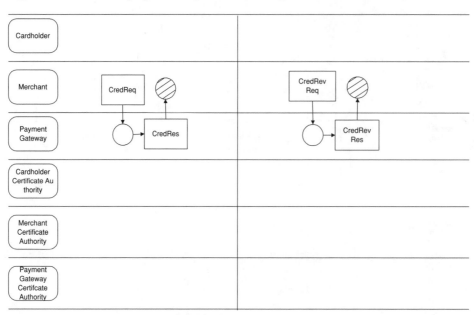

be sent at any time. InqRes is similar to the PRes message, but a PRes would indicate the Merchant's final disposition of a transaction.

Capture Reversal and Credit messages are identical in syntax and perform the same functions. Data structures defined by SET are identical for both sets of messages.

The Capture Reversal Request (CapRevReq) message is sent by the Merchant to the Payment Gateway to change or eliminate a previously successful transaction capture. The message may be sent at any time after completion of a capture request to reduce or remove the amount of capture. The Capture Reversal Response (CapRevRes) message indicates the outcome of the request processing. This message is not directly performed within any formal phase of a SET transaction, rather it's used to correct information from Phase 8.

Figure 11.6 illustrates two other message flows that SET considers optional.

Credit Request (CredReq) messages are sent from the Merchant to the Payment Gateway requesting a return credit on a previously captured transaction. This pair is used when CapReq/CapRes information for the original transaction has aged and is no longer available on the Merchant or Payment Gateway transaction logs. While that information is still available, the CapRevReq/CapRevRes message pairs may be used instead.

Credit Reversal Request (CredRevReq) and Credit Reversal Response (CredRevRes) processing are used between the Merchant and the Payment Gateway to reverse a previously granted credit on a transaction. This might occur when a Cardholder elects to return goods to the Merchant, but the goods fail to show up within a certain time period, or when a disputed charge is determined to be a legitimate one, and the goods remain in the Cardholder's possession.

Completion success for the messages illustrated varies with the type of processing requested. For a detailed explanation of what these messages contain, see Chapter 12 for the specific message pair.

Gateway Certificate Request and Batch Administration Protocols

Figure 11.7 illustrates two (unrelated) message pairs that are used between Merchants and Payment Gateways.

The Payment Gateway Certificate Request (PCertReq) is sent by the Merchant to request the most current certificate chains from her Acquiring Payment Gateway for the card Brands she accepts. The Payment Gateway Certificate Response (PCertRes) returns the requested certificate status codes and thumbprints to correspond to the Brand and BIN sequences requested. Payment Gateway certificates are required by the Merchant to encrypt all communications intended for future processing. This message

Figure 11.7 Gateway Certificate Request and Batch Administration message flows.

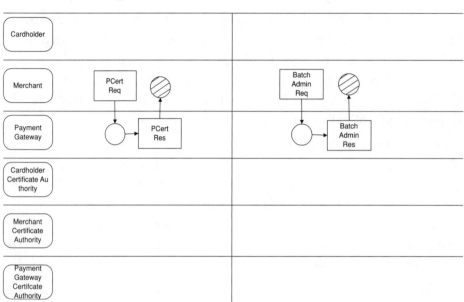

pair wili normally be used at the start of each business day, but could also be used multiple times during the day as well.

Batch Administration Request (BatchAdminReq) and Batch Administration Response (BatchAdminReq) processing is used to manage batches of transactions awaiting capture and settlement processing. Chapter 2 discusses some of the details in the section "Phase 8: Capture and Settlement." Batch Administration includes requests to open a batch, close a batch (settle it), purge a batch, and return the totals, status, and/or the details of a batch for reconciliation and batch balancing purposes. These requests and responses help both Merchants and Payment Gateways to identify any discrepancies between their sets of transactional data.

Error Messages

The process maps illustrated in the preceding sections show request and response processing that proceeds normally. Sometimes request messages are met with an Error response message due to various SET-related problems. Conditions that the SET Specification identifies as errors occur when message responders cannot reliably identify an incoming message request. *Error* messages are in response to incoming SET-defined messages, and never in response to other *Error* messages. Furthermore, they typically deal with errors at the communication level—not at the business level, such as authorization declines or back-end host system-identified errors.

Error message categories include:

- Parsable but malformed messages that do not follow the SET Protocol message format requirements
- Illegal values for message components
- Failures in cryptography

SET states that *Error* messages should only be used for low-level processing errors on SET request messages. The ErrorCode component of the *Error* message can contain any of the values shown in Table 11.1.

Table 11.1 ErrorCode Values for SET *Error* Message

ErrorCode Value	Description
unspecifiedFailure	Used when no other failure condition can be identified.
messageNotSupported	Message type is not supported by the recipient. This could occur if a Cardholder E-wallet accidentally received a message intended for a Payment Gateway.
decodingFailure	Error detected on the DER encoding process on a message.
invalidCertificate	A certificate needed for message processing was deemed invalid.
expiredCertificate	A certificate needed for message processing was deemed expired.

Table 11.1 (continued)

revokedCertificate	A certificate needed for message processing was deemed revoked.
missingCertificate	A certificate needed for message processing was not included in the message.
signatureFailure	Digital signature for the message could not be verified.
badMessageHeader	Message Header could not be processed by the recipient.
wrapperMsgMismatch	The contents of the message wrapper are inconsistent with the internal contents of the message. For example, the Request/Response Pair ID does not match.
versionTooOld	Version number of the message is too old for the recipient to process.
versionTooNew	Version number of the message is too new for the recipient to process.
unrecognizedExtension	A message or a certificate contains an extension that the recipient cannot process.
messageTooBig	Message size is too large for the recipient to process.
signatureRequired	An unsigned version of the request message is not valid.
messageTooOld	The date on the message indicates that it's too old to process.
messageTooNew	The date on the message indicates that it's too new to process.

thumbsMismatch	The thumbprints sent within an unsigned message do not match the thumbprints returned to a requester that's checking for message substitution attack.
unknownRRPID	An unknown Request/Response Pair ID was received.
unknownLID	An unknown Local ID was received.
unknownXID	An unknown Transaction ID was received.
challengeMismatch	A challenge sent in a request message does not match the challenge in the response message. Indicates a failure of a freshness challenge for a message.

In this chapter we've seen how SET defines several normal and optional flow processes that implement payment card transaction processing and certificate management services.

All the messages described here consist of several components, and often several layers of components, representing information that's needed at processing time. Detailed descriptions of these message pairs are found in Chapter 12, arranged alphabetically by message-pair name.

SET MESSAGE PAIRS

12

SET's implementation relies on pairs of Request/Response messages between end-entities to accomplish useful work. SET enables the insecure Internet to *behave as though* it's the same type of private virtual network that banks use for POS transactions. These message pairs are, in fact, the same operations that POS terminal and Acquirer payment systems perform, only SET first "wraps" them up so securely in cryptography as to render them indistinguishable from gibberish, except to the intended recipient. As these messages travel over the open communication channels of the Internet, it behaves as a virtual private network between the sender and receiver. This security rivals that of the private leased-line networks in use today.

While the mechanics of these message pairs may not seem critical to understand, many of the data elements contained in these messages will use your Merchant Server and/or back-office accounting systems as their source or their destination. To help you build interfaces to those systems, it's vital to understand the mapping between your legacy systems and your SET POS System.

In Chapter 11, we mapped out SET's protocols by looking at how message pairs are exchanged by end-entities. In this chapter, we'll take a look at the details of each SET message pair. These messages, arranged alphabetically, are described along these dimensions:

- Identifier—name of the message pair
- Purpose—uses for the message pair
- Protocol involved—reference to Chapter 11 protocol that contains the message pair

- Request portion components—formats and content of the request message

- Response portion components—formats and content of the response message

The goal of this chapter is not to offer a comprehensive look at the cryptography that's used within SET messages. Those alone could fill a book. Rather, the goal is to help you understand what each message pair does and how the messages implement POS System–like functionality for payment card processing.

Readers with a further interest in SET-specific applications of cryptography are encouraged to refer to SET Specification Book 3 (Formal Protocol Definition). You can obtain copies at the Visa or MasterCard Web sites. Values for some message fields will vary by payment card Brand. Consult your bank's Merchant Services Department and your Acquirer for their specific requirements prior to configuring your systems.

SET Message Pair Overview

Arranged in alphabetical order, below you'll find the details for each SET message pair. For a review of the message notations and conventions, please refer to Chapter 5.

Components often recur from one SET message to another. Some of these components represent data structures, control structures, and other common conventions used within SET.

Common Data Components and Structures

For the message pairs defined in the main portion of this chapter, you may see some of these components often. Rather than bog down the details of each message description, those recurring components are defined here, listed in alphabetical order.

AcqCardMsg. A mechanism that permits Payment Gateways to send a message back to the Cardholder without allowing the Merchant to see the contents. This is used to implement the concept of *tunneling* information between the Issuer and the Cardholder. This is an optional field in SET. Its use is defined by the policies contained in the Payment Gateway Encryption Certificate.

Amount Fields. Amounts in SET transactions are expressed using a structure of three fields: currency, amount, and amtExp10. They appear in that specific order separated by commas. Currency is a three-digit code defined by ISO 4217. Amount is a numeric ASCII string representing the amount of payment in the stated currency. amtExp10 defines the decimal position for the payment amount. For example, to represent $100 in U.S. currency, the PurchAmt field would read: 840 (code for U.S. dollars), 10000, -2 (moves decimal point two places to the left).

AuthToken. Contains data that's required by the Payment Gateway for subsequent authorizations for a transaction. Used for split shipments of goods or recurring charges.

BatchStatus. Component used to return the status of a batch of transactions to the Merchant or to reconcile the value of a batch of transactions between the Merchant and the Payment Gateway.

CapPayload. Contains data that's required by the Payment Gateway to capture a previously authorized transaction at batch settlement time. It's generated by the Payment Gateway and passed back to the Merchant in an AuthRes message.

CapToken. Contains data that's required by the Payment Gateway to capture a previously authorized transaction at batch settlement time. It's generated by the Payment Gateway and passed back to the Merchant in an AuthRes message.

Date Fields. Dates are represented under SET in the form:

```
YYYYMMDDHHMM[SS[.f[.f[.f]]]]Z
```

where:

YYYY is the four-digit year

MM is the two-digit month

DD is the two-digit day

MM is the two-digit minute

SS is the optional number of seconds

.f are the optional fractions of seconds

Z is the literal "Z" that ends the character string

A simple example of Jan 1 1999 at noon would read: 199901011200Z

InstallRecurData. Used in authorizing installment payments or recurring charges as dictated in the PI AuthToken component.

OIData. Order Information data that's common to both forms of Purchase Request messages (dual signed and unsigned). It contains Order Description (OD) data that are exchanged between the Merchant and the Cardholder out-of-band to SET. This information will typically include goods ordered, quantity, size, price, shipping address information, Cardholder's billing address, and so on. OIData will also contain the amount of the transaction agreed upon by the Cardholder and various other components.

PANData. Contains the data that identifies a specific payment card account number. Its structure is such that it may be broken apart and superencrypted as separate components.

PANToken. Used in instances where superencryption of Payment Account Number (PAN) data is not a requirement for blinding the data from the Merchant.

PI (Payment Instructions). The most sensitive data structure under SET. It implements the concept of Dual Signatures (see Chapter 5) to hide the payment account number (PAN) from the Merchant, while allowing the Payment Gateway to process the authorization request sent by the Merchant using the hidden data that only the Payment Gateway can decipher.

There are three versions of PI:

- *Unsigned.* Created by Cardholder without signature certificates. Used within a PReqUnsigned message (see PReq/PRes).

- *DualSigned.* Created by the Cardholder using signature certificate. Used for PReqSigned messages (see PReq/PRes).

- *AuthToken.* Used to support split shipments of goods that require subsequent authorizations each time another shipment is to occur. An example of use might include purchase of a series of Time/Life Books, where the payment card is charged for each separate volume in the series.

RRTags. Contain request-response (RR) message identification data that serve as a unique identifier for a message pair.

SaleDetail. Contains all sale-related data for a transaction. It's generated in the settlement process between the Merchant and the Payment Gateway. The uses of the Sale Detail fields are dictated by the card brands, not by the SET Specification itself.

TransIDs. Unique transaction identifiers that enable a payment system participant (end-entity) to tag every message used within a complete transaction. All message pairs involved in the transaction will share the same unique ID, thus serving as an aid to audit trails for transactions.

TransactionDetail. Provides the details needed by the Merchant Server to reconcile a batch of transactions submitted to the Payment Gateway. The Payment Gateway returns these transaction details for a given batch when requested to do so by the Merchant Server.

SET Message Pair Definitions

Listed in alphabetical order, you'll find 17 SET message pairs that are used to implement POS System–like functionality or certificate management services. Boldface type indicates the message notation (from Chapter 5) and the top-level components to each message. Dots (.) are used to indicate nesting levels.

Authorization Request/Response Pair: AuthReq/AuthRes

Table 12.1 describes the Authorization Request/Response message pair. These are used by Merchants to obtain the authorization for a sale from a Payment Gateway. They're used for both authorization-only transactions (with a later capture request) and for authorization with capture (sale) transactions where permitted by Acquirer rules.

Merchant POS software creates an AuthReq using data about the purchase, signs it, encrypts it, combines it with the Payment Instructions (PI) component from the Cardholder, and forwards it to the Payment Gateway for processing and response. This message pair is found in Figure 11.4 (illustrating normal purchase flow).

Table 12.1 AuthReq/AuthRes Message Pair

Request Portion: AuthRes	Message Contents EncB(M, P, AuthReqData, PI)
where:	
AuthReqData	{ AuthReqItem, [Mthumbs], CaptureNow, [SaleDetail] }
.AuthReqItem	{ AuthTags, [CheckDigests], AuthReqPayload }
..AuthTags	{ AuthRRTags, TransIDs, [AuthRetNum] }
...AuthRRTags	RRTags. See beginning of Chapter 12 for common components.
...TransIDs	Copied from Order Information Data (OIData).
...AuthRetNum	Identification of authorization request used within the financial network.
..CheckDigests	Hashes of the Order Information Data computed twice, once by the Cardholder

.	and once by the Merchant; used by the Payment Gateway to compare and verify the linkage between Payment Instructions and Order Information.
..AuthReqPayload	{ SubsequentAuthInd, AuthReqAmt, [AVS-Data], [SpecialProcessing], [CardSuspect], RequestCardTypeInd, [InstallRecurData], [MarketSpecAuthData], MerchData, [ARqExtensions] }
...SubsequentAuthInd	Boolean expression indicating that Merchant requires additional authorizations due to split shipments.
...AuthReqAmt	Authorization request amount. May differ from PurchAmt because of taxes, shipping fees, etc.
...AVSData	{ [StreetAddress], Location }
....StreetAddress	Mailing address of the Cardholder.
....Location	Location data from SaleDetail component; includes country code, city name, state or province, postal code, and a location code for a Merchant.
...SpecialProcessing	Boolean expression indicating any type of special processing requested from the Payment Gateway.
...CardSuspect	An enumerated code that indicates that the Merchant is suspicious of the Cardholder data along with the reason for the suspicion.
...RequestCardTypeInd	Indicates that the Merchant is requesting the type of card being used and wishes it returned in the response message from the Payment Gateway.

Table 12.1 (continued)

...InstallRecurData	See beginning of chapter for common components.
...MarketSpecAuthData	Market-specific authorization data (hotel, car rental, etc.).
...MerchData	{ [MerchCatCode], [MerchGroup] }
....MerchCatCode	4-byte code describing Merchant's type of business, products, or service. Defined by ANSI X9.10.
....MerchGroup	Numeric code identifying the general category of the Merchant.
.MThumbs	Thumbprints of certificates, CRLs, and CRL Identifiers held by Merchant cache.
.CaptureNow	Boolean expression indicating that a capture should be performed if the authorization is approved.
.SaleDetail	See beginning of chapter for common components.
PI	See beginning of chapter for common components.

Response Portion:	**Message Contents**
AuthRes (two forms: only one or the other is used in a transaction)	< EncB(P, M, AuthResData, AuthResBaggage), EncBX(P, M, AuthResData, AuthResBaggage, PANToken >
AuthResData	{ AuthTags, [BrandCRLIdentifier], [PEThumb], AuthResPayload }

where:

.AuthTags	Copied from corresponding AuthReq; see beginning of chapter for common components.
.BrandCRLIdentifier	List of current CRLs for all CAs under the brand.
.PEThumb	Thumbprint of Payment Gateway certificate is indicated as required by Merchant.
.AuthResPayload	{ AuthHeader, [CapResPayload], [ARsExtensions] }
..AuthHeader	{ AuthAmt, AuthCode, ResponseData, [BatchStatus], [CurrConv] }
...AuthAmt	Copied from AuthReq Payload authorization amount.
...AuthCode	Numeric code indicating the result of the request processing.
...ResponseData	{ [AuthValCodes], [RespReason], [CardType], [AVSResult], [LogRefID] }
....AuthValCodes	{ [ApprovalCode], [AuthCharInd], [ValidationCode], [MarketSpecDataID] }
.....ApprovalCode	Approval code assigned to the transaction by the Card Issuer.
.....AuthCharInd	Numeric code indicating the conditions under which the authorization was performed.
.....ValidationCode	4-byte code computed to ensure that the required fields in the authorization messages also appear in their subsequent clearing messages.
.....MarketSpecDataID	Numeric code that indicates the type of market-specific data supplied on the authorization as determined by the financial network.

Table 12.1 (continued)

....RespReason	Numeric code that identifies the authorization service entity and reason for decline if authorization was declined.
....CardType	Numeric code indicating the type of card used in the authorization.
....AVSResult	Numeric Address Verification Service response code.
....LogRefID	Alphanumeric data assigned to the authorization to match with a reversal if requested.
...BatchStatus	See beginning of chapter for common components.
...CurrConv	{ CurrConvRate, CardCurr }
....CurrConvRate	Currency conversion rate to multiply by the AuthReqAmt to convert to the currency used by the Cardholder.
....CardCurr	Currency code for the Cardholder as defined by ISO 4217.
..CapResPayload	See CapRes message for details.
..ARsExtensions	Extended data used only for processing authorization response or a subsequent authorization reversal or capture request.
AuthResBaggage	{ [CapToken], [AcqCardMsg], [AuthToken] }
.CapToken	See beginning of chapter for common components.
.AcqCardMsg	See beginning of chapter for common components.

| .AuthToken | See beginning of chapter for common components. |
| **PANToken** | See beginning of chapter for common components. |

Once an authorization request is processed, the result may be:

- Approved
- Declined
- Conditionally declined

A conditional decline, also called a referral, is indicated as a "callIssuer" response in the AuthCode field of the AuthRes message. Merchant software may allow the operator to enter an approval code to convert it into an approved authorization, or the Merchant may be requested to call the Issuer out-of-band using the telephone. With this phone call, a Merchant may be given an approval code to proceed with the transaction, which would be entered directly into the POS software.

AuthReq/AuthRes are used in Phase 5 of the on-line payment transaction, described in Chapter 2. This message pair, with its use of cryptography and dual signatures, represents one of the most complex of those found within SET.

Authorization Reversal Request/Response: AuthRevReq/AuthRevRes

Table 12.2 describes the Authorization Reversal message pair. It's used to reduce or cancel a previously approved authorization response (AuthRes). The use of this message pair is optional under SET. It can be sent by the Merchant to a Payment Gateway anytime after an approved authorization, but before the capture step for that transaction. It may be used to change an authorized amount or remove it entirely. It can also be used to split a previously unsplit order, as might occur with a back-order situation.

When a Merchant realizes that a shipment cannot be made in its entirety, he can use an AuthRevReq to split the order, with the new authorization amount representing the total value of the goods he's able to ship, and any subsequent authorizations representing the value of the order balance.

This message pair is found in Figure 11.5 (Other payment system message flows, Part One).

Table 12.2 AuthRevReq/AuthRevRes

Request Portion:	Message Contents
AuthRevReq	EncB(M, P, AuthRevReqData, AuthRevReqBaggage)
AuthRevReqData	{ AuthRevTags, [MThumbs], [AuthReqData], [AuthResPayload], AuthNewAmt,[ArvRqExtensions] }
where:	
.AuthRevTags	[AuthRevRRTags, [AuthRetNum] }
..AuthRevRRTags	RRTags. See beginning of Chapter 12 for common components.
..AuthRetNum	Identification of the authorization request used for the financial network.
.MThumbs	Thumbprints of certificates, CRLs, and CRL Identifiers held in the Merchant's cache.
.AuthReqData	Copied from previous corresponding AuthReq message. See AuthReq/AuthRes message pair.
.AuthResPayload	Copied from previous corresponding AuthRes message. See AuthReq/AuthRes message pair.
.AuthNewAmt	New authorization amount requested by the Merchant; a value of zero indicates a complete reversal of the previous approved authorization request.

.ArvRqExtensions	Extended data that's related to an authorization reversal process as indicated by the financial institution.
AuthRevReqBaggage	{ PI, [CapToken] }
.PI	See beginning of chapter for common components.
.CapToken	See beginning of chapter for common components.

Response Portion:	**Message Contents**
AuthRevRes (two forms: Encapsulation and Encapsulation with extra Baggage, depending on whether request is for full or partial reversal	<EncB(P, M, AuthRevResData, AuthRevResBaggage), Enc(P, M, AuthRevResData) >

where:

AuthRevResData	{ AuthRevCode, AuthRevTags, [BrandCRL Identifier], [PEThumb], AuthNewAmt, AuthResDataNew, [ARvRsExtensions] }
.AuthRevCode	Numeric code indicating the outcome of authorization reversal processing.
.AuthRevTags	Copied from corresponsing AuthRevReq message.
.BrandCRLIdentifier	List of current CRLs for all CAs within the Brand.
.PEThumb	Thumbprint of Payment Gateway certificate if Merchant had indicated the need for one.
.AuthNewAmt	Copied from corresponding AuthRevReq message.

Table 12.2 (continued)

.AuthResDataNew	{ TransIDs, [AuthResPayloadNew] }
..TransIDs	Copied from corresponding AuthRevReq message.
..AuthResPayloadNew	If AuthAmtNew is not zero, the Payment Gateway creates a new instance of AuthResData and places the AuthResPayload component here. See AuthReq/AuthRes message pair.
.ArvRsExtensions	Extended data that's related to an authorization reversal process as indicated by the financial institution.
AuthRevResBaggage	**{ [CapTokenNew], [AuthTokenNew] }**
.CapTokenNew	New capture token with updated fields that replaces the previous CapToken when the AuthNewAmt is not zero.
.AuthTokenNew	New authorization token with updated fields that replaces the previous AuthToken when the AuthNewAmt is not zero. Merchant uses this as the PI component in subsequent AuthReq messages, as needed for split shipments.

AuthRevReq/AuthRevRes are used in Phase 5 of the on-line payment transaction, described in Chapter 2.

Batch Administration Request/Response: BatchAdminReq/BatchAdminRes

Table 12.3 describes the Batch Administration Request/Response message pair. Batch Administration Requests, sent from the Merchant to the Payment Gateway, are used to administer batches of transactions awaiting capture. Instructions might indicate to open a new batch, purge a batch, close a batch, transfer a copy of the batch contents, or return the status of the batch. The response portion of the message indicates the completion status for the request, along with the results, if any. The protocol that covers the use of BatchAdminReq/BatchAdminRes is shown in Figure 11.7 (Gateway Certificate Request and Batch Administration message flows).

Table 12.3 BatchAdminReq/BatchAdminRes

Request Portion:	Message Contents
BatchAdminReq	Enc(M, P, BatchAdminReqData)
BatchAdminReqData	{ BatchAdminRRTags, [BatchID], [BrandAndBINSeq], [BatchOperation], ReturnBatchSummaryInd, [ReturnTransactionDetail], [BatchStatus], [TransDetails], {BARqExtensions] }
where:	
.BatchAdminRRTags	RRTags (fresh RRPID and Date). See beginning of chapter for common components.
.BatchID	Identification of the batch for Merchant and Acquirer accounting purposes.
.BrandAndBINSeq	{ BrandAndBIN + }
..BrandAndBIN	{ BrandID, [BIN] }
...BrandID	Payment card brand ID without product type.
...BIN	Bank Identification Number needed for processing of the Merchant's transactions by the Acquirer.
.BatchOperation	Numeric value indicating the activity to be performed on the batch (values are not defined by SET).

Table 12.3 (continued)

.ReturnBatchSummaryInd	Indicator that instructs the Payment Gateway to return batch summary data in BatchReqRes message.
.ReturnTransactionDetail	{ StartingPoint, MaximumItems, ErrorsOnlyInd, [BrandID} } If BrandID is specified, only those transactions for the identifed brand are returned.
..StartingPoint	If nonzero, this number represents the NextStartingPoint value from a previous BatchAdminRes. If zero, it indicates to send the detail of the first group of transaction details.
..MaximumItems	A number representing the maximum number of transaction details to return in the group.
..ErrorOnlyInd	Boolean expression to indicate if error-only transactions are returned in this group.
..BrandID	Payment card brand ID without product type.
.BatchStatus	See beginning of chapter for common components.
.TransDetails	{ NextStartingPoint, TransactionDetailSeq }
..NextStartingPoint	A zero indicates that the group of transactions returned with the last BatchAdminRes is the last of the batch. Opaque values are otherwise placed there by the Payment Gateway to be copied into the next BatchAdminReq message from the Merchant.
..TransactionDetailSeq	{ TransactionDetail + }

...TransactionDetail	See beginning of chapter for common components.
.BARqExtensions	Extended data that may be used for batch administration purposes.
Response Portion:	**Message Contents**
BatchAdminRes	Enc(P, M, BatchAdminResData)
BatchAdminResData	{ BatchAdminTags, BatchID, [BAStatus], [BatchStatus], [TransmissionStatus], [SettlementInfo], [TransDetails], [BARsExtensions] }

where:

.BatchAdminTags	RRTags, copied from previous BatchAdminReq message.
.BatchID	Identification of the batch for Merchant and Acquirer accounting purposes.
.BAStatus	Numeric code indicating status of batch open.
.BatchStatus	See beginning of chapter for common components.
.TransmissionStatus	Numeric code indicating the status of the transmission from the payment gateway to the next upstream system.
.SettlementInfo	{ SettlementAmount, SettlementType, SettlementAccount, SettlementDepositDate }
..SettlementAmount	The net settlement amount for the Merchant's account.
..SettlementType	Numeric code indicating the type of settlement.
..SettlementAccount	The Merchant account number to be settled.

Table 12.3 (continued)

..SettlementDepositDate	The date that the Merchant's account will be credited or debited with SettlementAmount.
.TransDetails	{ NextStartingPoint, TransactionDetailSeq }
..NextStartingPoint	A zero indicates that this group of transactions returned is the last of the batch. Opaque values are otherwise placed here by the Payment Gateway to be copied into the next BatchAdminReq message from the Merchant.
..TransactionDetailSeq	{ TransactionDetail + }
...TransactionDetail	See beginning of chapter for common components.
.BARqExtensions	Extended data that may be used for batch administration purposes.

BatchAdminReq/BatchAdminRes are used in Phase 8 of the on-line payment transaction to correct discrepancies between record-keeping systems, as described in Chapter 2.

Capture Request/Response: CapReq/CapRes

Table 12.4 defines the Capture Request/Response message pair. These messages are sent from the Merchant to the Payment Gateway to complete those transactions having a previous successful authorization response. This message pair may be found in Figures 11.4 and Figure 11.5 (Normal purchase flow, and Other payment system message flows, Part One).

Table 12.4 CapReq/CapRes

Request Portion:	Message Contents
CapReq (two forms: Encapsulated with extra baggage if PANToken is required)	< EncB(M, P, CapReqData, CapTokenSeq), EncBX(M, P, CapReqData, CapTokenSeq, PanToken) >

CapReqData	{ CapRRTags, [Mthumbs], CapItemSeq, [CRqExtensions] }

where:

.CapRRTags	RRTags. Fresh RRPID and Date. See beginning of chapter for common components.
.MThumbs	Thumbprints of certificates, CRLs, and CRL Identifiers currently held in the Merchant's cache.
.CapItemSeq	{ CapItem + }
..CapItem	[TransIDs, AuthRRPID, CapPayload }
...TransIDs	Copied from corresponding AuthRes or AuthRevRes message.
...AuthRRPID	RRPID copied from corresponding AuthReq or AuthRevReq.
...CapPayload	{ CapDate, CapReqAmt, [AuthReqItem], [AuthResPayload], [SaleDetail], [CPayExtensions] }
....CapDate	Date of capture that will appear on Cardholder's billing statement.
....CapReqAmt	Capture amount being requested by the Merchant.
....AuthReqItem	See AuthReq message for details.
....AuthResPayload	See AuthReq message for details.
....SaleDetail	See beginning of chapter for common components.
....CPayExtensions	Extended financial data related to individual items in the capture request.
.CRqExtensions	Extended financial data related to the entire sequence of capture request items.

Table 12.4 (continued)

CapTokenSeq	{ [CapToken] + }
CapToken	See beginning of chapter for common components.
PANToken	See beginning of chapter for common components.
Response Portion:	**Message Contents**
CapRes	Enc(P, M, CapResData)
CapResData	{ CapRRTags, [BrandCRLIdentifier], [PEThumb], [BatchStatusSeq], CapResItemSeq, [CRsExtensions] }

where:

.CapRRTags	RRTags, copied from CapReq message.
.BrandCRLIdentifier	List of current CRLs for all Brand CAs.
.PEThumb	Payment Gateway certificate thumbprint if Merchant indicates the need for a copy.
.BatchStatusSeq	{ BatchStatus + }
..BatchStatus	See beginning of chapter for common components.
.CapResItemSeq	{ CapResItem + }
..CapResItem	{ TransIDs, AuthRRPID, CapResPayload }
...TransIDs	Copied from previous CapReq.
...AuthRRPID	RRPID copied from corresponding CapReq.
...CapResPayload	{ CapCode, CapAmt, [BatchID], [BatchSequenceNum}, {CRsPayExtensions] }
....CapCode	Numeric code indicating the status of the capture.

....CapAmt	Copied from corresponsing CapReq message.
....BatchID	Identification of the settlement batch for accounting purposes. Copied from corresponding CapReq message.
....BatchSequenceNum	Sequence number of the item within the batch. Copied from corresponding CapReq message.
....CRsPayExtensions	Extended financial data related to individual items in the capture response.
.CRsExtensions	Extended financial data related to the entire sequence of capture request items.

Return values defined for CapCode are:

success, unspecifiedFailure, duplicateRequest, authExpired, authDataMissing, invalidAuthData, capTokenMissing, invalidCapToken, batchUnknown, batchClosed, unknownXid, unknownLID

CapReq/CapRes are used in Phase 8 of the on-line payment transaction, as described in Chapter 2.

Capture Reversal Request/Response: CapRevReq/CapRevRes

Table 12.5 defines the Capture Reversal Request and Response messages, sent from the Merchant to a Payment Gateway, to reverse a previously successful Capture Request. These may be used to cancel a captured sale where a customer has changed her mind before accepting delivery of goods, or has returned those goods within a certain (short) period of time following the sale. When a Capture Reverse cannot be used (after a period of time subsequent to original capture), the Credit Request/Response pair may be used instead. This message pair may be found in Figure 11.5 (Other payment system message flows, Part One).

Table 12.5 CapRevReq/CapRevRes

Request Portion:	Message Contents
CapRevReq (two forms: Encapsulated with extra baggage if PANToken is required)	< EncB(M, P, CapRevData, CapTokenSeq), EncBX(M, P, CapRevData, CapTokenSeq, PANToken) >
where:	
CapRevData	CapRevOrCredReqData
.CapRevOrCredReqData	{ CapRevOrCredRRTags, [MThumbs], CapRevOrCredReqItemSeq, [CRvRqExtensions] }
.. CapRevOrCredRRTags	RRTags. Fresh RRPID and Date. See beginning of chapter for common components.
..MThumbs	Thumbprints of certificates, CRLs, and CRL Identifiers currently held in the Merchant's cache.
..CapRevOrCredReqItemSeq	{ CapRevOrCredReqItem + }
... CapRevOrCredReqItem	{ TransIDs, AuthRRPID, CapPayload, [NewBatchID], CapRevOrCredReqDate, [CapRevOrCredReqAmt], NewAccountInd, [CRvRqItemExtensions] }
....TransIDs	Copied from corresponding CapRes.
....AuthRRPID	Request-response pair ID copied from corresponding AuthReq or AuthRevReq.
....CapPayload	{ CapDate, CapReqAmt, [AuthReqItem], [AuthResPayload], [SaleDetail], [CPayExtensions] }
.....CapDate	Date of capture that will appear on Cardholder's billing statement.

.....CapReqAmt	Capture amount being requested by the Merchant.
.....AuthReqItem	See AuthReq message for details.
.....AuthResPayload	See AuthReq message for details.
.....SaleDetail	See beginning of chapter for common components.
.....CPayExtensions	Extended financial data related to individual items in the capture reversal request.
....NewBatchID	Specifies a new batch ID number used for reversal requests for items submitted in a batch that was already closed. BatchID in CapPayload identifies the original batch ID number.
....CapRevOrCredReqDate	The date of the request.
....CapRevOrCredReqAmt	Capture reversal or credit request amount.
....NewAccountInd	Indicates that a new account number is present in PANToken. If this information is present, it will override the account information from the coresponding CaptureToken. Use of this is subject to Acquirer and brand policies.
....CRvRqItemExtensions	Extended financial data related to individual items in the capture reversal request.
CapTokenSeq	{ [CapToken] + }
CapToken	See beginning of chapter for common components.
PANToken	See beginning of chapter for common components.

Table 12.5 (continued)

Response Portion:	Message Contents
CapRevRes	Enc(P, M, CapRevResData)
where:	
CapRevResData	CapRevOrCredResData
.CapRevOrCredResData	{ CapRevOrCredRRTags, [BrandCRLIdentifier], [PEThumb], [BatchStatusSeq], CapRevOrCredResItemSeq, [CrvRsExtensions] }
..CapRevOrCredRRTags	RRTags. Copy of CapRevOrCredRRTags from corresponding CapRevReq.
..BrandCRLIdentifier	List of current CRLs for all CAs within the Brand ID.
..PEThumb	Thumbprint of Payment Gateway certificate is provided if Merchant indicates the need for one.
..BatchStatusSeq	{ BatchStatus + }
...BatchStatus	See beginning of chapter for common components.
..CapRevOrCredResItemSeq	{ CapRevOrCredResItem + }
...CapRevOrCredResItem	{ TransIDs, AuthRRPID, CapRevOrCredResPayload }
....TransIDs	Copied from corresponding CapRevOrCredReqData.AuthReqData.AuthTags.
....AuthRRPID	RRPID from corresponding AuthReq or AuthRevReq.
....CapRevOrCredResPayload	{ CapRevOrCredCode, CapRevOrCredActualAmt, [BatchID], {BatchSequenceNum}, [CrvRsPayExtensions] }

.....CapRevOrCredCode	Number indicating cature reversal or credit status.
.....CapRevOrCredActualAmt	Copied from the corresponding CapRevOrCredReqItem.
.....BatchID	ID number of the settlement batch for accounting purposes.
.....BatchSequenceNum	Sequence number of the item within the BatchID.
.....CRvRsPayExtensions	Extended financial data related to individual items in the capture reversal request.
CrvRsExtensions	Extended financial data related to the entire in the capture reversal request.

CapRevReq/CapRevRes are used to reverse work that was performed earlier during Phase 8 of the on-line payment transaction, as described in Chapter 2.

Card Certificate Initialization Request/Response: CardCInitReq/CardCInitRes

Table 12.6 describes the Cardholder Certificate Initialization Request and Response message pair. These messages begin the process of a Cardholder Certificate Request. They're sent between Cardholder E-wallets and Cardholder CAs (CCAs). The protocol that contains this message pair may be found in Figure 11.1.

Table 12.6 CardCInitReq/CardCInitRes

Request Portion:	Message Contents
CardCInitReq	{ RRPID, LID-EE, Chall-EE, BrandID, [Thumbs] }
where:	
RRPID	Request/Response pair ID

Table 12.6 (continued)

LID-EE	Local ID that's generated by the Cardholder's system.
Chall-EE	Challenge by the Cardholder to the freshness of the CCA's signature.
BrandID	BrandID of the certificate requested.
Thumbs	List of certificate, CRL, and CRL Identifier thumbprints already held by the Cardholder (if present these will cut down the number of certificates the CCA returns to the Cardholder's E-wallet).
Response Portion:	**Message Contents**
CardCInitRes	**S (CA, CardInitResTBS)**
CardCInitResTBS	{ RRPID, LID-EE, Chall-EE, [LID-CA], CAEThumb, [BrandCRLIdentifier], [Thumbs] }
where:	
.RRPID	Request/Response pair ID.
.LID-EE	Copied from previous CardCInitReq.
.Chall-EE	Copied from previous CardCInitReq.
.LID-CA	Local ID that's generated by the CCA for its use.
.CAEThumb	Thumbprint of CCA Key-Exchange Certificate that Cardholder will use to encrypt the data in the Registration Form in the ReFormReq message.
.BrandCRLIdentifier	Separate structure defined by SET to identify the list of known CRLs for the Brand

	(see Chapter 7) and maintained by the Brand CA (BCA).
.Thumbs	Copied from previous CardCInitReq. CardCInitReq/CardCInitRes are used by Cardholders to prepare for Phase 0 of the on-line payment card transaction, as discussed in Chapter 2.

Certificate Request/Response: CertReq/CertRes

Table 12.7 describes the Certificate Request and Response message pair. This pair is used by all end-entities in the last phase of certificate issuance and renewal processing. It appears in Figures 11.1, 11.2, and 11.3 as the final step for requesting the completed certificate from any Certificate Authority.

Table 12.7 CertReq/CertRes

Request Portion:	Message Contents
CertReq (two forms: EncX used where AcctInfo is present)	< EncX(EE, CA, CertReqData, AcctInfo), Enc(EE, CA, CertReqdata) >
where:	
CertReqData	{ RRPID, LID-EE, Chall-EE3, [LID-CA], [Chall-CA], RequestType, RequestDate, [IDData], RegFormID, [RegForm], [CaBackKeyData], PublicKeySorE, [EEThumb], [Thumbs] }
.RRPID	Request-response pair ID number.
.LID-EE	Copied from corresponding RegFormRes or Me-AqCInitRes.
.Chall-EE3	End entity's challenge to CA signature freshness.

Table 12.7 (continued)

.LID-CA	Copied from corresponding RegFormRes or Me-AqCInitRes.
.Chall-CA	Copied from corresponding RegFormRes or Me-AqCInitRes.
.RequestType	See Table 12.8 for RequestType possible values.
.RequestDate	Date of this certificate request.
.IDData (omitted by Cardholders)	< MerchantAcquirerID, AcquirerID >
..MerchantAcquirerID	{ MerchantBIN, MerchantID }
...MerchantBIN	Bank Identification Number used to process the Merchant's transaction at the Acquiring Bank or card company. Used for Merchant certificate requests.
...MerchantID	Merchant number assigned by the Acquirer. Used for Merchant certificate requests.
..AcquirerID	{ AcquirerBIN, [AcquirerBusinessID] }
...AcquirerBIN	Bank Identification Number for the Acquirer requesting a certificate.
...AcquirerBusinessID	Business Identification Code for the Acquirer requesting a certificate.
.RegFormID	Assigned number by the CA.
.RegForm	{ RegFormItems + } These are the field names copied from the corresponding RegFormRes or Me-AqCInitRes messages, now filled in with values supplied by the end-entity.

..RegFormItems	{ FieldName, FieldValue }
...FieldName	One or more of the registration form field names that appeared on the RegFormRes or Me-AqCInitRes.
	One or more of the registration form field values now entered by the end-entity from the RegFormRes or Me-AqCInitiRes.
.CABackKeyData	{ CAAlgId, CAKey }
..CAAlgId	Symmetric key algorithm identifier.
..CAKey	Secret key associated with the algorithm above.
.PublicKeySorE	{ [PublicKeyS], [PublicKeyE] }
..PublicKeyS	Proposed public signature key to certify.
..PublicKeyE	Proposed public encryption key to certify.
.EEThumb	Thumbprint of entity's key encryption certificate that is being renewed (for renewal requests only).
.Thumbs	List of certificates (including Root), CRL, and BrandCRLIdentifiers currently held in cache by the end-entity.
AcctInfo	< PANData0, AcctData >
.PANData0	{ PAN, CardExpiry, CardSecret, EXNonce }
..PAN	Primary Account Number. This is typically the account number on the payment card.
..CardExpiry	Expiration date on the payment card.
..CardSecret	Cardholder's proposed half of the shared secret, PANSecret.

Table 12.7 (continued)

..EXNonce	A fresh nonce to foil dictionary attacks on PANData0.
.AcctData	{ AcctIdentification, EXNonce }
..AcctIdentification	Merchant ID assigned by the Acquirer if request is from a Merchant. Unique Acquirer ID assigned by the payment card brand if request is for an Acquirer.
..EXNonce	A fresh nonce to foil dictionary attacks on AcctIdentification.
Response Portion:	**Message Contents**
CertRes. Two forms. Second form is used for Cardholder, first form for others.	< S(CA, CertResData), EncK(CABackKeyData, CA, CertResData) >
where:	
CertResData	{ RRPID, LID-EE, Chall-EE3, LID-CA, CertStatus, [CertThumbs], [BrandCRLIdentifier], [Thumbs} }
.RRPID	Request-response pair ID.
.LID-EE	Copied from prior CertReq.
.Chall-EE3	Copied from prior CertReq. Requestor will check for a match with previously stored value.
.LID-CA	Copied from prior CertReq.
.CertStatus	{ CertStatusCode, [Nonce-CCA], [EEMessage], [CAMsg], [FailedItemSeq] }

..CertStatusCode	See Table 12.9 for Certificate Status Codes.
..Nonce-CCA	If a Cardholder request is complete, this will contain the other half of the shared secret between the Cardholder and the Cardholder Certificate Authority. Not used by other end-entites.
..EEMessage	Message from the CA that will be displayed on the end-entity's system.
..CAMsg (for completed Cardholder requests only)	{ [CardLogoURL], [BrandLogoURL], [CardCurrency], [CardholderMsg] }
...CardLogoURL	URL for the card logo artwork (specific to an issuer).
...BrandLogoURL	URL for the payment card brand logo.
...CardCurrency	Currency for Cardholder billing purposes.
...CardholderMsg	A message for the Cardholder that will be displayed on Cardholder's system.
..FailedItemSeq	{ FailedItem + }
...FailedItem	{ ItemNumber, ItemReason }
....ItemNumber	Indicates the position of the field from the registration form that failed verification.
....ItemReason	A text description of the reason for the failure of ItemNumber above.
.CertThumbs	Thumbprints of the enclosed signature or encryption certificate if response is complete.
.BrandCRLIdentifier	BCIs for the brand.
.Thumbs	Copied from corresponding CertReq.
CABackKeyData	Copied from corresponding CertReq.

CertReq/CertRes are used by all end-entities to prepare for Phase 0 of the on-line payment card transaction, as discussed in Chapter 2.

Table 12.8 lists the values for the RequestType tuple in the CertReq message.

Table 12.8 RequestType Codes for CertReq Message

Request Type	Signature-Only Certificate	Encryption Certificate Only	Both Certificates
Cardholder Initial	1	2*	3*
Cardholder Renewal	10	11*	12*
Merchant Initial	4	5	6
Payment Gateway Initial	7	8	9
Merchant Renewal	13	14	15
Payment Gateway Renewal	16	17	18

Options that are reserved for future versions of SET.

Table 12.9 indicates the CertStatus Code possible values, along with their meanings and the source of the completion code.

Table 12.9 Certificate Request Status Codes

CertStatus Code	Meaning	Source
requestComplete	Certificate request was approved.	CA
invalidLanguage	Invalid language code in certificate initiation request.	CA
invalidBIN	Request rejected due to an invalid BIN.	Issuer or Acquirer
sigValidationFail	Request rejected because of signature validation failure.	CA

decryptionError	Request rejected because of a decryption error.	CA
requestInProgress	Request is in progress.	CA, Issuer, or Acquirer
rejectedByIssuer	Request was rejected by Issuer.	Issuer
requestPending	Request is pending action.	CA, Issuer, or Acquirer
rejectedByAcquirer	Request was rejected by Acquirer.	Acquirer
regFormAnswer Malformed	Request was rejected because of malformed data on the registration form.	CA
rejectedByCA	Request was rejected by Certificate Authority.	CA
unableToEncrypt CertRes	If the CA did not receive a key, it's unable to encrypt the response to the Cardholder.	CA

Certificate Inquiry Request/Response: CertInqReq/CertInqRes

Table 12.10 describes the Certificate Inquiry Request and Response message pair. These may be used by end-entities to determine the status of the certificates they've requested from their CAs. This message pair appears in Figures 11.1, 11.2, and 11.3 as an optional message pair, used as needed.

Table 12.10 CertInqReq/CertInqRes

Request Portion:	Message Contents
CertInqReq	S(EE, CertInqReqTBS)
where:	
CertInqReqTBS	{ RRPID, LID-EE, Chall-EE3, LID-CA }

Table 12.10 (continued)

.RRPID	Request-response pair identifier.
.LID-EE	Copied from CertRes.
.Chall-EE3	End-entity's challenge to CA's signature freshness.
.LID-CA	Copied from CertRes.
Response Portion:	**Message Contents**
CertInqRes	Identical to CertRes. See CertRes message.

CertInqReq/CertInqRes may be used by all end-entities to check on certificate issuance requests while preparing for Phase 0 of the on-line payment card transaction, as discussed in Chapter 2.

Credit Request/Response: CredReq/CredRes

Table 12.11 describes the Credit Request and Response message pair. It's used by the Merchant to request a credit for a previously authorized and captured transaction, when goods are returned by the Cardholder and a credit on his payment card is desired. This message pair is defined in Figure 11.6.

Table 12.11 CredReq/CredRes

Request Portion:	**Message Contents**
CredReq (two forms: Encapsulated with extra baggage if PANToken is required)	< EncB(M, P, CredReqData, CapTokenSeq), EncBX(M, P, CredReqData, CapTokenSeq, PANToken) >
where:	
CredReqData	CapRevOrCredReqData
.CapRevOrCredReqData	{ CapRevOrCredRRTags, [MThumbs], CapRevOrCredReqItemSeq, [CRvRqExtensions] }

.. CapRevOrCredRRTags	RRTags. Fresh RRPID and Date. See beginning of chapter for common components.
..MThumbs	Thumbprints of certificates, CRLs, and CRL Identifiers currently held in the Merchant's cache.
..CapRevOrCredReqItemSeq	{ CapRevOrCredReqItem + }
... CapRevOrCredReqItem	{ TransIDs, AuthRRPID, CapPayload, [NewBatchID], CapRevOrCredReqDate, [CapRevorCredReqAmt], NewAccountInd, [CRvRqItemExtensions] }
....TransIDs	Copied from corresponding CapRes.
....AuthRRPID	Request-response pair ID copied from corresponding AuthReq or AuthRevReq.
....CapPayload	{ CapDate, CapReqAmt, [AuthReqItem], [AuthResPayload], [SaleDetail], [CPayExtensions] }
.....CapDate	Date of capture that will appear on Cardholder's billing statement.
.....CapReqAmt	Capture amount being requested by the Merchant.
.....AuthReqItem	See AuthReq message for details.
.....AuthResPayload	See AuthReq message for details.
.....SaleDetail	See beginning of chapter for common components.
.....CPayExtensions	Extended financial data related to individual items in the capture reversal request.
....NewBatchID	Specifies a new batch ID number used for reversal requests for items submitted in a batch that was already closed. BatchID in CapPayload identifies the original batch ID number.

Table 12.11 (continued)

....CapRevOrCredReqDate	The date of the request.
....CapRevOrCredReqAmt	Capture reversal or credit request amount.
....NewAccountInd	Indicates that a new account number is present in PANToken. If this information is present, it will override the account information from the corresponding CaptureToken. Use of this is subject to Acquirer and Brand policies.
....CRvRqItemExtensions	Extended financial data related to individual items in the capture reversal request.
CapTokenSeq	{ [CapToken] + }
CapToken	See beginning of chapter for common components.
PANToken	See beginning of chapter for common components.
Response Portion:	**Message Contents**
CredRes	**Enc(P, M, CredResData)**
where:	
CredResData	CapRevOrCredResData
.CapRevOrCredResData	{ CapRevOrCredRRTags, [BrandCRLIdentifier], [PEThumb], [BatchStatusSeq], CapRevOrCredResItemSeq, [CrvRsExtensions] }
..CapRevOrCredRRTags	RRTags. Copy of CapRevOrCredRRTags from corresponding CapRevReq.
..BrandCRLIdentifier	List of current CRLs for all CAs within the Brand ID.

..PEThumb	Thumbprint of Payment Gateway certificate is provided if Merchant indicates the need for one.
..BatchStatusSeq	{ BatchStatus + }
...BatchStatus	See beginning of chapter for common components.
..CapRevOrCredResItemSeq	{ CapRevOrCredResItem + }
...CapRevOrCredResItem	{ TransIDs, AuthRRPID, CapRevOrCred ResPayload }
....TransIDs	Copied from corresponding CapRevOrCred ReqData.AuthReqData.AuthTags.
....AuthRRPID	RRPID from corresponding AuthReq or AuthRevReq.
....CapRevOrCredResPayload	{ CapRevOrCredCode, CapRevOrCredActualAmt, [BatchID], {BatchSequenceNum}, [CrvRsPayExtensions] }
.....CapRevOrCredCode	Number indicating capture reversal or credit status.
.....CapRevOrCredActualAmt	Copied from the corresponding Cap RevOrRedReqItem.
.....BatchID	ID number of the settlement batch for accounting purposes.
.....BatchSequenceNum	Sequence number of the item within the BatchID.
.....CRvRsPayExtensions	Extended financial data related to individual items in the capture reversal request.
CrvRsExtensions	Extended financial data related to the batch of capture reversal requests.

CredReq/CredRes are used by Merchants to request credit for earlier completed sales. The messages are not directly associated with any normal phase of the on-line payment card transaction.

Credit Reversal Request/Response: CredRevReq/CredRevRes

Table 12.12 defines the Credit Reversal Request Response message pair. This pair is used by a Merchant to request a reversal of a previously approved Credit Request/Response from a Payment Gateway. It may be needed when a Cardholder receives credit from a purchase with a promise to return the goods to the Merchant, but the goods never show up. This message pair can be found in Figure 11.6.

Table 12.12 CredRevReq/CredRevRes

Request Portion:	Message Contents
CredRevReq (two forms: Encapsulated with extra baggage if PANToken is required)	< EncB(M, P, CredRevReqData, CapTokenSeq), EncBX(M, P, CredRevReqData, CapTokenSeq, PANToken) >
where:	
CredRevReqData	CapRevOrCredReqData
.CapRevOrCredReqData	{ CapRevOrCredRRTags, [MThumbs], CapRevOrCredReqItemSeq, [CRvRqExtensions] }
..CapRevOrCredRRTags	RRTags. Fresh RRPID and Date. See beginning of chapter for common components.
..MThumbs	Thumbprints of certificates, CRLs, and CRL Identifiers currently held in the Merchant's cache.
..CapRevOrCredReqItemSeq	{ CapRevOrCredReqItem + }

... CapRevOrCredReqItem	{ TransIDs, AuthRRPID, CapPayload, [NewBatchID], CapRevOrCredReqDate, [CapRevorCredReqAmt], NewAccountInd, [CRvRqItemExtensions] }
....TransIDs	Copied from corresponding CapRes.
....AuthRRPID	Request-response pair ID copied from corresponding AuthReq or AuthRevReq.
....CapPayload	{ CapDate, CapReqAmt, [AuthReqItem], [AuthResPayload], [SaleDetail], [CPayExtensions] }
.....CapDate	Date of capture that will appear on Cardholder's billing statement.
.....CapReqAmt	Capture amount being requested by the Merchant.
.....AuthReqItem	See AuthReq message for details.
.....AuthResPayload	See AuthReq message for details.
.....SaleDetail	See beginning of chapter for common components.
.....CPayExtensions	Extended financial data related to individual items in the capture reversal request.
....NewBatchID	Specifies a new batch ID number used for reversal requests for items submitted in a batch that was already closed. BatchID in CapPayload identifies the original batch ID number.
....CapRevOrCredReqDate	The date of the request.
....CapRevOrCredReqAmt	Capture reversal or credit request amount.
....NewAccountInd	Indicates that a new account number is present in PANToken. If this information is

Table 12.12 (continued)

	present, it will override the account information from the corresponding CaptureToken. Use of this is subject to Acquirer and Brand policies.
....CRvRqItemExtensions	Extended financial data related to the batch of transactions in the capture reversal request.
CapTokenSeq	{ [CapToken] + }
CapToken	See beginning of chapter for common components.
PANToken	See beginning of chapter for common components.
Response Portion:	**Message Contents**
CredRevRes	**Enc(P, M, CredRevResData)**
where:	
CredRevResData	CapRevOrCredResData
.CapRevOrCredResData	{ CapRevOrCredRRTags, [BrandCRLIdentifier], [PEThumb], [BatchStatusSeq], CapRevOrCredResItemSeq, [CrvRsExtensions] }
..CapRevOrCredRRTags	RRTags. Copy of CapRevOrCredRRTags from corresponding CapRevReq.
..BrandCRLIdentifier	List of current CRLs for all CAs within the Brand ID.
..PEThumb	Thumbprint of Payment Gateway certificate is provided if Merchant indicates the need for one.

..BatchStatusSeq	{ BatchStatus + }
...BatchStatus	See beginning of chapter for common components.
..CapRevOrCredResItemSeq	{ CapRevOrCredResItem + }
...CapRevOrCredResItem	{ TransIDs, AuthRRPID, CapRevOrCredResPayload }
....TransIDs	Copied from corresponding CapRevOrCredReqData.AuthReqData.AuthTags.
....AuthRRPID	RRPID from corresponding AuthReq or AuthRevReq.
....CapRevOrCredResPayload	{ CapRevOrCredCode, CapRevOrCredActualAmt, [BatchID], {BatchSequenceNum], [CrvRsPayExtensions] }
.....CapRevOrCredCode	Number indicating capture reversal or credit status.
.....CapRevOrCredActualAmt	Copied from the corresponding CapRevOrRedReqItem.
.....BatchID	ID number of the settlement batch for accounting purposes.
.....BatchSequenceNum	Sequence number of the item within the BatchID.
.....CRvRsPayExtensions	Extended financial data related to individual items in the capture reversal request.
.CrvRsExtensions	Extended financial data related to the entire batch in the capture reversal request.

CredRevReq/CredRevRes are used by Merchants to request a reversal for a credit issued to a Cardholder from an earlier completed sale. The messages are not directly associated with any normal phase of the on-line payment card transaction.

Error

Table 12.13 describes the components of the Error message. Error messages are returned when a receiver of a request message cannot process the request due to some SET-related problem. Error messages are not used to return information about a failed business operation, only for SET-specific problems. Values for ErrorCode are defined in Table 11.1 in the preceding chapter.

Table 12.13 Error Message Definition

Message Format:	Message Contents
Error	< SignedError, UnSignedError >
where:	
SignedError	S(EE, ErrorTBS)
.ErrorTBS	{ ErrorCode, ErrorNonce, [ErrorOID], [ErrorThumb], ErrorMsg }
..ErrorCode	Numeric code for the error that occurred. See Chapter 11 for details.
..ErrorNonce	A nonce that ensures that the signature is generated over unpredictable data.
..ErrorOID	If an error occurred because the application did not know how to process a critical extension, this will contain the object identifier of the extension in question.
..ErrorThumb	The thumbprint of the certificate that produced the error or the hash value of the certificate if signature verification failed.
..ErrorMsg	< MessageHeader, BadWrapper >
...MessageHeader	The message header of the message that produced the error.

...BadWrapper	The message wrapper for the message that produced the error.
UnSignedError	ErrorTBS (unsigned version is only used if the end-entity does not have a signature certificate). See above for contents.

Inquiry Request/Response: InqReq/InqRes

Table 12.14 defines the Inquiry Request and Response message pair. These messages are used by the Cardholder to request the status of a transaction from the Merchant. This message pair can be found in Figure 11.5.

Table 12.14 InqRes/InqRes

Request Portion:	Message Contents
InqReq	< InqReqSigned, InqReqData >
where:	
InqReqSigned	S(C, InqReqData)
.InqReqData	{ TransIDs, RRPID, Chall-C2, [InqRqExtensions] }
..TransIDs	Copied from the most recent Purchase Request (PReq), Purchase Response (PRes), or previous Inquiry Response (InqReq).
..RRPID	Request-response pair ID.
..Chall-C2	Fresh Cardholder's challenge to Merchant's signature.
..InqRqExtensions	Inquiry request message extensions.
Response Portion:	**Message Contents**
InqRes	Identical to Purchase Response (PRes) message. See PRes for details.

InqRes/InqRes may be used by Cardholders any time after Phase 4 of the on-line payment card transaction, as discussed in Chapter 2.

Merchant-Acquirer Certificate Initialization Request/Response: Me-AqCInitReq/Me-AqCInitRes

Table 12.15 describes the Merchant and Acquirer Certificate Initialization Request and Response message pair. These messages begin the process of a Merchant or Acquirer (Payment Gateway) Certificate Request. They're sent between either end-entity and their corresponding CA (MCA or PCA). The protocol that contains this message pair may be found in Figures 11.2 and 11.3.

Table 12.15 Me-AqCInitReq/Me-AqCInitRes

Request Portion:	Message Contents
Me-AcCInitReq	{ RRPID, LID-EE, Chall-EE, RequestType, IDData BrandID, Language, [Thumbs] }
where:	
RRPID	Request/Response pair ID.
LID-EE	Local ID that's generated by the end-entity's system.
Chall-EE	Challenge by the end-entity to the freshness of the CA's signature.
RequestType	See table following Certificate Request/Response CertReq/CertRes) message pair.
IDData	< MerchantAcquirerID, AcquirerID >
.MerchantAcquirerID	{ MerchantBIN, MerchantID }
..MerchantBIN	Bank Identification Number used to process the Merchant's transaction at the

	Acquiring Bank or card company. Used for Merchant certificate requests.
..MerchantID	Merchant number assigned by the Acquirer. Used for Merchant certificate requests.
.AcquirerID	{ AcquirerBIN, [AcquirerBusinessID] }
..AcquirerBIN	Bank Identification Number for the Acquirer requesting a certificate.
..AcquirerBusinessID	Business Identification Code for the Acquirer requesting a certificate.
BrandID	BrandID of the certificate requested.
Language	Desired language for the rest of the certificate request flow process.
Thumbs	List of certificate, CRL, and CRL Identifier thumbprints already held by the end-entity.

Response Portion:	**Message Contents**
Me-AqCInitRes	**S (CA, Me-AqCInitResTBS)**
Me-AqCInitResTBS	{ RRPID, LID-EE, Chall-EE, [LID-CA], Chall-CA, RequestType, RegFormOrReferral, [AcctDataField], CAEThumb, [Brand-CRLIdentifier], [Thumbs] }

where:

.RRPID	Request/Response pair ID.
.LID-EE	Copied from previous Me-AqCInitReq.
.Chall-EE	Copied from previous Me-AqCInitReq.
.LID-CA	Local ID that's generated by the CA for its use.
.Chall-CA	CA's challenge to end-entity's signature freshness.

Table 12.15 (continued)

.RequestType	See Table 12.8.
.RegFormOrReferral	< RegFormData, ReferralData >
..RegFormData	{ [RegTemplate], PolicyText }
...RegTemplate	{ RegFormID, [BrandLogoURL], [CardLogoURL], RegFieldSeq }
....RegFormID	Number assigned by CA for specific registration form.
....BrandLogoURL	URL for the payment card logo.
....CardLogoURL	URL for the financial institution logo.
....RegFieldSeq	{ RegField + }
.....RegField	{ [FieldID], FieldName, [FieldDesc], [FieldLen], FieldRequired, FieldInvisible }
......FieldID	Object identifier for registration form field.
......FieldName	Field names to be used as labels for a fill-in form on the requestor's system.
......FieldDesc	Description of content required for the field. Used when help is requested by end-entity.
......FieldLen	Maximum length of the field.
......FieldRequired	Boolean expression indicating when data in the field is required or not.
......FieldInvisible	Boolean expression indicating that the field should not be displayed to the requestor.
...PolicyText	Statement that will be displayed along with the registration form on the requestor's system.

..ReferralData	{ [Reason], [ReferralURLSeq] }
...Reason	Statement concerning the request (will be displayed on the requestor's system).
...ReferralURLSeq	{ ReferralURL + }
....ReferralURL	URL to an alternate CA that may be used for processing certificate requests.
.AcctDataField	Defined as **RegField** (see above) to collect the values for AcctData in a certificate request (CertReq) message.
.CAEThumb	Thumbprint of CA Key-Exchange Certificate that end-entity will use to encrypt the contents of CertReq.
.BrandCRLIdentifier	Separate structure defined by SET to identify the list of known CRLs for the Brand (see Chapter 6) and maintained by the Brand CA (BCA).
.Thumbs	Copied from previous Me-AcCInitReq.

Me-AqCInitReq/Me-AqCInitRes are used by Merchants and Payment Gateway operators to prepare for Phase 0 of the on-line payment card transaction, as discussed in Chapter 2.

Payment Gateway Certificate Request/Response: PCertReq/PCertRes

Table 12.16 describes the Payment Gateway Certificate Request and Response message pair. These are used by Merchants to request a copy of a Payment Gateway's encryption certificate which they'll use in sending subsequent messages to the Payment Gateway. This pair can be found in Figure 11.7 (Gateway Certificate Request and Batch Administration message flows).

Table 12.16 PCertReq/PCertRes

Request Portion:	Message Contents
PCertReq	S(M, PCertReqData)
where:	
PCertReqData	{ PCertTags, [MThumbs], BrandAndBIN-Seq, [PCRqExtensions] }
.PCertTags	RRTags. Fresh RRPID for this message.
.MThumbs	Thumbprints of Payment Gateway certificates currently held in Merchant's cache.
.BrandAndBINSeq	{ BrandAndBIN + }
..BrandAndBIN	{ BrandID, [BIN] }
...BrandID	Payment card brand ID (without card product type).
...BIN	Bank Identification Number for the processing of the Merchant's transactions by the Payment Gateway.
.PCRqExtensions	Extensions to the PCertReq message as required by Merchants and Payment Gateways.
Response Portion:	**Message Contents**
PCertRes	S(P, PCertResTBS)
where:	
PCertResTBS	{ PCertTags, [BrandCRLIdentifierSeq], PCertResItems, [PCRsExtensions] }
.PCertTags	RRTags. Copied from corresponding PCertReq.

.BrandCRLIdentifierSeq	{ BrandCRLIdentifier + }
..BrandCRLIdentifier	List of CRLs for all CAs within the Brand ID.
.PCertResItems	{ PCertCode, [CertThumb] }
..PCertCode	Value that indicates the result of PCertReq. See Table 12.17.
..CertThumb	Thumbprint of returned certificate.
.PCRsExtensions	Extensions to the PCertRes message as required by Merchants and Payment Gateways.

Table 12.17 PCertCode Values and Meanings

PCertCode Value	Meaning
success	The request was processed successfully.
unspecifiedFailure	The request failed because of some other problems not defined as a different PCertCode.
brandNotSupported	The request failed because the Brand ID supplied in the request is not supported by the Payment Gateway.
unknownBIN	The request failed because the BIN supplied in the request is not supported by the Payment Gateway.

PCertReq/PCertRes are used by Merchants to obtain the most current copy of Payment Gateway certificates to use in all SET phases of the on-line payment card transaction, as discussed in Chapter 2.

Payment Initialization Request/Response: PInitReq/PInitRes

Table 12.18 defines the Purchase Initialization Request and Response message pair. It's used by the Cardholder to initiate a purchase request from a

Merchant. This message pair may be found in Figure 11.4 (Normal purchase flow).

Table 12.18 PInitReq/PInitRes

Request Portion:	Message Contents
PInitReq	{ RRPID, Language, LID-C, [LID-M], Chall-C, BrandID, BIN, [Thumbs], {PIRqExtensions] }
where:	
RRPID	Request-response pair ID.
Language	Cardholder's language code.
LID-C	Local ID generated by the Cardholder's system.
LID-M	Local ID for the Merchant copied from SET initiation message (if used).
Chall-C	Cardholder's challenge to Merchant's signature freshness.
BrandID	Cardholder's chosen payment card brand ID.
BIN	Bank Identification Number from the first six digits of the Cardholder's payment card account number.
Thumbs	List of certificate, CRL, and BrandCRL Identifier thumbprints held in the Cardholder's cache.
PIRqExtensions	Message extensions to Purchase Initialization Request message.
Response Portion:	**Message Contents**
PInitRes	S(M,PInitResData)

where:

PInitResData	{ TransIDs, RRPID, Chall-C, Chall-M, [BrandCRLIdentifier], PEThumb, [Thumbs], [PIRsExtensions] }
.TransIDs	See beginning of chapter for common components.
.RRPID	Request-response pair ID.
.Chall-C	Copied from corresponding PInitReq.
.Chall-M	Merchant's challenge to Cardholder's signature freshness.
.BrandCRLIdentifier	List of current CRLs for all CAs under the Brand CA.
.PEThumb	Thumbprint of Payment Gateway Key-Exchange Certificate.
.Thumbs	Copied from corresponding PInitReq.
.PIRsExtensions	Message extensions to Purchase Initialization Response message.

PInitReq/PInitRes are used by Cardholders to initiate Phase 4 of the online payment card transaction, as discussed in Chapter 2.

Purchase Request/Response: PReq/PRes

Table 12.19 describes the Purchase Request and Response message pair. It's used by the Cardholder to send Purchase Order data to a Merchant. This message pair is considered the heart of the SET payment protocol. It is the most complex of all SET messages. It consists of two parts: an Order Instructions (OI) piece and a Payment Instructions (PI) piece. Order Instructions is intended for processing by the Merchant. Payment Instructions are intended to be tunneled through the Merchant to the Payment Gateway for processing. Each item is signed separately using a dual signature (see Chapters 4 and 5). There is typically a delay period between a Purchase Request and a Purchase Response during which the Merchant will communicate with the Payment Gateway to authorize the transaction. Afterward, a response is sent back to the Cardholder.

Table 12.19 PReq/PRes

Request Portion:	Message Contents
PReq	<PReqDualSigned, PReqUnsigned >
where:	
PReqDualSigned	{ PIDualSigned, OIDualSigned } Used where Cardholder certificates are present.
.PIDualSigned	PI. See beginning of chapter for common components.
.OIDualSigned	L(OIData, PIData)
..OIData	See beginning of chapter for common components.
..PIData	See beginning of chapter for common components.
PReqUnsigned	{ PIUnsigned, OIUnsigned } Used where Cardholder certificates are not present.
.PIUnsigned	PI. See beginning of chapter for common components.
.OIUnsigned	L(OIData, PIDataUnsigned)
..OIData	See beginning of chapter for common components.
..PIDataUnsigned	{ PIHead, PANToken }
...PIHead	See beginning of chapter for common components.
...PANToken	See beginning of chapter for common components.

Response Portion:	Message Contents
PRes	S(M, PResData)
where:	
PResData	{ TransIDs, RRPID, Chall-C, [BrandCRL Identifier], PResPayloadSeq }
.TransIDs	Copied from corresponding PReq.
.RRPID	Request-response pair ID.
.Chall-C	Copied from corresponding PInitReq.
.BrandCRLIdentifier	List of current CRLs for all CAs within payment card Brand.
.PResPayloadSeq	{ PResPayload + } One entry per authorization performed, or status information if no authorization was performed.
..PResPayload	{ CompletionCode, [Results], [PRsExtensions] }
...CompletionCode	Enumerated code indicating the result of the transaction. See Table 12.20.
...Results	{ [AcqCardMsg], [AuthStatus], [CapStatus], [CredStatusSeq] }
...AcqCardMsg	Copied from interim AuthRes message between Merchant and Payment Gateway.
...AuthStatus	{ AuthDate, AuthCode, AuthRatio, [Curr Conv] }
....AuthDate	Date of the authorization. Copied from AuthRRTags.
....AuthCode	Code that indicates the result of the authorization request processing. Copied from corresponding AuthResPayload.
....AuthRatio	AuthReqAmt divided by PurchAmt.

Table 12.19 (continued)

....CurrConv	{ CurrConvRate, CardCurr }
.....CurrConvRate	Currency conversion rate. Copied from AuthResPayload.
.....CardCurr	Cardholder's payment card currency code. Copied from AuthResPayload.
...CapStatus	{ CapDate, CapCode, CapRatio }
....CapDate	Date of capture. Copied from CapPayload.
....CapCode	Code that indicates the status of capture request. Copied from CapResPayload.
....CapRatio	CapReqAmt divided by PurchAmt.
...CredStatusSeq	{ CreditStatus + } Data will appear only if a Credit Request (CredReq) that corresponds to the Authorization Response has been performed.
....CreditStatus	{ CreditDate, CreditCode, CreditRatio }
.....CreditDate	Date of credit. Copied from the CapRev OrCredReqData component.
.....CreditCode	Code that indicates the status of the Credit Request. Copied from the CapRevOrCred ReqData component.
.....CreditRatio	CapRevOrCredReqAmt divided by Purch Amt.
...PRsExtensions	Message extensions to Purchase Response message as required by Cardholder or Payment Gateway software.

Table 12.20 CompletionCode Values

CompletionCode Value	Meaning
meaninglessRatio	If PurchAmt = 0 the ratio cannot be computed.
orderRejected	Merchant cannot process the order.
orderReceived	No authorization information to report back to Cardholder yet.
orderNotReceived	Inquiry message about order was received before order itself was received by the Merchant.
authorizationPerformed	Code defined by AuthStatus in AuthRes.
capturePerformed	Code defined by CapStatus in CapRes.
creditPerformed	Code defined by CreditStatus in CredRes.

Table 12.20 lists values defined for CompletionCode.

PReq/PRes are used by Cardholders to initiate Phase 5 of the on-line payment card transaction, as discussed in Chapter 2.

Registration Form Request/Response: RegFormReq/RegFormRes

Table 12.21 defines the Registration Form Request/Response message pair. It's used by Cardholders in the Certificate Request protocol, defined in Figure 11.1.

Table 12.21 RegFormReq/RegFormRes

Request Portion:	Message Contents
RegFormReq	EXH(C, RegFormReqData, PANOnly)
where:	
RegFormReqData	{ RRPID, LID-EE, Chall-EE2, [LID-CA], RequestType, Language, [Thumbs] }

Table 12.21 (continued)

.RRPID	Request-response pair ID.
.LID-EE	Copied from corresponding CardCInitRes.
.Chall-EE2	End-entity's challenge to CA's signature freshness.
.LID-CA	Copied from CardCInitRes.
.RequestType	See Table 12.8 for RequestType possible values.
.Language	Language code desired for the rest of the certificate request flow.
.Thumbs	Lists of certificates, CRLs, and BrandCRL Identifiers currently held in Cardholder's cache.
PANOnly	{ PAN, ExNonce }
.PAN	Cardholder's payment account number.
.ExNonce	Random number used to mask the PAN.
Response Portion:	**Message Contents**
RegFormRes	S(CA, RegFormResTBS)
where:	
RegFormResTBS	{ RRPID, LID-EE, Chall-EE2, [LID-CA], Chall-CA, [CAEThumb], RequestType, RegFormOrReferral, [BrandCRLIdentifier], [Thumbs] }
.RRPID	Request/Response pair ID.
.LID-EE	Copied from previous RegFormReq.
.Chall-EE2	Copied from previous RegFormReq.

.LID-CA	Local ID that's generated by the CA for its use.
.Chall-CA	CA's challenge to requestor's signature freshness.
.CAEThumb	Thumbprint of CA Key-Exchange Certificate that end-entity will use to encrypt the contents of CertReq.
.RequestType	See Table 12.8.
.RegFormOrReferral	< RegFormData, ReferralData >
..RegFormData	{ [RegTemplate], PolicyText }
...RegTemplate	{ RegFormID, [BrandLogoURL], [CardLogoURL], RegFieldSeq }
....RegFormID	Number assigned by CA for specific registration form.
....BrandLogoURL	URL for the payment card logo.
....CardLogoURL	URL for the financial institution logo.
....RegFieldSeq	{ RegField + }
.....RegField	{ [FieldID], FieldName, [FieldDesc], [FieldLen], FieldRequired, FieldInvisible }
......FieldID	Object identifier for registration form field.
......FieldName	Field names to be used as labels for a fill-in form on the requestor's system.
......FieldDesc	Description of content required for the field. Used when help is requested by end-entity.
......FieldLen	Maximum length of the field.
......FieldRequired	Boolean expression indicating whether data in the field are required or not.

Table 12.21 (continued)

......FieldInvisible	Boolean expression indicating that the field should not be displayed to the requestor.
...PolicyText	Statement that will be displayed along with the registration form on the requestor's system.
..ReferralData	{ [Reason], [ReferralURLSeq] }
...Reason	Statement concerning the request that will be displayed on the requestor's system.
...ReferralURLSeq	{ ReferralURL + }
....ReferralURL	URL to an alternate CA that may be used for processing certificate requests.
.BrandCRLIdentifier	Separate structure defined by SET to identify the list of known CRLs for the Brand (see Chapter 6) and maintained by the Brand CA (BCA).
.Thumbs	Copied from previous RegFormReq.

RegFormReq/RegFormRes are used by Cardholders during the certificate issuance process to prepare for Phase 0 of the on-line payment card transaction, as discussed in Chapter 2.

With all SET message details in hand, you should be better prepared to determine how your systems will need to interface properly to your SET POS System. Many of the data elements are already present somewhere in your back-office operations, but will need to be made available as required. Furthermore, information returned to your POS System will be used in updating some of your other systems. With the complete details of what information is needed or obtained in which process, your analysis work should be simpler.

In the next section of the book we begin the planning, analysis, design, and implementation steps to bolting on SET. In Chapter 13, we first look at some high-level planning work that you'll perform to understand your project and its scope.

PLANNING

Similar to any other information systems projects, building a SET-enabled e-commerce site should follow some software engineering development model that includes the steps of planning, analysis, design, implementation, and testing. The following five chapters will help you through these efforts. The methodology that you use will depend on your specific situation; over the course of these chapters we'll use a hybrid of development methodologies that you can adapt to your particular needs. In this chapter, we start out with some planning steps.

Without adequate levels of up-front planning, your chances for success are relatively slim. Each business opportunity is unique, and your relationships with the banks and your customers introduce complexities that require adequate understanding if they're to be nurtured.

This chapter lays the groundwork for the next four chapters by outlining what's required for a SET-enabled Merchant e-commerce site. We'll look at these needs from the perspective of using commercially available (packaged) SET-compliant Merchant POS software.

To help with understanding the other, non-SET-related requirements for any e-commerce system, you're encouraged to pick up and read *Creating the Virtual Store* by Magdelena Yesil (Wiley, 1997).

To aid in the efforts of planning and preliminary analysis, we cover these topics in this chapter:

- Organizing your project team
- First-pass cost estimates for your site

- Shopping for a SET-compliant Acquiring (Merchant) Bank
- Different processing options for your SET POS System
- Moving into detailed analysis and design work

A Call to Arms

Successful software projects always start out with the right mix of people in the right place at the right time. This is especially true where SET-related projects are concerned. A single person can never accomplish what a committed team of skillful professionals can accomplish, but it's essential to select your team wisely and carefully.

Here are a few suggestions to help you build your team and organize your project. Find those people who can best perform these tasks, and you tremendously increase your chances for project success:

- **Project sponsorship.** Make certain that your employees and co-workers understand the level of management commitment that's in place to see the project through completion. No other single factor is more responsible for disillusionment than a lack of visible and constant management support.

- **Understand your customer.** Since the ultimate goal of your SET-enabled system is to process as many lucrative transactions as possible, you must first be aware of your customer's needs. Since your Marketing and Sales personnel are the closest to your customer, make certain they're a part of the team.

- **Understand your systems.** A SET-enabled Merchant System will place tremendous demands for processing on your computer systems. Make certain that you've included systems personnel who know your computing environment thoroughly. You can bank on adding new computer resources as you approach the implementation phase, so early Information Technology staff involvement and buy-in will increase your odds for success.

- **Understand your back-office processes.** A SET implementation will force you to take a close and hard look at your existing processes. As we discussed in Chapter 1, a first-generation e-commerce approach will not stand up to the transactional nature of SET. Your business users and systems operators are in the best position to help you understand where information processing gaps exist and how to fill them in to provide seamless on-line transaction processing.

- **Understand your budgets and capital resources.** We can't stress this point enough—SET will not come cheaply! Be prepared for significant investments of time, capital, and labor. To help you justify the project to those who hold the purse strings, you'll need sufficient detailed analysis to build your business case. Bring in those people from your organization who can best offer their services here. This will include systems analysts, financial analysts—even your external CPA if you use one.

Justify Yourself

With your project team in place and ready to conquer, it's time to look at some investment decisions. As we've said over and over, SET is no slam dunk and there are no shortcuts along the way. Investments in hardware, software, services, time, and labor are certain to become significant, so it's imperative that you convince your company that it's worthwhile to make such investments. Here's where your financial analysis experts will help you most.

Prepare a cost-benefit analysis for your project that includes as many of the following items as possible:

- Good-faith estimates of costs for the duration of the project (time, materials, software, travel, maintenance, etc.). Consider these costs as a cash outflow in the years they occur.

- Estimates of capital expenditure costs throughout the lifetime of the project (hardware, network upgrades, etc.). Consider these costs as a cash outflow in the years they occur. As an example, if you expect additional investments in hardware three years from now to upgrade what you're buying now, record these cash outflows in both Year 0 and Year 2 for cost-benefit determination purposes. Use the operating environment example in Chapter 15 to help you decide which hardware you'll need to purchase and to estimate its costs.

- Estimates of development costs for personnel (both full-time and contract employees). These costs are another cash outflow. Record them in the period in which they'll occur. Include labor costs associated with system maintenance too.

- Estimates of new revenues by year following project implementation. These represent the first of your cash inflows for cost-benefit determination purposes.

- Reduction in costs due to improvements in process following project implementation, enumerated by year. These should be treated as cash inflows as well.

- Any other costs that you can foresee to implement the system. Include these with the other costs mentioned above.

- Any other costs savings that you can foresee after system implementation. Include these with the other savings mentioned above.

With these numbers in hand, you're ready to compute the project's overall estimated value to the company. You'll want to determine the project's Net Present Value (NPV), Simple Rate of Return, Internal Rate of Return (IRR), payback period in years (or months), and any other measures that your Finance Department may require for project justification.

Make sure you do your homework here. Without the commitment to resources, both human and capital, your project will die on the vine. Don't let that happen.

Since your project will force you to examine your internal operations carefully, you might consider taking full advantage of this, using the opportunity to reengineer certain related business processes associated with transaction processing and fulfillment. Before your SET implementation project gets out of hand, you may want to discuss this idea with your project team to decide what's best for your company. You may decide to begin several concurrent projects using other teams to assure timely completion, but you don't want those efforts to muddle your SET implementation project. To prevent that type of problem, define your project's scope very clearly, and stick to your plans. Projects of this nature tend to involve many different systems, business processes, outside relationships, and other factors. Any scope creep on your project will only lead to delays and frustration. On the other hand, you need to remain flexible enough to uncover *all* system-related requirements from everyone and everything that's affected by the new system. By spending more of your team's time up front in the planning, analysis, and design work, you're better positioned to track down all these potential effects. Remember that errors made in the early phases of a project can be corrected for free. Once they become defects in later phases, the costs to correct them become exorbitant.

Plan now to avoid surprises later on.

Shopping for a SET Merchant Bank

As we've discussed throughout the book, a successful relationship with an Acquiring Bank is essential for SET. Without reliable access to the bank's Payment Gateway software, transaction processing stops dead in its tracks. Consequently, you want to be certain that your bank's Merchant Services operation is fully in support of SET for payment card processing. Currently, not all banks are properly prepared, so you'll need to shop around for one that is prepared.

Once you've selected a bank, the bank may point you in a specific direction for the SET POS software that they're prepared to support. Use the information or systems they offer you as a set of requirements to carry into the detailed analysis phase of your project.

Where to Look

Since SET is an Internet-based protocol, it's natural that those banks that support SET will show a significant presence on the Internet. Your shopping adventure should start there. Multistate or national banks are far likelier to offer SET support than smaller local banks in your city or town.

MasterCard has been working with Mellon Bank and Chase Manhattan Bank in the United States to offer SET to their Merchants. In Canada MasterCard has been pilot testing SET with Credit Union Electronic Transaction Services (CUETS). Several other MasterCard pilots have also been conducted across Japan, China, Europe, and South Africa.

Visa has been pilot testing SET in the United States with First Union National Bank, Bank of America, and several others. Like MasterCard, Visa is conducting SET pilot tests with member banks across the world.

Many of the U.S. pilot tests rely on First Data Merchant Services for operation of the SET Payment Gateway on behalf of the banks. You may want to start your search here, especially if you've already established a Merchant account at a different Acquiring Bank.

Transaction Processing and Fulfillment Options

One ongoing cost component of any payment card–accepting site is transaction fulfillment. As we discussed in Chapter 2, transaction fulfillment includes the steps of payment capture, credit processing, batch settlement, and batch administration work.

Your SET POS System gives you two transaction fulfillment options. Deciding which to use will be based on your business and your relationship with your Merchant Bank. Consider these as you move toward more detailed analysis and design, since one choice will lead to a different set of system requirements than the other.

Option 1: Authorization-Only Processing

Under this option, you'll use your SET POS System to communicate with your customer Cardholders and Acquirer Payment Gateway to authorize charges as cards are presented for payment. Subsequent to successful authorization, you'll move that data into other systems that you may already operate to capture and settle all charges from all sources in one place. This option may make the most sense if your e-commerce site is simply another channel for selling your goods or services, and your systems are already in place to process payment card charges. Figure 13.1 illustrates this option.

Option 2: Use the Full Complement of SET POS Services

With this option, your Merchant POS System will perform all the work necessary for payment card acceptance and transaction fulfillment. Here you'll need interfaces to the system for all those parts of the company that modify transaction information. These will include your shipping department to indicate those transactions ready to capture, your accounting department for reconciliation and reporting purposes, and any others that might be

Figure 13.1 Using SET POS software for authorization-only processing.

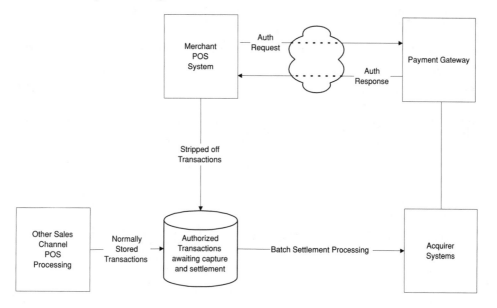

affected. This option may make the most sense for retailers who consider their Web-based sales site as a separate business (for record-keeping reasons), or where a business is exclusively operated via the Web. Figure 13.2 illustrates how this option would work.

Dependent on your choice, your system needs will differ, often dramatically. It's critical that decisions of this nature be made early in the project to avoid significant amounts of rework later on.

One other consideration for your SET POS System relates to the nature of your business itself. Recall that payment card association rules prevent you from capturing a transaction until it's been authorized and shipped to the customer. If what you're selling may be delivered on-line, you might be able to both authorize and capture the sale at the same time. Wherever products can be delivered during the course of transaction (downloadable software, clip-art or other libraries, publications, etc.), you might consider this approach.

Preparing for Detailed Analysis and Design

With the course of your project established, decisions related to transaction processing made, a fully funded budget, adequate personnel resources, and a commitment to success, you're ready to proceed into defining the detailed

Figure 13.2 Full use of SET messaging.

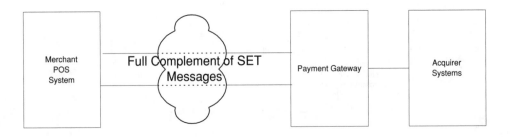

requirements for your new system and new processes. At the conclusion of your preliminary planning phase, you should have in hand sufficient lists of high-level requirements. You should also now understand the impacts and effects on your existing systems, existing processes, and existing computing environments.

In Chapter 14, we'll take these high-level requirements down to their next level by analyzing what SET-related processing will be added to your environment and how this may affect the work you're already performing.

ANALYSIS

In Chapter 13, we looked at some planning steps to help organize your team, estimate the work and resources required for the project, locate a suitable SET-compliant Acquiring (Merchant) Bank, decide on some options for system use, and extract some high-level needs. Those needs define the scope and some aspects of the system, along with identifying the associated business processes that require deeper examination.

With this high-level understanding in place, we can move forward into further detailed analysis to collect sufficient information that will move you into design work. The goal of this analysis is to extract *what's required* of the system without regard to its specific implementation at this point.

The degree of this analysis work will vary depending on your specific situation. If you're starting from scratch, broader analysis will be needed. If you only wish to add SET to an existing Merchant e-commerce site, narrower analysis will be needed. It's through this analysis that the work and the costs that lie ahead will be better understood.

In taking this understanding to the next level, it's important that we place the project into its proper perspective from the start. Since contemporary Web-based projects, including e-commerce software projects, are implemented through Object-Oriented Programming principles, its seems natural to use some Object-Oriented (OO) approaches to analysis and design for them as well. Internet projects rely on several of these key concepts and development tools, including:

- Distributed processing and associated standards (CORBA/IIOP and DCOM)

- Three- or *n*-tier client-server computing

- Uses of middleware

- Object-Oriented or Object-Relational database management systems

SET especially benefits from these approaches because of its need for a highly modular and highly secure environment. Many of the components that you'll collect and assemble for your SET-compliant system depend on modularity. Let's take a look at how the use of Object-Oriented Analysis and Design (OOA&D) techniques help you achieve project successes.

Topics we'll cover in this chapter include:

- Object-Oriented Analysis and Design principles

- Distributed object computing principles

- Application of principles to SET-related Merchant Server components

Object-Oriented Analysis and Design

For some of you, the following might be a review of techniques you already know. For many of you who aren't often involved in the work from earlier phases of systems development (programmers, webmasters, and systems administrators), it's important to adopt an object-centric view of the entire process, from start to finish.

However important programming is, the greatest benefits of the Object-Oriented (OO) approaches are found during the analysis and design phases of development when the components of a business problem can be identified and modeled. Programming these components can then be performed appropriately, and reusability can be achieved. This gives birth to a systems development process that's a matter of reassembling components into new structures that provide new services which can, in turn, be reused later.

OO approaches are rooted in the concept of *information hiding*, where shared public data areas are eliminated. Objects communicate through message passing mechanisms rather than sharing common variables. An object is a package of all of the functions needed to maintain data, along with an interface for each of these services.

How an object implements its services is irrelevant to a requesting object. All it needs to know is that a service is available and how to request it. Even if the method in how a service is implemented changes, no other object will even realize that it changed, since the message format to request the service remains consistent. Because of this, changes that might otherwise affect many parts of a traditionally developed system are localized into a single point when OO techniques are used.

Figure 14.1 offers a conceptual view of an object.

When you view your SET-enabled Merchant commerce site as a series of collaborating abstract objects, you remain focused on what's being accom-

Figure 14.1 An object.

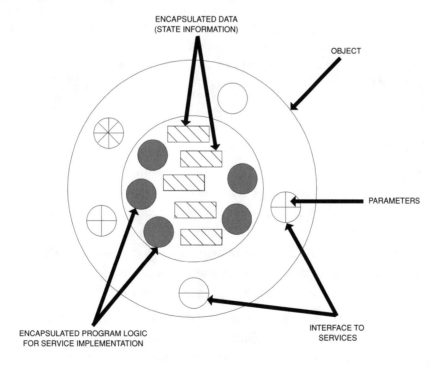

plished rather than how it's being accomplished, enriching the analysis phase with vital information.

OOA&D Tools

While a formal methodology for OOA&D is helpful, it's not essential to success. The goal of this analysis phase is to build understanding of what's needed.

You can easily perform the work with blank sheets of paper and pencil, as long as you're consistent and complete. Or you may want to use commercial Computer-Aided Software Engineering (CASE) tools that support the concepts instead. One example of this type of tool is Rational Rose from Rational Software Corp. It uses the methodology defined by the "Three Amigos," Grady Booch, James Rumbaugh, and Ivar Jacobson. Under their approach, they've developed what's called the Unified Modeling Language (UML), which graphically depicts OO systems. UML relies upon a syntax that expresses ideas and uses diagrams. These diagrams include use-cases, classes, sequences of steps, components, deployment, state-transition charts, and collaboration diagrams. The models created by these diagrams are helpful to everyone involved in the systems development life cycle by simplifying otherwise complex ideas. You may also find the book *The UML Tookit* from Hans-Erik Eriksson (Wiley, 1997) useful in your efforts.

OO Systems

Development techniques based on Object-Oriented Analysis and Design (OOA&D) are most valuable where large or complex systems are custom developed, as with information-processing Web sites, and especially with e-commerce and SET that will likely become mission-critical applications. An important feature of OO is its modularity, where processing is invoked only when it's needed. You can think of this in terms of Just-In-Time processing, where the right process is in the right place, at the right time.

In summary, an object is a conceptual creation that relates to things found in the real world. Using OO techniques, you'll *create* computerized versions of entities (persons, places, things, events) by combining behavior (methods or services) and associated information (attributes) into a single point with which other objects communicate by passing generic messages. Objects know about other objects through message standards that are developed to request an object's services. Objects are identifiable as objects only when they're created using the fundamental OO principles for systems development.

OO Programming

In simple terms, object-oriented programming is the application of object-oriented principles to computer programming. For SET's development, the relevant OO languages you'll encounter are C++ and Java. Vendor-supplied Software Development Kits (SDKs) for SET POS Systems include class libraries to access the services that support either or both languages.

Object-oriented programming languages do not guarantee object-oriented systems. It's possible to use traditional analysis and design techniques and use C++, for example, to develop the system, but the work becomes self-defeating. In order to create an OO system, you *must* use an OO approach during the entire project.

Because these techniques often presume a networked environment consisting of computers from a variety of manufacturers, it's useful to look briefly at distributed system concepts too.

What Are Class Libraries?

Class libraries are collections of classes (prebuilt objects) that provide certain functionality and can be reused in program development. Class libraries are roughly the same as libraries in the traditional programming sense, but are in the form of classes and can be subclassed or used directly. For example, an accounting class library could be purchased from a supplier of accounting software and modified to meet specific needs without modifying the vendor-supplied code. Several class libraries are available commercially that implement graphical user interfaces (GUIs), relational database processing, and communications. SET class libraries offer access to POS services through message-passing from other non-SET objects in the system.

Distributed Systems

Three- and *n*-tier client-server architectures, like the one you'll construct to operate your SET environment, use these object-oriented technologies that hide the inner details of programs *and* make their location within the system irrelevant, at least to all other objects.

Distributed object computing is a breakthrough in computing that resulted from the convergence of OO and client-server technologies. It blends the distribution advantages of client-server technology with the richness of living information contained in OO systems. Distributed objects fundamentally change the information processing landscape of businesses, and something totally new begins to happen. The methods by which business software is developed changes forever.

Distributed object computing is used to distribute objects across mixed-computer networks. It allows objects to interoperate as a unified whole, like a symphonic band. The network *becomes* the computer where distributed objects are at play.

Object Request Brokers

Objects interact by passing messages to one another. These messages represent requests for information or services. During any given interaction, objects dynamically assume the roles of clients and servers. The physical glue that ties the distributed objects together is an Object Request Broker (ORB). ORBs provide the means for objects to locate and activate other objects on a network, regardless of their location, the processor for which they're written, or the programming language used to develop them. ORBs are the *middleware* of distributed object computing that allows interoperability of objects.

What Is Middleware?

Middleware generally describes the glue that holds client applications and server applications together. Middleware takes care of all the details when a client requests a server-based service—a database query, for example. This not only makes system development easier, but allows a "high-level" view of the system that, for the most part, ignores the physical details of the implementation. This is significant because, in theory, it's possible to replace back-end services with similar ones without affecting client applications.

Middleware can be categorized in a variety of ways, often with considerable overlap. As viewed by function, five basic categories appear:

- Database middleware handles communication between client applications and database server engines.

- Network middleware enables workstations using virtually any network protocol to connect to servers operating on entirely different network protocols. With these tools, it's possible for applications to bridge dissimilar network architectures, which maximizes the use of existing resources.

- Custom server applications may be made accessible by desktop systems through the use of application processing middleware. Typically this is accomplished with server-based applications allowing access via Remote Procedure Calls (RPCs) that can be invoked by custom-written applications running on the workstation. A typical use might be a desktop program that creates custom letters, but requires information from a mainframe-based host system. RPCs might be used as the mechanism to obtain the information from the legacy systems.

- Object Request Brokers (ORBs) use OO development techniques and allow client applications to invoke server functions through message-passing mechanisms that are simpler to use and help to reduce development efforts.

- Specialized middleware is used to offer services such as transaction processing monitors, printing, faxing, or other services not specific to existing products.

When objects are distributed across a network, clients can be servers and conversely, servers can be clients. It doesn't matter, since they work in cooperation with each other. Essentially you can view the whole concept of distributed object computing as simply a global network of mixed clients and servers or, more precisely, cooperative business objects.

Legacy (already written) system processes and data can also be *wrapped up* to appear as objects. Once wrapped, these legacy system functions can participate in a distributed object environment. Wrapping is a technique of creating an OO interface that can access specific functionality contained in one or more existing computer applications.

Objects only know what services other objects provide (their interfaces), not how they provide those services (their implementation). The hiding of implementation details within objects is one of the key contributions of object-oriented technology to managing complexity in distributed computing environments.

Distributed Object Standards

The Object Management Group (OMG) defined the CORBA/IIOP standard for distributed object systems in mixed computer environments. In 1992, OMG approved a standard architecture called the Common Object Request Broker Architecture (CORBA) that defines the services that an ORB needs to provide. CORBA Internet Inter ORB Protocol (IIOP) guarantees CORBA interoperability over the Internet.

Other major software vendors offer their own, often competing, distributed object technologies. Some commercial implementations of distributed object computing products include Expersoft's PowerBroker, IBM's DSOM, Sun's NEO, Iona's Orbix, and HP's ORB+. A complete ORB implementation offers C++ and Java developers the ability to fully distribute application objects among various platforms and provides client access to distributed objects from Windows 3.1 and NT programs. Distributed Component Object Model (DCOM) is Microsoft's contribution to the Object Request Broker debate. DCOM describes an ORB for use with ActiveX, formerly known as OLE (Object Linking and Embedding), as Microsoft's proprietary model for component software within Microsoft Windows, and is currently being extended to support other platforms. Its intent is to create object-based standards that promote the use of Microsoft products.

Benefits Galore

In summary, Object-Oriented Analysis and Design helps your SET project in the following ways:

- Abstraction of processing enables you to understand functionality without requiring you to understand specific implementation details (e.g., cryptographic processing).

- Similar processing is collected into a single object.

- Low-coupling between objects eliminates shared data areas and corresponding threats to security.

- Easy to integrate with developer support and production management tools.

- Simplifies testing procedures.

- Improves system documentation.

- Reduces system maintenance and administration costs.

- Improves system scalability.

- Allows reuse of existing processing.

- Allows access to legacy system processes and data using object-wrapping techniques.

- Reduces overall development costs.

With these ideas in mind, let's turn our attention to their application, looking at the specific areas of Merchant Server SET-compliant POS software.

Applying OOA&D to Your SET Project

In this section, we'll identify objects to describe what's happening within the system by looking at relevant services needed for SET, some possible attributes for those services, and which services rely on others. Later, you can decide how to best implement these objects—through purchasing them, developing them yourself, or assembling them from existing objects. You can also better decide how to distribute them to maximize processing speed, implement the necessary security, and scale them to fit growing needs. These steps are further discussed in the next chapter on design.

At the end of this analysis phase, you'll have a complete set of business and processing requirements in the form of a model that a designer can use to determine the best approach to their implementation, deciding on *how* the system should be built. Recall that the tasks here are to determine *what's* needed, not how to solve the needs.

Let's begin by taking a context-level view of the SET POS operating environment. Figure 14.2 shows one way to view the high-level context for the SET payment process. It illustrates the overall interaction between Card-

Figure 14.2 Payment system context diagram.

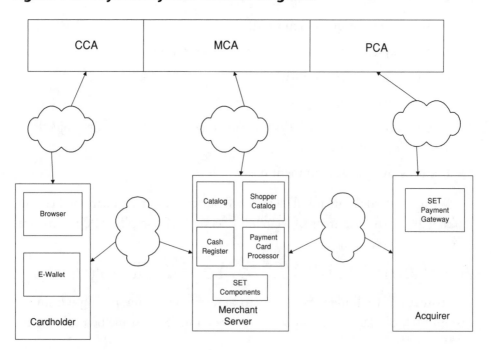

holder systems, Merchant systems, Acquirer systems, and CA systems to meet SET's overall processing requirements. We'll focus on the center of the diagram, where the Merchant Server and SET POS System reside.

To begin, let's look at each phase of the on-line payment card transaction from Chapter 2 and see which services will be needed for each phase. Some of these services will be part and parcel of the SET software that you'll select later. At this point we're mainly concerned with determining all the services and information needs. Even if you don't wind up writing your own software for every service identified, their identification is still essential for an overall understanding that a designer requires in the next phase.

Phase 0: Digital Certificates in Place for Transacting. Services needed here require processing to support certificate requests from several Merchant Certificate Authorities, storage of received certificates, renewal and maintenance processing, security to assure private key protection, etc.

Phase 1: The Shopping Experience. Here you'll need the services that provide access to catalog information, determining the availability of merchandise for sale, possible customization of the customer's interface to meet the customer's preferences or historical buying patterns, dynamic generation of Web pages based on stored information, etc.

Phase 2: Item Selection. Services here include accumulating the information about products selected for purchase, determining the sale's running total, and other services that typical shopping cart software provides.

Phase 3: Check Out. In this phase, the services needed include order-totaling, determining applicable charges and taxes, and presenting the completed order to the customer, requesting her approval for the order, and any subsequent processing to handle changes in the order.

Phase 4: Payment Selection. Here you'll need services that permit your customer to choose from a variety of payment options. In the case where a SET-enabled payment card is chosen, you'll need a service that invokes SET POS processing (wake-up messages to the POS).

Phase 5: Payment Initialization Processing. Services required here include receiving and processing SET messages for purchase initialization, certificate distribution to Cardholder E-wallets in response, receipt of signed purchase order data and handling of payment instructions that will pass through to the Payment Gateway.

Phase 6: Payment Authorization Request. Here you'll need services for preparing authorization requests from information presented combined with information on your systems, processing for receipt of authorization responses and handling of both success and decline conditions, and preparation of return messages to your customer.

Phase 7: Delivery of Goods. Services here include pulling up authorized orders that require shipment, shipping information entry, and preparation of previously stored authorization requests for capture processing.

Phase 8: Capture and Settlement. Services for this phase include batching of capture requests, preparing capture messages, handling capture responses, batch reconciliation, and services to permit adjustments to orders, capture requests, and so on.

As you're defining these services and their associated attributes, your model may reveal similar services required for several areas of processing. You can abstract these into a single object that other objects can use as necessary. As you continually refine the model and determine the dependencies of objects upon each other, you're building the architecture or hierarchy of operations for the entire system.

Subsequent layers to the analysis will reveal more detail about each subcomponent, and define any additional subcomponents that are present to implement a service. Eventually all primitive components will be identified along with each set of services they'll provide, what attributes of data are required for those services, and so on. An OOA&D tool may help you in these efforts by keeping track of layers, components, and all associated data (attributes). Some OOA&D CASE tools will even help by creating source code once the components are fully defined. The beauty of this approach is that no work is sacrificed between phases as development progresses. The approach lends itself to any systems development life cycle—traditional waterfall development environments (analysis, design, build, test, rollout), as well as Rapid Application Development (RAD) environments.

Once you're satisfied that you've analyzed the "to be" environment thoroughly, you'll want to share your model with everyone from those areas of the business that will be affected to ascertain both the completeness and correctness of your model. Since OO analysis techniques build models that virtually anyone can understand in native terms, be sure they're comfortable with your work and they're ready to proceed into detail design. Remember, errors found and corrected during the analysis phase won't creep into subsequent phases as defects. Eliminating any errors now will spare you from tremendous time, effort, and frustration later.

At completion, your object model will contain a validated roadmap of what objects are present, what services they'll provide, and what data elements are needed by each service.

You can see how defining these layers of modularity helps you to design their placement within the network under which they'll operate. In Chapter 15, we look to how a system designer uses the model to select those mixes of technology and hardware architecture to best implement the services required.

DESIGNING YOUR SET SYSTEM

15

Building on the analysis in Chapter 14, we move into system design using the same modular approaches. Here we look at how to best distribute the system's hardware and software components throughout the network. Based on the object models that you created through your analysis, now is the time to decide if and what you'll buy or build. Based on these choices, you'll then select the appropriate combinations of hardware and software to support them. Several sets of decisions are made in this phase. Here you'll act primarily as a systems integrator, defining customized software components, conceptual layouts, and physical architecture layouts.

In this chapter we offer a recommended architecture in which a Web-based SET environment is best implemented. Topics covered here include:

- Defining software and hardware components to support SET and other processing needs

- Designing the elements of the logical and physical environment

- Benefits of using a distributed processing approach to SET

Designing the Components for SET

Effective design is critical to security, to scalability, and to the ultimate success of your site.

With the validated object hierarchy from Chapter 14 and sufficient understanding of your budget and processing requirements, you can now begin to map the conceptual view to a real-world implementation.

Software Design and Development Considerations

Each software design is going to vary because of differences in types of business, existing information systems, variations in business size, and other factors. Because of this, no single solution can possibly meet everyone's software needs.

During the object definition processes in the analysis phase, several SET-specific components were identified. Typically you'll purchase these as an off-the-shelf system that you'll customize with interfaces to your existing back-office operations. These interfaces should also be identifiable as objects that you'll construct using development languages such as C++ or Java, which will extend some classes that you purchase with your SET POS software.

Your design work should begin with a detailed understanding of your selected POS to best determine how these interfaces must be built to work properly. These interfaces will include:

- Access to legacy systems and data

- Update mechanisms to legacy systems and data

- Interfaces to existing DBMS products

- Interfaces to Merchant Server components (catalogs, shopping cart software, etc.)

- Interfaces to existing non-Internet-based payment card processing (for out-of-band) capture purposes

- Interfaces to shipping systems

- Interfaces to inventory adjustment systems to handle returns, credits, and exchanges

Your design work for these machine interfaces will likely include these activities:

- Design of user interfaces for all data entry and data maintenance processing (a prototype approach might be valuable here)

- Data management strategy development for overall access to back-office systems

- Designs for databases and tables or persistent objects to physically store the new information identified during your analysis work

- Design of message interfaces for all discrete objects

- Definition of state transitions for message-passing between objects to bring your object model to life

If you've used a CASE tool in your analysis work, you should be able to continue using it through the design phase, adding further details for implementation purposes.

Operating Environment Design

With software design approaches in hand, we can now turn the attention to the hardware and infrastructure necessary for operating your SET-compliant Merchant Commerce System. Hardware elements requiring specific attention include:

- Internal networks (LANs and WANs)

- Firewall(s)

- Web (HTTP) Server(s)

- Application Server(s)

- Database Server(s)

- Security Server(s)

While it's technically possible to operate all components on a single, monolithic computer, SET's security, processing, and reliability requirements mandate that you distribute the work over multiple, well-defined systems. This is a good time to review the list of environmental assumptions we describe in Chapters 8 and 10 . These will help you to better understand the context for certain design choices made in this chapter.

Figure 15.1 illustrates one design choice using multiple dedicated servers to implement SET's processing needs. The principles behind this design include meeting security requirements, distributing the work to assure the highest availability of resources, meeting scalability needs, and collecting common services into one place.

Figure 15.1 Multiple servers for SET.

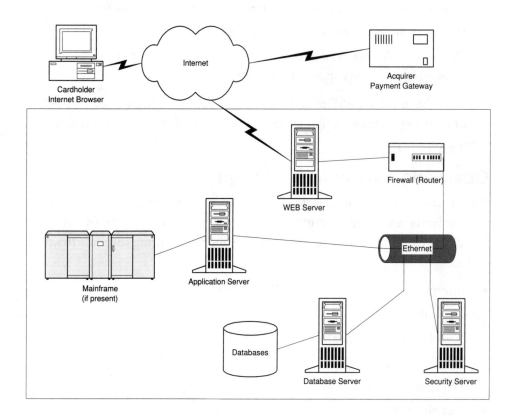

This diagram illustrates the complete operating environment for SET, showing where the Merchant network will interface with Cardholder and Payment Gateway systems via the public Internet. The boxed-in area of the drawing represents the Merchant network you'll need to build or enhance to meet SET's security and processing requirements.

Specific Servers for Specific Needs

The modular approach to design calls for the segregation of work on dedicated servers. The following describes the purposes and functions for each type of server you'll need.

- The Web Server (HTTP Server) responds to HTTP requests for HTML pages, which it delivers to customer browsers over the Internet. It's the only server that sits in front of the firewall and allows direct controlled access to the public Internet. It's on this server you may want to store static Web page content and graphic images. All information processing that the Web Server needs from Application or Database Servers can only be accessed through the firewall.

- The firewall controls the access to the internal (back-office) corporate networks. It serves as the mechanism under which the Web Server accesses applications and data that's found behind them. The firewall will typically run monitoring software to detect and thwart external attacks on the site, and is needed to protect internal corporate networks. Common firewall services are implemented as routers that sit in between two domains (subnets), and are selective about IP addresses from which the firewall receives packets before it permits their routing to the other domain (subnet). These select IP addresses are considered *trusted hosts*. Figure 15.2 illustrates how the firewall protects the internal back-office network from the public Internet.

- The Security Servers is where SET-related work is performed. This is the computer in which you'll load the SET POS software that you've purchased. In placing these components onto a separate server, you eliminate the need for multiple copies of SET Merchant digital certificates, and you permit their shared use by any Merchant Server software on the network. Security Servers handle the required cryptography, either through software or hardware implementations (see Chapter 6), manage your SET Merchant digital certificates, and rely on the Database Servers to log transaction and processing steps.

- The Database Server stores your product, purchase, and customer data in addition to all other distributed processing data already in place. It may use Object-Oriented Database Management products, traditional relational database products, or hybrids of the two. Choices of Database Server software include Oracle, MS SQL Server, Sybase, DB/2,

Figure 15.2 Firewall between back-office network and Merchant Web Server.

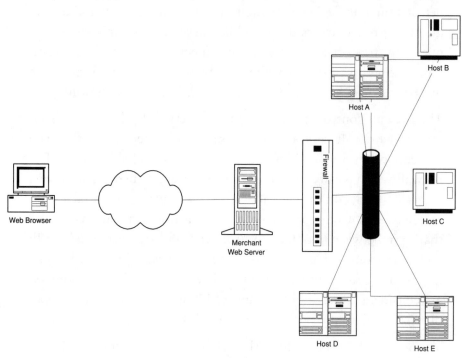

Informix, and ObjectStore. Be sure that your SET POS software is compatible with the DBMS product you select. In securing your database systems and software through a separate Database Server you ensure several benefits—most notably reducing the workload on the Application Server.

- The Application Server stores, manages, and operates those software components relevant to the business, including Merchant Server software, back-office accounting systems, customer information systems, and order-entry and fulfillment systems. You may opt for multiple Application Servers as your needs dictate. Any links to other legacy systems (e.g., mainframe-based systems) may be made through the Application Servers as well.

- If present, Mainframe systems can also be used in the distributed processing environment through the notion of object wrappers (discussed in Chapter 14), which preserve existing processing and leave the work where it may best be suited for operations or data storage.

Although Figure 15.1 shows a single instance of each server type, you may in fact want multiple, similar servers to distribute the work further. A distributed architecture naturally supports this. Over time, you may find that one or more servers become saturated with work, holding up processing elsewhere. Symptoms of saturated processors include unexpected waiting times despite normal server operation, inability to log in because too many processes are running simultaneously, or processes that appear hung up. You can solve these problems by adding more processors (e.g., symmetric multiprocessing), adding new servers, or upgrading existing servers.

With an understanding of the types of servers you'll need, we can now look at specific considerations for your design.

Designing Your Networks

SET environment network design is a critical element to ensure adequate throughput of secured processing. Choices here take into account such factors as current networks in place, corporate standards, projections of volume, and types of information traversing the network. Often your selection of server hardware dictates the network configurations that you'll implement. You'll also want to consider network management software tools to aid in supporting the network's operation later. Again, your choices of hardware may lead you to a native monitoring software. You may want to dedicate a PC or workstation to provide a constant view of your network's operation. These monitoring devices may also serve as an early detection of processor saturation. Some choices for software that perform network monitoring include these three:

- BMC's Patrol Knowledge Module for Internet Servers is an application management tool that covers Web servers as well as DNS, mail, FTP, and other services that are often found together. It concentrates on monitoring performance and looks for problems that might cause downtime. BMC also uses a Java-based browser interface to its Patrol product.

- AIM's Sharpshooter uses systems distributed across the network to monitor the traffic on each network segment, and correlates this with the traffic on the server. Samples of packets are taken and analyzed, and per-protocol statistics are generated and correlated with more conventional measurements. Preconfigured intelligent alarms and a GUI-based distributed installation process simplify setup and use.

- BGS has extended the capacity management capabilities of Best/1 to the network by collecting network protocol data on network segments (using dedicated PCs) and analyzing traffic patterns by users, applications, and protocols. It then feeds this data into a capacity planning model so that the impact of future changes can be predicted.

Often it's best to consult with network design experts who are familiar with your line of business and your e-commerce goals. These experts can help you design the most cost-effective and internally maintainable networks so that outside help should be needed only in the event of total network failure.

Designing Your Firewall(s)

Firewalls secure all back-office servers and networks from public access via the Internet. There are several types of firewall implementations available on the market. Your choice for a specific implementation will depend on your existing networks and your business needs. Companies that use a combination of intranets and extranets (see Chapter 19) will need extra security to protect systems from attacks on back-office subnetworks.

With a *dual-homed gateway* firewall (illustrated in Figure 15.1), the Web Server sits in between the Internet and your private internal network. It separates the Web Server from all other servers in the environment. All calls to CGI scripts, calls to other application programs, and calls through

APIs are directed from the Web Server to the firewall. The configuration illustrated offers significant levels of security for your SET and other related data and processes.

Designing Your Web Servers

Chapter 10 outlined some steps to secure your payment processing environment. This is a good time to review those steps as they apply to your Web Server. All unused services should be removed or turned off.

Because your Web Server acts as the front line to both your customers and would-be attackers, you'll want to be certain it's not vulnerable, but at the same time you want to be sure it's available with sufficient robustness to prevent undue wait times for your customers.

Follow your Web Server installation guidelines to maximize site security. As your site grows, you might consider mirrored Web Servers to ensure the highest degree of availability and throughput for any visitor browsing your merchandise catalog.

In addition, follow the Web Server installation instructions to configure the server for both System and Web log generation. You can use these logs to detect if attacks on your site are occurring. Analyze them periodically to determine if you're being subjected to attack.

Designing Your Application Servers

Application Servers store and operate your application programs and communicate with all other servers on the network as needed to access services located on them. Some of the application programs you'll operate here include:

- Accounting systems and other application software, including programs you've developed and the interfaces to SET's services that we discussed earlier in this chapter

- Merchant Server software (Netscape Commerce Server, Microsoft's IIS and SiteServer, Open Market, etc.)

- Database client access components (e.g., Open Client, ODBC)

• Links to mainframe systems via API calls or object wrappers

From your software design work, you'll need to decide which objects are best operated from the Application Servers and which on other servers within the network.

Application Software

The application software that runs on the Application Server is typically where the "business rules" are found. If you place too much work on one Application Server you may adversely affect performance or find later scalability problems. Consider the volume of work you're trying to perform, the length of time it takes to run particular processes, and the frequency of such work.

If you begin to experience the symptoms of saturation (discussed earlier), you might consider scaling your Application Servers to meet the demand for processing. You may be able to off-load some of the work to other Application Servers on the network. You might also consider scheduling certain processor-intensive work at times when demand for processing is lighter (early morning hours, weekends, etc.).

Merchant Server Software

Merchant Server applications such as Net.Commerce, Netscape Commerce Server, OpenMarket Server, or other shopping site components will operate on your Application Server. These components will implement the catalog functions using dynamically generated data from the Database Servers, shopping-cart software to permit selection of products, customer-centric processing such as profiles, and all other non-SET-specific components. SET processing is invoked from this server via client calls to SET POS APIs that operate on your Security Server.

Database Client Access Components

Application Servers access, update, and store data via client calls that initiate a process on the Database Servers. Common implementations here include Open Database Connectivity (ODBC), Open Client, and others. With these components, customized configurations establish access control lists to the databases. These lists ensure data protection by establishing which client host systems can communicate with which databases, and what access privileges are permitted from them.

Object Wrappers

If you're using a mainframe system for existing systems and need to continue using them, you may want to explore the use of object wrappers for mainframe application programs. As we discussed in Chapter 14, using object technology you can create interfaces to mainframe systems that other objects can invoke as needed for access to information.

The most common approach uses the High Level Language Application Program Interface (HLLAPI) utilities that are commonly found in mainframe terminal emulation software, such as Dynacomm, Attachmate, Netware for SAA, and Microsoft SNA Server. With HLLAPI, you can write programs using languages like C or C++ that serve as stand-ins for human operators at a terminal's keyboard. These programs can both enter information onto terminal screens and extract information that's displayed to use in other programs you may write. These *screen-scraping* applications can further be wrapped up in object message interface formats that other objects can invoke through simple message passing. You can use these techniques to locate information that helps to pre-fill-in browser forms, determine inventory availability, or any other process that must remain within a mainframe processing environment.

Designing Your Security Server

The Security Server is where SET-related processing occurs. You'll install most of your SET POS system software on this server to isolate the system from the rest of the network. Here you'll operate the Cash Register functions, payment card processing functions as needed by the Cash Register software, and SET processing work as requested by the Payment Card Processing components. The software here will manage the access to your Acquirer Payment Gateways, perform the required cryptography processing, manage your digital certificates, and use the Database Servers to store all related processing data.

Look at the detailed directions for your POS system to help you understand what work occurs where so that you can best decide the placement of
the system's components. Each vendor's implementation for each operating
system may work differently.

If you opt to use hardware-assisted cryptography, it's on this server
you'll install the boards and related software. If you use a separate stand-
alone cryptographic processor, your SET POS software will need configuration changes to access its services. Consult your installation and user's guide
for detailed instructions for the products you select.

Designing Your Database Servers

Effective design of your Database Servers is a critical factor in the overall
performance of your systems. Here you'll want to balance your transaction-
processing needs with your information reporting needs. Typically database
systems are optimized for one type of work or another. Transaction processing requirements are far different than Online Analytical Processing
(OLAP) requirements. Attempting to mix those two operations on the same
server often leads to problems.

Take these factors into account when you select your DBMS and its
architecture. You may want distinct Database Servers for distinct processing, recognizing that the distributed system approach enables you to split
the work among multiple physical devices while maintaining a single logical view of all data relationships throughout the network.

Use extra care to ensure that your SET POS retains exclusive access
rights to all SET-related databases and tables. Consult your POS system
installation guide for the details pertaining to your DBMS software.

Selecting Your Middleware

Middleware is identified through the presence of APIs that expose offered
services to other applications and defines the communication parameters
needed (see Chapter 14). Middleware encourages system development to
occur at the highest logical view of a system, almost without regard to its

physical implementation. There are several families of middleware you might need within this distributed processing model:

- Data-oriented middleware is thought of as "Fat-client" partitioning. Fat-clients typically store the business logic (rules) and the user interface components on desktop computers with the database requests and responses traveling over the network to the Database Servers. You might use this type of middleware if your shipping department is remote to your other operations or has no dedicated connections into your network. For example, you could develop a desktop database application (MS Access, etc.) that allows shipping personnel to enter information throughout the day that you upload via batch processing at night.

- Function-oriented middleware uses Remote Procedure Calls (RPCs) to perform work. RPCs may be thought of as remote subroutines that are located on Application Servers across the network, used when needed by other Application Servers or desktop systems. Many of the UNIX systems rely on RPC for interprogram communications.

- Event-oriented middleware, also known as Message-Oriented Middleware (MOM), works by offering message request and response queues that stack up requests, perform the operations, and return the results through messages passed back to the application. The main feature of MOM systems is that asynchronous (untimed) access is available, permitting applications to continue on with other processing without waiting for replies in between messages sent. By simply *reacting* to return messages whenever they arrive, the work can continue, maximizing resource uses. An example of message-oriented middleware is IBM's MQSeries, which simplifies and standardizes development work for a variety of applications, notably Web-based application software.

- Object-oriented middleware uses Object Request Brokers (ORBs) and behaves in a manner similar to MOM systems in that it works by handling the arrival of service requests as events. See Chapter 14 for a discussion of ORBs.

- Screen-oriented middleware describes the "Thin-client" approach to application partitioning. With Thin-clients, application logic resides on the host systems, with only the user interface components residing on the client (desktop) system. Thin-clients are often developed using Java applets that are downloaded from network servers and run within a browser window. You might consider this approach in developing the interface for your shipping department to enter order fulfillment data.

Benefits from Distributing SET Processing

You'll find that a modular design of your SET environment offers a variety of benefits that you'll realize immediately and continue to realize while it's operating. These benefits include the following:

- Centralization permits you to control and secure programs and servers under a mainframe-like environment that's scalable, predictable, and easily monitored.

- Reliability is enhanced, since equipment resides in a controlled environment that can be easily replicated or moved onto fault-tolerant systems.

- Scalability is easier, since servers or processors can be added to achieve acceptable levels of performance. Centralized database services tend to be more optimal, since constant monitoring leads to prevention and quick detection of server or network problems.

- Flexible, well-defined software layers permit the highest degrees of responsiveness to changing business needs, allowing you to quickly adopt improvements in technology. Additionally, non-PC clients (POS devices, voice-response units, hand-held devices, etc.) can be added at any time, since the interfaces to them are based on open industry standards and are well defined to developers.

- Existing mainframe services can be reused through the virtue of a flexible data layer. Mainframe services made to look just like any other data service layer preserve the transaction processing capabilities of the mainframe. This is significant, since mainframes tend to be optimal environments for high-volume transaction processing.

- Systems based on open industry standards allow you to rapidly incorporate new technologies into the operation without the concern of interoperability problems that exist with products based on proprietary approaches.

When you view your entire system (software and hardware) as a set of collaborating objects, you assure yourself the highest degree of flexibility for development, implementation, operation, and maintenance. With a detailed blueprint for your system's architecture, you can better plan the work for the next phases of implementation, installation, and testing.

Because hardware purchases often take time, you may want to consider using a critical path method (CPM) and project scheduling tool to plan these next tasks, taking into account order lead times, cabling requirements, network-related activities, and so on. Working with a single value added reseller (VAR), you may be able to accelerate some of this work.

In Chapter 16, we shift the focus from design activity to actual system installation and configuration work as it relates to implementing SET.

SET Installation and Configuration

It's time to discuss how to install and configure your Merchant SET POS software. We continue to refer to these systems generically as POS, since their closest counterpart in the *real* world is the POS device. Here we examine the general tasks of installation, using IBM's CommercePOINT eTill and GlobeSet's POS software as examples. This POS system functionality is required for all the phases of the on-line payment transaction in which SET is active.

In this chapter, we cover the following topics:

- Another view of the POS system architecture
- The basic components of the payment system software
- A sample checklist of preinstallation activities
- Installation steps for the payment system software
- Obtaining a Merchant Certificate
- Configuring the system
- Running and maintaining the payment system
- Managing databases

Another View of the SET POS Architecture

POS software performs all the same functions as the card-swiping machines used pervasively at Merchant locations today, with the additional security of a SET implementation to protect private and confidential information while it's traversing the Internet. Figure 16.1 takes a view of the SET operational environment from the perspective of POS software.

The diagram in Figure 16.1 corresponds to work conducted in those phases of the on-line payment transaction where SET is operating. It also corresponds to the normal purchase flow protocols, as described in Chapter 11.

Figure 16.1 POS architecture overview.

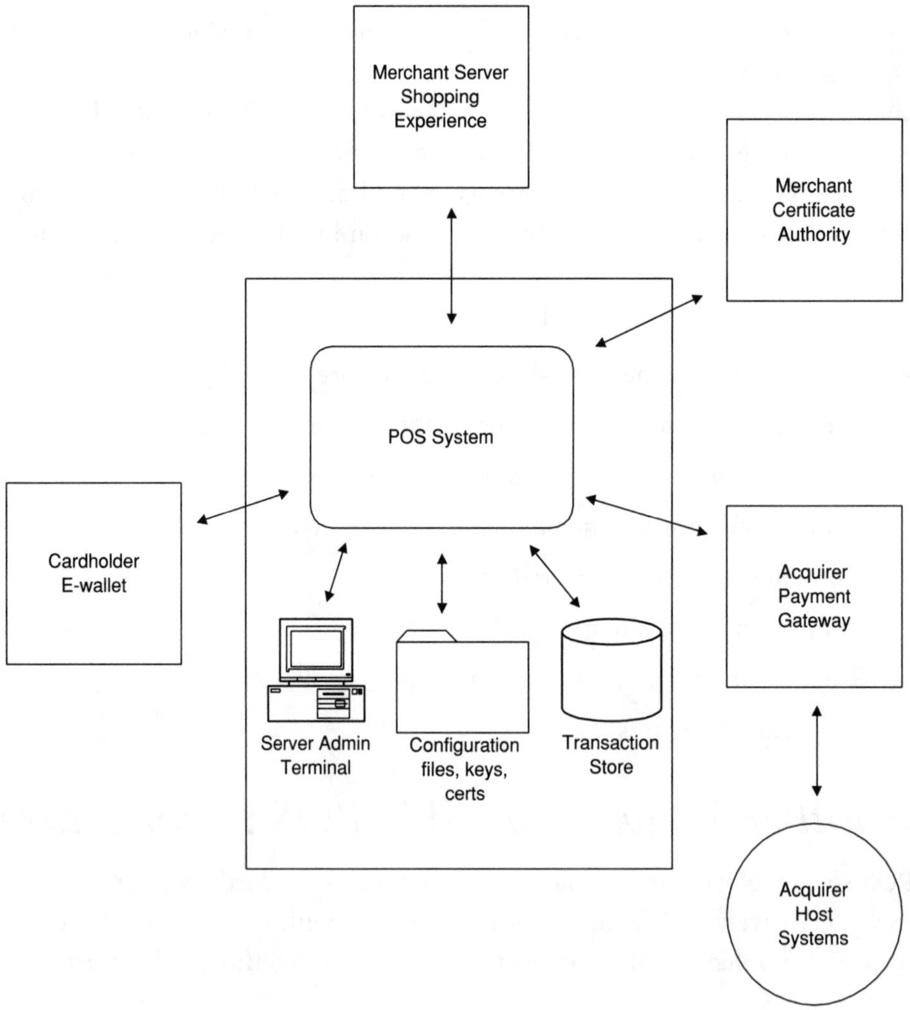

There are nine steps in this process. The Cardholder who has already installed the E-wallet software on her PC and has obtained a certificate for each card brand she wants (Phase 0—doesn't count as a step), makes the first step and selects some merchandise (Phase 1), clicks the BUY button (Phase 2), proceeds to check-out processing (Phase 3), and selects a payment card for the purchase (Phase 4).

The Merchant Server sends a message to the POS system through an API that a payment card transaction has been initiated. The POS sends a wake-up message through the Merchant Server back to the Cardholder's wallet to initiate SET processing for the payment (start of Phase 5).

- The wake-up message launches the Cardholder's E-wallet.

- The Cardholder enters her secret password after reviewing the transaction data and clicks OK.

- The purchase details, along with the Cardholder's certificate, are sent to the Merchant POS software, which returns a response to the E-wallet. The Cardholder can now verify the Merchant's identity.

- The Cardholder's E-wallet sends a purchase request message to the Merchant POS which notifies the POS that the Cardholder has proceeded with the purchase (end of Phase 5).

- The Merchant POS sends a payment card authorization request message to the Payment Gateway, which returns a response indicating whether or not the payment is authorized (Phase 6).

- Assuming that the payment is authorized, the POS sends a message to the Merchant Server indicating that the Cardholder request has been approved and the server can proceed with completing the transaction.

- The Cardholder receives an acknowledgment message indicating success or failure of the transaction.

Phases 8 and 9 are assumed to occur at some point in the future. What's described here is only the on-line interaction from order to purchase completion.

Figure 16.2 SET and non-SET messaging between all SET entities.

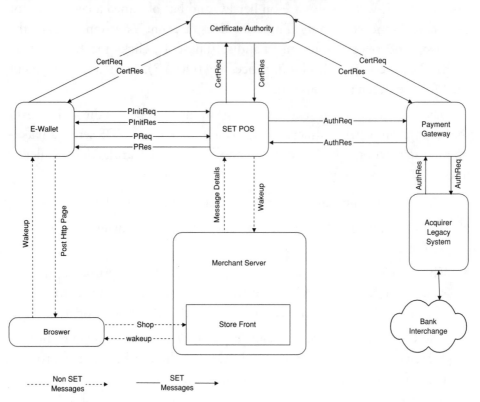

We've discussed SET-specific messages all along, but non-SET messages are also required to fulfill a transaction. These messages include those necessary to access the data required to transact. They also include E-wallet wake-up-type messages, which SET does not explicitly define, but which are required to make SET work.

The relationship between two types of messages (both SET and non-SET), and between the Cardholder, the Merchant, the Acquirer Payment Gateway, and the Certificate Authorities within the POS system, are shown in Figure 16.2. The broken lines indicate the flow of non-SET messages. Solid lines indicate SET messages.

In Chapter 10 we looked at various commercial implementations of SET POS Systems, including those from IBM, GlobeSet, VeriFone, and Cyber-Cash. Here we begin to dissect some of these products to see what's required to install and configure them properly.

POS Components

Merchant SET POS products vary in their implementation, but we can talk generally about the basic components of the system. Webmasters can expect to find the following components in any SET Merchant product:

- A Java-based application that receives payment messages from both the Merchant Server and the Cardholder and sends messages to the Payment Gateway.

- An Application Programming Interface (API) for C or C++, which enables the Merchant Server software to communicate with the POS.

- A modifiable User Exit library that permits callback functions, allowing the Merchant Server administrator to view payment processing information dynamically during the course of a transaction.

- Configuration databases and transaction databases, typically relational in structure (e.g., DB2, Oracle, Sybase, MS SQL Server), that contain information about Merchant Digital Certificates, private keys, transaction logs, authorization responses, and so on.

- User interface forms to configure, administer, report, and allow manual intervention to the POS Systems.

- A SET digital certificate registration utility to obtain and store certificates.

Preinstallation Checklist

Prior to installing the POS system, the webmaster must gather certain site configuration information that's needed by the configuration database. This information includes:

- Database and systems administrator information. This will include server IP addresses, gateway addresses, and other local information.

- Hostname and IP addresses of the server where the POS will reside. You can obtain this information most commonly from the /etc/hosts file on UNIX-based servers.

- POS database name(s). These you'll define through your database management software.

- Merchant ID for obtaining a Merchant certificate. Your Acquirer will supply you with this information.

- Brand ID for each card brand (supplied by the Acquiring Bank). You'll need these for every card product that you wish to accept through the POS System.

- Merchant's six-digit BIN (again, supplied by the Acquiring Bank). Each Acquirer relationship that you maintain will use a unique Bank Identification Number.

- Brand URL for each card (again, supplied by the Acquiring Bank). Each Card Brand will provide a URL for Merchant Servers to obtain the artwork, policies, etc. for their brand(s).

- Location of the certificate key file(s) on the server's storage device.

- Valid server port IDs if other than the default. These settings help you limit access to outsiders by restricting the port numbers on which the servers communicate.

- IP addresses for Payment Gateways. Your Acquirer will supply you with this information.

- Terminal ID for the Merchant. Your Acquirer will also supply you with this information.

- Chain IDs (if multiple locations or lines of business) for the Merchant. You might need this information if your specific location is one of many and has been assigned a unique number in addition to your unique Merchant ID number.

- Store number for the Merchant. Your Acquirer will supply you with this information.

- Agent number for the Merchant. Your Acquirer will supply you with this information.

- Acquirer's business hours, holidays, etc. Your Acquirer will supply you with this information.

- Scheduled Payment Gateway maintenance downtimes, to prevent communications while under maintenance. Your Acquirer will supply you with this information.

With the above information in hand, you're ready to proceed to preparing the strategy for your installation. In the next section we look at the steps to installing a POS System, using IBM's eTill as an example.

Installation Steps for the POS System Software

The installation and configuration of your POS Merchant software involve a number of preinstallation tasks and the development of administrative procedures to support the software once you have installed it. The webmaster should consider the following activities and thoroughly understand their importance before beginning the actual installation of the POS System:

System requirements. The minimum configuration for hardware and software in order to run the POS System correctly.

Security considerations. Precautions you should take to secure the POS System and the security server (see Chapter 15) where you plan to install the POS software.

Backup and recovery procedures. The obligatory steps to ensure recovery of critical programs and data in the event of a system failure.

Database configuration and maintenance. Selecting the appropriate relational DBMS and steps to maintain it.

Preinstallation tasks. Common tasks you might need to perform before installing your POS software.

Separation of duties. Let common generally accepted accounting practices and systems administration duties be your guide here.

System Requirements

Your hardware and software needs will vary based on your operating platform and the POS system that you choose. You'll need to read the configuration recommendations from the vendor for your specific environment. However, you can expect to find a discussion of these operational needs:

- A Pentium processor, a desktop workstation, and a dedicated Security Server
- A supported operating system (AIX, Windows NT, etc.)
- Database software that supports Java Database Connectivity (JDBC)
- A Web browser
- A minimum amount of RAM
- Disk space requirements for logging, for error reporting, and for the POS databases

Security Considerations

You will never hear the final word on the importance of securing your equipment and your data, nor should you. You *must* make sure that you have taken every possible precaution to protect your equipment, your network, and your data.

Place your POS server and all backup media in a secure room with controlled access. This server should be dedicated to POS operations exclusively.

Next, look at the login accounts currently on the server. The only valid account should be for the systems administrator. You should delete all other accounts, including all guest accounts. Name your administrator account something other than "administrator." Also, set the password security options for your system by specifying a minimum password length, enforcing password uniqueness, and setting a low threshold for failed password attempts. Finally, enable event auditing for failed operations. Event auditing could prove useful in identifying attacks on the system or general system failures.

Protecting your network is also critical. You should use only TCP/IP and remove any other unused networking protocol stacks (NETBIOS-over-TCP/IP in particular may pose a major security risk). Block all TCP/IP ports except those used by the POS System. Finally, remove network access for everyone, including remote logins using telnet or rlogin, and configure the firewall enabling only those ports used by the Merchant Server and the POS software. Chapter 15 discusses these concerns as well.

Backup and Recovery Procedures

As with any hardware/software installation, you should put in place all the appropriate backup and recovery procedures to prevent downtime and significant loss of data. You need to decide what the minimum period of recovery for your system is. Backing up your POS registry settings and hardware cryptographic devices is critical. You should also be prepared to restore your databases with forward recovery, and to reinstall the POS software, registry settings, hardware cryptographic devices and associated data; and you should be able to verify all data integrity.

Database Configuration and Maintenance

You will probably have to decide whether or not to run your POS system and your database on the same machine. We recommend using a separate Database Server. Figure 16.3 shows two different implementations for your Database Server. If you do install the databases on a separate server, you will also have to configure the server on which you install your POS to communicate properly with the Database Server.

However you implement the Database Server, you will need to enable it for data encryption to support SET's processing. You should also use separate physical disks for recovering your database, not logical partitions of the same physical disk. Also, create a special user account for POS tables and remove all other access permissions for any other groups and users. Finally,

Figure 16.3 Options for installing the Database Server.

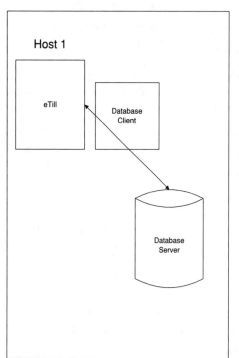

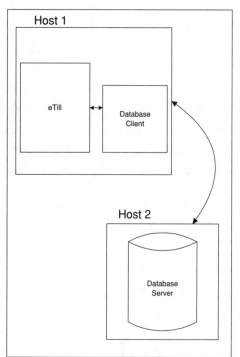

define a complete set of database backup procedures, including a full backup of user account tables, on-line daily backups, incremental on-line backups between full backups, and complete weekly backups for off-line storage.

Your POS database will also store your private keys, the state of your certificate requests, and records of certificates it stores and uses. Without access to its database, the POS will not run, nor will your on-line business.

Preinstallation Tasks

You will need to perform several other tasks, including the installation of the database software, before actually installing the POS software. Some of these tasks vary with the products involved, but you can generally expect the following:

- Your DBA will need to create a POS user account in the database that is maintained separately from the other tables and kept safe from all other users. The POS user must have the ability to create tables (permanent and temporary) with complete table processing capabilities.

- If you are running ODBC to a Microsoft SQL Server database, you will need to install an ODBC client on your POS Security Server.

- Determine whether your POS uses software-only or hardware-assisted cryptography, or both. There may be additional steps required to set it up appropriately.

- Create the preinstallation configuration file. This requires entering data specific to your POS product. You will likely have to enter information about port settings for receiving payment, error, and trace setting messages.

- Define the SET Configuration Profile, including the valid available TCP port where your POS will accept SET payment messages, the inquiry port for SET messages, and an indication of whether or not the SET messaging system issues trace messages.

- Enter the Acquirer profile information. This will include information about a specific acquirer and a Payment Gateway as they relate to a specific Merchant. Each profile will define a one-to-one relationship between an Acquirer and a Merchant account, and will include batch configuration information, business hours, and communication settings.

Obtaining a Merchant Certificate

Before running your POS system, you will have to request a separate certificate for every payment card Brand that you accept. You will need to obtain the following information from your Acquirer before obtaining these certificates (see Chapter 10 for more information):

- Merchant ID
- Brand ID
- Six-digit Bank Identification Number (BIN)
- Request URL for your Acquirer's Merchant CA site

With this information you can now run the appropriate utility to request a Merchant certificate. For example, the CommercePOINT utility uses *eecertreq*. You may need to enter a root hash to obtain a certificate—your Acquirer can provide this.

Starting the POS Software

Start-up procedures will vary depending upon the POS system you choose and the operating platform. In general, you'll locate the start-up directory for the start-up script and make sure it is in the path for the administrator's login. You will also have to start the database if it is not already running, log in using the administrator's ID, and start the POS using the appropriate command as specified by the vendor's systems administration guide.

Administering the POS Software

Ongoing administration of your POS system requires certain periodic intervention. A further discussion of these tasks may be found in Chapter 18. At a high level, these tasks include:

- *Pruning* the transaction data.

- Monitoring POS server statistics. This includes the server status, the number of SET-based purchase transactions attempted, SET-based certificate transactions attempted, and the number of SET-based batch transactions attempted.

- Adjusting POS timeout settings to regulate communication between the POS and the Cardholder, Payment Gateway, and Merchant CA.

- Monitoring message logs for system aberrations.

- Monitoring all aspects of system operation including the batching of transactions and the use of certificates. Your POS should include administration software that allows you to easily monitor its performance.

What Are the Next Steps?

Before you go *live*, you will have to thoroughly test and certify the installation and the daily processing cycle required for card authorization, capture, settlement, and reporting. Chapter 17 discusses the certification work you must perform, and Chapter 18 discusses how to keep your SET environment humming and ringing up sales.

TESTING AND CERTIFYING YOUR SET ENVIRONMENT

In Chapter 16, we outlined the installation and configuration steps to help you prepare your Merchant POS software for daily operations. Because your system is completely reliant on communications with external partners (Cardholders and Payment Gateways), it needs to be certified for proper performance under SET rules. This is where interoperability should be your predominant concern. Until all software components, regardless of their origin or their commercial status, are deemed effective in communications and operations with all other SET software components, SET simply won't work in the marketplace.

For example, if your IBM CommercePOINT E-wallet fails to send properly formatted and "decryptable" messages to your GlobeSet POS system or vice versa, you'll lock out customers or payment processors to all but those who use the same software as you do—creating an intolerable situation. While any given SET suite may work flawlessly across all its own components, it's of little use if it can't also work with components from other SET software developers. It's the same problem as when a Web site owner insists that you use one brand of browser to the exclusion of all other browsers. You'll never be certain which E-wallets your shoppers will use, nor can you be certain which Payment Gateway software your Acquirer uses. More important, it shouldn't matter and you shouldn't care. There's no room for proprietary implementations under the SET umbrella.

SET software testing must occur on three levels—specification compliance, compatibility, and end-user testing—after successful integration into the Merchant Server and legacy data sources. You will perform the end-user tests, but it's worthwhile to see how the SET industry polices itself to ensure that the other two forms of testing occur and succeed.

In this chapter we look at testing and certifying steps from compliance with SET specifications to interoperability to end-user integration testing points of view. In the first section, we'll look at some of the roles for SETCo in ensuring specification compliance. Next we'll look at some interoperability testing initiatives sponsored by members of the developer community. Finally, we'll look at the types of testing you'll need to perform before you ring up sales under SET.

While it's clear that you'll purchase SET POS software that's deemed compatible with all others, you need to be sure that your specific installation operates under the proper form, fit, and function defined by SET. Without these steps, your system will remain an island with no hopes for reaching into the pockets of the outside world.

Underwriting the SET Standard

Since SET is an open and neutral protocol, in theory you're able to purchase any implementation from anyone who offers it without concern for proprietary ingredients. To turn this theory into a reality, testing is required to ensure compliance as defined by the specification.

SET Version 1.0 is the baseline standard that developers use to build their systems, given the knowledge that later versions will most certainly supersede it. As SET versions evolve, software must be tested and retested for compliance with the new standards.

Developer interpretation of the specification is the root of the problem here. There must be a single, unambiguous understanding among developers that eliminates the possibility of proprietary implementations of SET. That's one of the major tasks of Secure Electronic Transaction, LLP, also known as SETCo. Just as Underwriter's Laboratories (UL) certifies that electrical products comply with their high sets of standards, SETCo does the same for SET's high standards.

Compliance Testing and Certification

SETCo, established shortly after the release of SET Version 1.0, operates under the sponsorship of the card companies, but independently of them. They assume the responsibilities for SET's development, maintenance, evolution, and market acceptance, and they regulate the use of the SETMark (discussed in Chapter 1) for products that successfully pass their rigorous compliance testing program. SETCo also maintains a dispute resolution board that decides how to best handle disputes or questions regarding an implementation. The SET Compliance Administrator (SCA) serves the administrative functions for SETCo, evaluating test results submitted by software developers and maintaining SET testing tool suites.

Upon signing SETCo's Master License Agreement and paying their fees, developers are given testing tools and scripts. These testing tools run through various permutations of SET messages, monitor and log the results, and assist in identifying noncompliance (if it occurs). Once a developer is satisfied that her product is compliant, she sends the test results back to SETCo for verification. After SETCo is satisfied, they'll permit the developer to use the SETMark on her software. Each compliant component of SET will bear its own SETMark, attesting that the component itself passed the battery of tests. The SETMark, however, does not assure you that the component will work properly with other counterpart SET components. At present, SETCo does not offer end-to-end testing services, nor do they offer interoperability testing services.

Baseline vs. Derivative Systems

Since developers will often produce SET software for a variety of computer operating systems, SETCo has established rules separating the products that must be tested and certified from the ones that need not be. Each unrelated operating system implementation is considered a baseline product, and must undergo full testing with submission of test results to SETCo. Derivative products are adaptations of baseline products intended for use on a similar operating system. An example of a derivative is a port from Solaris to AIX.

The derivative must be documented for SETCo's purposes, and testing is strongly encouraged, but test results need not be submitted and no additional fees are charged. Developers decide which products they consider the baselines, and which ones the derivatives.

In addition to the initial testing of the baseline version, SETCo requires developers to retest their products every six months. In the reevaluation process, retesting is performed using the latest testing scripts, with the results resubmitted to SETCo for evaluation. If recertification is not performed, the developer risks losing the use of the SETMark. Periodically, SETCo may decide to audit completed software compliance tests. Some reasons for these audits include random selection to ensure conformance or reports from the field indicating suspected failures or compromises of security. To remain in the compliance testing program, developers must pay an annual fee to continue licensing SETCo's services.

While SETCo oversees the testing that ensures direct compliance of distinct components, the interoperability testing between components and between products from different companies remains the domain of SET developers.

Two of the vendor-initiated approaches to interoperability testing are described below.

Interoperability Testing

Recognizing that interoperability is a critical hurdle, most SET developers agree that their products must be tested for interoperability before they're introduced into the marketplace. In answer to this, IBM and VeriFone produced the "Interoperability Reference Guide for SET Version 1.0," based on experiences culled from the testing they're performing. The document describes test scenarios, assumptions in use, configurations for environments, and other related information. Some of the problems experienced are also documented, along with some recommended solutions to them. The guide remains in an evolutionary state with its latest release in January 1998. It describes the testing between Cardholder to Merchant Systems, namely between VeriFone vPOS and IBM CommercePOINT E-Wallet and between VeriFone vWallet and CommercePOINT eTill. Testing between Merchant System and Payment Gateway System and complete end-to-end testing will be covered in future releases of the guide. They hope that the SET development community will adopt the Interoperability Guide as a uniform approach to testing that helps streamline the process of bringing new products to market.

As IBM's and VeriFone's testing progressed, they grouped incompatibility errors and problems into six categories:

Application layer inconsistencies. These problems usually stem from outdated DLLs and socket interface bugs.

Communication problems. These relate to time-outs using the Internet.

ASN.1 constraints. Various problems were found with field sizes that exceed maximum size ranges.

Conflicting interpretations of the standard. One example of this problem is the failure of an E-wallet to send data that the Merchant POS System software expects to be present.

Certificate chain validation errors. Failures in using the same root key certificates (different hash values) cause Tree of Trust traversal problems.

Differences in certificate propagation. Incomplete certificate chains also leads to Tree of Trust traversal problems.

The guide suggests that developers obtain and use certain debugging tools that aid in testing efforts. Merchants may also want to consider using these tools too to help identify or eliminate certain problems in their own installations. These tools include a TCP/IP protocol analyzer and a Protocol Data Unit (PDU) debugger. Both of these are available through shareware software channels.

RSA's SET 1.0 Interoperability Test Plan

RSA Data Security Inc. has also developed interoperability documentation to assist developers. The SET 1.0 Interoperability Test Plan defines a certificate infrastructure, data, and business scenarios that vendors may use to test their applications among themselves. The plan establishes the I14Y committee to manage the ongoing maintenance and management of the plan. RSA is working in conjunction with SETCo to help build upon their compliance testing program with interoperability testing, using similar business scenarios and data.

Another aid in the interoperability quest is the SET External Interface Guide (sometimes called SET Book 4). It contains useful information to help understand the core of SET, interoperability issues, and application interface design issues.

What All This Means to You

As the SET development community works out interoperability problems among themselves, you must decide for yourself which products you think you can trust and which ones you think are best avoided. Currently, no single authority exists to help you with your selection. Take into consideration your specific needs, and any experiences with vendors you've had, and use your common sense to help point you in the right direction for your POS System. Additionally, keep an eye on new developments surrounding SET software interoperability as you find them in the press, and join a local users group with which you can share experiences.

End-user SET Testing and Certification

Let's assume that you've found and installed a POS System you believe will do the job for you. You'll certainly want to be sure that the product bears the SETMark and has undergone sufficient end-to-end interoperability testing. Let's further assume that your installation work from Chapter 16 has progressed smoothly and you're prepared to *link up* for a complete end-to-end test for your customized installation. This end-to-end testing from Cardholder E-wallets to your POS System and from your POS System to your Acquirer Payment Gateway should run the entire gamut of messages that you expect your Merchant Server to process.

The following steps will help guide you through the process.

Step 1: Establish a Testbed

As previously mentioned, you want to make sure that your POS software will communicate with any commercially viable E-wallets that your customers might use. To help make certain that it will, consider establishing a testbed for a variety of E-wallets that you're able to find on the market. Several examples of these are described in Chapter 9, and more may show up on the market over time. Because you won't know (and shouldn't care) which E-wallets your customers use, you'll want to be prepared for anything. The moment you turn someone away because of E-wallet problems, you'll likely never see them at your site again.

Dedicate individual PCs for each E-wallet, just like your customers would. Obtain actual or test Cardholder digital certificates for each card product that you accept on your server. Load each wallet with all certificates to isolate card-specific problems or issues. Also, use an ISP for remote access to your Merchant Server. Avoid using your intranet for testing, since it won't fully simulate the effects of communications over the Internet. You may consider placing these test machines in the homes of your employees to help you run through all types of testing scenarios faster.

Try to use the same test cases for all E-wallets and all card charges. Doing so permits you to compare the results on an equal footing. Take the time up front to create these test cases, knowing what the correct results should be when everything works properly. Document your findings thoroughly and report problems to the vendors who developed the software. To help your shoppers, you may want to list the brands and versions of E-wallets that you know work correctly with your POS software, and update this list regularly. You may also consider adding hypertext links to E-wallet vendors to aid those shoppers who aren't yet ready for SET payment processing. The easier you make it for your customers, the easier they'll make it for you.

In addition, offer as much evidence of SET compliance on your shopping site as the industry makes available to you. For example, MasterCard

Figure 17.1 MasterCard's Shop Smart logo.

provides the Shop Smart logo (shown in Figure 17.1), which you may wish to display when your site is ready for public access.

Once you're prepared for any E-wallet messaging that may come your way, it's time to look at your POS System to Payment Gateway messaging.

Step 2: Test Your SET POS System with Your Acquirer's Payment Gateway

Payment Gateway testing of your POS System is far more comprehensive—and complex—than testing with E-wallets alone. Beyond real-time payment processing, you'll also need to be certain that capture processing and batch administration processing operate properly. Your bank or acquirer may provide you with testing suites to use. Often, Acquirers will perform your testing on their SET testbed. They'll provide you with their test system IP address and the parameters they expect, which you'll need to customize the POS settings (discussed in Chapter 16).

Beyond their standard testing suites, you'll also want to include your earlier E-wallet test cases to ensure smooth operation the entire way through. If you're only using your Acquirer's Payment Gateway for authorizations (see Chapter 18), your testing will be complete after you're both satisfied that the POS software performs its job. If you're also using the POS System for capture and batch administration, further testing will be needed.

Another consideration for testing is the number of Acquirers you're using. Try to arrange the testing with them serially—don't try all the testing at once. Changes that one may require you to make could affect the testing or production uses of another. Before you move on to the next Acquirer, be sure that the previous one is stable. If you need to make changes due to a subsequent set of tests, go back and retest earlier successful test results (regression tests). Furthermore, don't try and rush through the testing process. There are *no* shortcuts to SET—don't try to find any. The more rigor you put forth earlier, the fewer headaches you'll experience later on.

Once all your POS System to Payment Gateway testing has been successful, your Acquirer will provide you with the right settings for its production systems. You'll use these settings to customize the POS software for final production setup. Once that's in place and you're confident in your installation, it's time to tell the world your doors are open for business.

A caveat remains however, one which neither the E-wallet vendors nor your Acquirer will help with: you must do system security testing.

Step 3: Perform a Comprehensive Security Examination of Your Site

In Chapters 8 and 10 we described the environment that SET assumes will be present for its operation. Now's the time to ensure that you meet these requirements. Try to use every trick in the book to break your security. If you don't, someone else most certainly will. Consider hiring a consulting company that specializes in such work to help you ascertain a secure installation. A single well-publicized breach of security may be all that's needed to keep customers far away from you. Several dimensions of security should be tested and several types of tests within each one should be performed. Refer to the guidelines that we provide to help you test them all.

The gamut of testing described in this chapter not only ensures that your installation will perform as it should, it also offers you something that money cannot buy—peace of mind! If any doubts remain, just keep on testing till you're absolutely *sure* your system is ready.

In Chapter 18, we'll look at what your SET POS System requires you to do on a daily basis to keep it secure, humming, and racking up sales.

Operating Your SET Environment

Throughout this section of the book we've looked at how to analyze your system in terms of its components. We've offered an approach to designing your system that maximizes resource utilization while providing the highest degrees of security, simplified installation, maintenance, and operation. In Chapter 17, we looked at the process of testing your site to uncover any bugs in the tasks it must perform daily. At this point, your system should be operational, stable, and ready for high-demand use.

Given that this is true, it's now the time to turn our attention to daily and periodic operations for your SET-compliant Merchant Server as they relate to the POS software. In this chapter we'll cover the following topics:

- Capture processing
- Batch settlement processing
- SET POS software administrative tasks
- Exception processing
- Pruning data
- Reporting
- Monitoring your SET environment

Capturing Transactions

As you may recall from earlier chapters, a transaction may not be captured (completing the sale) until the goods are shipped or the services are performed. This implies that authorized transactions must remain on file for a period of time before a capture request may be initiated. How this is specifically accomplished depends on a variety of factors, including:

- Interfaces to shipping and inventory management systems (if any)
- Physical processing at your warehouse
- Existing processing for other, non-SET charges

The SET Specification offers support for several mechanisms to capture previously authorized transactions, but it does not advocate any specific mechanism. Neither do any of the Merchant SET POS Systems available on the market. In this section, we'll look at some different scenarios of how capture operations might be performed. It's up to you to adapt to whatever model works best to suit your operations. There are never easy answers to complicated questions!

Authorization, Capture, and Settlement Payment Gateways

As each acquiring bank and card company implements SET, you'll find that it's done differently in accordance with their policies, their systems, their agreements with Merchants, and so on. A host of options for each arrangement only complicates matters further.

In the cases where you use your Acquirer's Payment Gateway to authorize, capture, and settle your transactions under SET, you're offered several different methods to perform the work.

Scenario 1: Manual Capture at Shipment Time

In this scenario, you'll put in place a PC with a Web browser and intranet connection to your POS System that permits a shipping clerk to indicate those transactions that have shipped or partially shipped. The GlobeSet POS implements this function through the interface shown in Figure 18.1.

Using the interface, your shipping clerk will locate the previously authorized transaction and change its state from authorized to captured, partially captured (in cases of back-ordered goods, partial shipments, recurring charges, etc.), or credits in cases of returned goods.

Figure 18.1 The GlobeSet POS Transaction Detail screen.

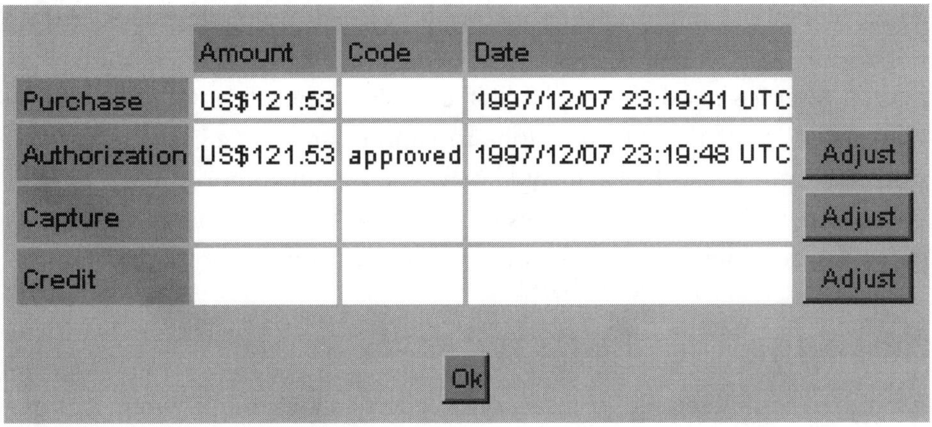

	Amount	Code	Date	
Purchase	US$121.53		1997/12/07 23:19:41 UTC	
Authorization	US$121.53	approved	1997/12/07 23:19:48 UTC	Adjust
Capture				Adjust
Credit				Adjust

Ok

This scenario may be most appropriate where few interfaces to order fulfillment systems exist. Depending on your volume of sales, full integration of all involved systems may be a desirable future enhancement. Here you can still benefit from offering SET with current manually intensive back-office operations.

Scenario 2: Automatic Capture at Shipment Time

In this scenario, you'll write an interface (via the API or Software Development Kit) that links your shipping system to the POS System, in either real-time or batch mode. Doing so eliminates the manual intervention steps described above and provides a tighter linkage to enable unattended processing. Your POS software will *not* offer you these interfaces directly—you'll have to build them yourself.

In the case where all your sales come through SET payments via the Internet, this may make the most sense for you. If your operation supports charges from other channels too (e.g., mail order, telephone order, or fax) you may want to capitalize on those existing systems that currently perform the same work. You can accomplish this by siphoning off successful transaction authorizations from your Web site and merging them with the others.

Authorization-only Payment Gateways

While SET offers complete support for all payment processing steps, it does not require you to use SET for all your transactions. Acquirers may insist that all Internet-based charges be SET compliant, but it may not be worthwhile to strip off those transactions to capture and settle them separately. You may want to use the Payment Gateway to obtain authorization approval codes, and route those transactions into existing systems that handle all your other charges, thus centralizing your charge processing operations.

Settling Your Differences!

As a batch of captured transactions collects in each of your Acquirer accounts, periodic processing is needed to settle the batch, transferring the funds to your Merchant Account at your Acquiring bank. This may occur at scheduled times throughout the day, once a day, or through manual intervention. Let's see how the GlobeSet POS Batch Administration Form (shown in Figure 18.2) helps you accomplish this work.

Batch processing and batch status reporting allow you to manage your operations in ways that best suit your needs. Batch processing work may be time consuming, especially when batches fail to balance or where the volume of charges is high.

Figure 18.2 The GlobeSet POS Batch Administration form.

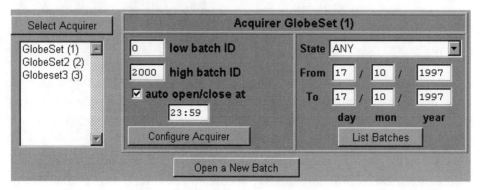

Once again, depending on your specific business environment, you're given several options, including *out-of-band* batch settlement which settles previously authorized charges from all sales channels. Refer back to Scenario 2 for ideas on how to approach this.

If you're using your POS system to manage your batches (i.e., Internet-only charges), you'll do this through an interface that may be similar (function-wise) to the one shown in Figure 18.2. With it, you can configure a search for a batch using date ranges or any of the various states that you're interested in viewing (All, New, Pending, Failed, Open, Settled, Closed, etc.) to see the details and manipulate the batch. This work may be performed by your Accounting Department or whomever you assign to perform charge processing work. Even with automatic batch settlement, you're bound to encounter situations where a batch is not in balance and investigation is required. This is typically *not* systems administrator work.

The closing of a batch initiates the settlement. Where the batch is deemed in balance, the Payment Gateway completes the work needed for exchanging the transactions and transferring funds. Where the numbers do not balance, further steps by the Merchant are required. Typically a reconciliation report is used to determine why the batch is out of balance and what needs to be done to make it balance. SET Batch Administration message pairs allow for a variety of request types to help you here.

Where you maintain different Merchant Accounts at various Acquirers (e.g., Visa and Mastercard at Bank of America, Diners Club through Citibank, and Discover Card through Novus), you'll need to settle open batches with the Acquiring Payment Gateway for each Acquirer, which may or may not be the same. Your POS terminal in the off-line world already supports what's referred to as *split-dial*, and your Merchant POS software needs to do the same.

In the cases where you're using an authorization-only Payment Gateway, your captured transactions will be processed along with your other captured charge requests through whatever means you're already using. You'll still need to indicate to your SET POS software that batch administration is not being conducted through the system. Each vendor of SET software may implement this differently.

What Is Split-Dial?

The split-dial feature, built into most POS terminals, allows Merchants to accept several card products without requiring them to use separate POS devices. Based on the intelligence (programmability) of them, when certain ranges of account numbers are read, a call is made to one processor; another card number range may call a separate number, and so forth. SET-compliant payment systems must include similar features if they're to fully replace POS terminals with Internet Web Server technology.

Care and Feeding of Your SET Server Environment

As we described in Chapter 17, POS software administration is required to establish your Acquirer relationship(s), obtain and install your digital certificates, and numerous other tasks. Here we revisit this work to ensure constant currency of information and any renewal processing for certificates ready to expire.

With any information processing system, especially a complex system like your SET environment, problems are bound to occur. At times, disk partitions fill up, communications may grind to a halt, or users may not be able to access software. As a systems administrator, you're the one most likely to be called for help.

To aid in the effort to deal with problems relating to your SET POS software, IBM supplies a systems administrative form for its CommercePOINT eTill product, shown in Figure 18.3.

With this interface, you can:

- Shut down the POS application for system maintenance. You may perform this periodically at strategic times (when traffic patterns indicate low usage times, etc.).

Figure 18.3 IBM CommercePOINT eTill Administration form.

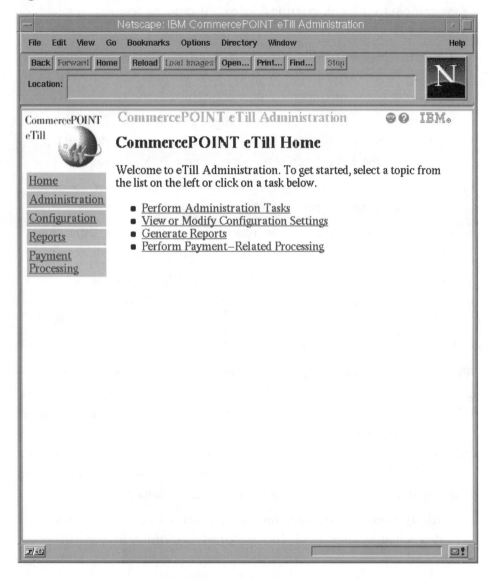

- Configure changes to the environment. Periodically you may need to update system settings, renew certificates, etc.

- Add new Acquirers. If you change your Acquiring Bank relationship, you'll need to adjust this information accordingly.

- Delete Acquirers no longer needed or used. Again, if you change your Acquiring Bank relationship, you'll need to remove outdated settings accordingly.

- Change Acquirer configurations. If your Acquiring Bank makes changes to its Payment Gateway, the new information will need to be reflected in your system's processing tables.

- Change timeout settings. Due to changes anywhere on the Internet, communications may begin to fail due to timeout problems. Here you can decrease the delay sensitivity of your POS System.

- Generate reports. Any POS-related reporting (custom or canned) may be requested via this interface selection.

- Perform exception transaction processing. Some of the situations that require exception processing are described in the next section.

While the actual interface you'll use may differ from the one shown above, similar processing selections will be available to you.

Exceptional Transactions!

While people generally think that exceptional means out-of-this-world, we use it here to mean out-of-the-ordinary. As we've seen in earlier chapters, SET provides message pairs to undo certain transactions and to correct batch balancing errors. Most of these require manual processing steps by whoever is appointed to perform them. As a systems administrator, your responsibility is to provide these operators the means with which to perform them when needed. Some of these unusual transactions include:

Authorization reversals that undo an authorization. Perhaps the customer changed his mind and canceled his order before you've shipped it.

Capture reversals that undo a sale. You might need to request a capture reversal in the event of returned goods within a certain time period (established between you and your Acquiring Bank).

Credits for returned goods. These may be required if returns occur after the period of time that still allows a capture reversal.

Credit reversals for goods not returned. These may be needed when you've issued the customer a credit for a return, but you never received the returned goods. Essentially this places the charge back on the customer's payment card account.

We've seen the interfaces that are used by the GlobeSet POS System (Figure 18.1) and IBM's eTill (Figure 18.3) to perform some of these tasks. Regardless of the interfaces used, your Accounting Department must have the ability to access the POS software to perform these tasks. You may also need custom software that interfaces your legacy systems to the POS System to permit automatic processing as it occurs. You may want to review the specific message pairs mentioned above to extract your system requirements for support purposes.

Pruning Your Databases

Your databases that support the POS software will require periodic pruning to eliminate messages that are only required for short periods of time. How much data you'll need to prune depends on how much disk space is available to the POS System, how many transactions are performed, and how long your policies allow customers to take actions on already-completed transactions (refunds, returns, etc.).

Three types of data require periodic pruning:

- Order table messages containing data about each individual order
- Short-lived messages containing several informational entries about transactions as they occur
- Long-lived messages that may be required for extended storage to enable later processing of a transaction

Each SET POS System will support the processing necessary to trim data that's not needed for continuous on-line processing. For purposes of example, we'll examine the IBM eTill system tables.

Order Table Messages

The eTill system logs information about each and every order it processes—merchant name, amount, currency type, order description data, and so on. You'll have to decide how often these data need to be removed or archived to another form of on-line or off-line storage. Factors in this decision include size of your server and database(s), volume of traffic, and type of business you're performing. You may want to keep these order data on file for the period of time you allow customers to make a change, or you may want to back them up into a restorable format until your customers contact you for changes. The driving factor here is your business policy. If you offer a money-back guarantee on all orders, you'll need to retain the data longer than if you don't have such a policy.

Short-lived Messages

eTill uses a table called ETSETMESSAGES to store in-process information about SET transactions. Most of the messages contained here are considered short-lived, that is, only needed while a transaction is processing. IBM's rule of thumb states that short-lived messages should be pruned away after one hour of their completion. To prune them, you may create a cron-type (automatically submitted) batch job that removes or archives the data, according to your needs. All SET messages other than those listed as long-lived messages below may be considered short-lived.

Long-lived Messages

Long-lived messages, also stored in the ETSETMESSAGES table for eTill, are needed for further processing. Your business model will determine if you use these message types, and how long they should remain on file. Specifically these are the long-lived message types that SET uses:

- Purchase Request (PReq) entries are needed until an authorization is complete (AuthRes received).

- The most recent authorization response (AuthRes) messages should remain on file until no further actions on the transaction are performed.

- The most recent authorization reverse response (AuthRevRes) messages should remain on file until no further actions on the transaction are performed.

- The most recent capture response items (CapResItem) and capture reverse response items (CapRevResItem) should be kept on file until no further processing action requires their use.

All other SET message responses may be considered short-lived and pruned hourly or as often as you deem appropriate for your installation.

System, processing, and MIS reporting from your POS System can provide you with valuable detail and summary information about your operations. Because your SET POS System's uses of databases is both open and flexible, reporting may be customized as much as you desire.

POS System Reporting

Reporting requirements will vary, again depending on the nature of your business, your accounting practices, and other factors. Since your system relies on relational databases for all data storage purposes, you can build whatever reports you might find useful. Canned and customizable reports may be supplied with your POS software for order information and for SET processing information. You can add your own, using a database access reporting package (Crystal Reports, Excel, MS-Access, or any other ODBC-compliant system). One of the steps in the analysis and design phase (see Chapter 14 and 15) will be defining those reports that your users need from the POS System. As a systems administrator, it's your duty to provide these reports and the means whereby users can select them. You'll want to offer users the ability to choose ranges of dates or other *interesting* sort or selection criteria that make the reports most useful for operational purposes.

For example, your accounting department may want to know about authorized transactions that await capture after 30 days. They may also wish to see trends in authorization and capture times for a specific customer, certain types of products, and so on.

From an operational point of view, management may be interested in viewing the activity resulting from high-volume or high-dollar transactions. They may also want to periodically audit the POS System to ensure that no Internet sales channel problems are occurring.

Monitoring the Environment

One of your extended responsibilities that goes hand-in-hand with systems administration work is the monitoring of the SET environment to ensure its smooth operation. In this section we're focused on the specific monitoring that's required for the POS software and the server on which it operates. Several dimensions of monitoring are required to ensure the highest degrees of availability and accuracy in processing:

- POS server statistics monitoring, including server status, the number of SET purchase transactions attempted, SET certificate transactions attempted, and the number of SET-based batch transactions attempted, successful, or failed

- Systems operation monitoring, including the batching of transactions and the uses of certificates

- Message logs monitoring for other troubleshooting and performance metrics

IBM offers two monitoring processes to help you in using their eTill POS software. Two logs are maintained that contain traceability data and error reporting. There are over 150 unique error conditions defined for eTill, along with error message context, description, severity level, and appropriate user responses.

GlobeSet uses a different approach for their POS. They provide administrators three functions (in the form of tabs) to help in monitoring the system's operation and use. The Process tab, shown in Figure 18.4, displays the statistics for the POS Server, including counts of all transaction types in process and completed since the last time the system was started. This facility is helpful when trying to diagnose communication problems with Payment Gateways and with Cardholder E-wallets. It

Figure 18.4 The GlobeSet POS Process tab.

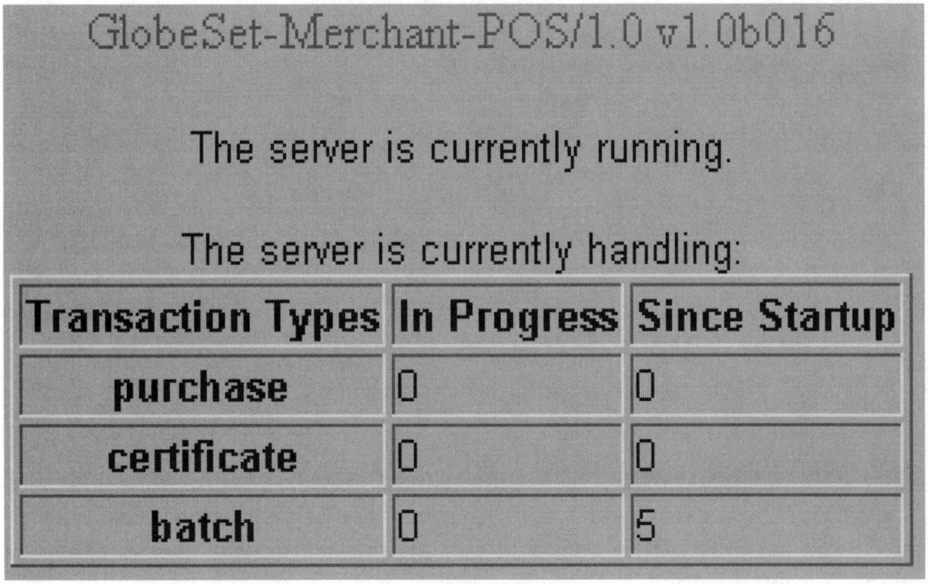

GlobeSet-Merchant-POS/1.0 v1.0b016

The server is currently running.

The server is currently handling:

Transaction Types	In Progress	Since Startup
purchase	0	0
certificate	0	0
batch	0	5

might be useful to point you in the right direction for solving various types of problems you may encounter.

The Certificates tab, shown in Figure 18.5, displays information about certificates being used by the POS System. This information will be useful in determining that all certificates that need to be present are in fact loaded and ready for use, and will aid renewal processing as certificates near their expiration dates.

The Logs tab for the GlobeSet POS System permits you to examine Event and Access Logs. You can specify the number of log entries to display, choose only certain item types to display, or omit lines that contain a value that you're not interested in viewing. You can also use this facility to update the logs with in-process transaction data to view activity while it's occurring, and you can clear and archive these logs as they become too full.

Between the tools that your vendor software provides you and those you can build yourself for general system monitoring, you should be well prepared to quickly detect and troubleshoot problems as they occur. Once you have

Figure 18.5 The GlobeSet POS Certificates tab.

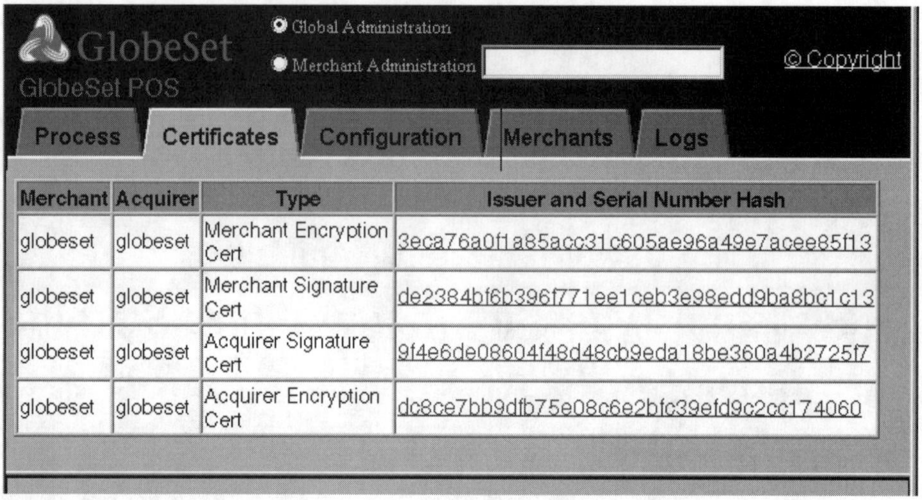

Merchant	Acquirer	Type	Issuer and Serial Number Hash
globeset	globeset	Merchant Encryption Cert	3eca76a0f1a85acc31c605ae96a49e7acee85f13
globeset	globeset	Merchant Signature Cert	de2384bf6b396f771ee1ceb3e98edd9ba8bc1c13
globeset	globeset	Acquirer Signature Cert	9f4e6de08604f48d48cb9eda18be360a4b2725f7
globeset	globeset	Acquirer Encryption Cert	dc8ce7bb9dfb75e08c6e2bfc39efd9c2cc174060

some experience in operating the environment, this information should also be invaluable in helping you prevent common problems from recurring.

Seasoned systems administrators will know what to expect in terms of how a normal networked environment should behave, but one thing is certain: users tend be to unpredictable, especially with a new system. Distributed networks are complicated. SET complicates them much further. Prepare yourself for a flurry of changes and potential hazards (crashes, strange behavior, etc.) before you actually get it completely right. Forewarned is forearmed!

With your SET-enabled Merchant Server operating and ringing up sales beyond all expectations, you can step back, take a deep breath, and smile at your success. The road is long, but certainly worth the journey. As customers beat a path to your virtual door, you can rest a little easier knowing that you're offering them the safest way to shop. They'll reward you in spades!

While the primary focus of this book is on consumer shopping, the next frontier that also benefits from SET is commercial or business-to-business

Figure 18.6 The GlobeSet POS Logs tab.

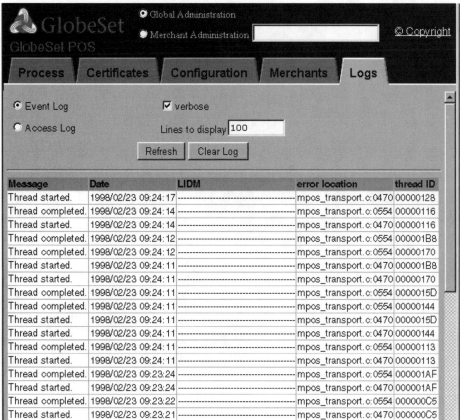

e-commerce. In the last section of the book we look at how companies can reap these rewards too.

We begin the discussion with those Web-based technologies that enable commercial e-business—intranets, extranets, and SET's roles in their uses.

INTRANETS, EXTRANETS, AND SET

Competitive forces, ease-of-use, low costs, and the pervasiveness of the Internet have all but mandated that businesses create the electronic storefronts that we've discussed over the last six chapters. In addition to creating sites on the Internet, many companies have used Internet technology to connect internal systems (creating *intranets*) and to bridge internal systems to external Web sites (creating *extranets*). This opportunity to change how employees communicate with one another inside the walls of a corporation and to support transactional sites for customers is unparalleled in the history of commerce.

This opportunity also raises concerns for both businesses and consumers about how secure their data really are over the Internet. SET answers many of these concerns.

In this chapter we'll discuss:

- Securing Internet resources
- A quick primer on intranets and extranets
- The role and benefits of SET in an intranet/extranet context
- Policy-setting guidelines to consider as you incorporate SET into your business

Three Kingdoms of Internet Security

In their book *Secure Electronic Commerce*, Warwick Ford and Michael Baum define three main areas of Internet security: network security, application security, and system security. The details of overall Internet security are outside the scope of this book, but a general understanding of Internet security places SET in its proper context and helps to explain its raison d'être.

Network Security

Network security refers to the safe transmission of data from one network-connected device to another. It does not refer to what happens to the data once it reaches its destination. As Ford and Baum point out, if a business does not secure its Internet connection, data it receives may be false or corrupted. The data may have been intentionally or unintentionally modified in transit or may not be from the advertised source. SET, as we have seen, addresses these concerns through certification, authentication, and message integrity services. Still, savvy network administrators recognize that additional security procedures may be needed to prevent certain threats to hardware and software.

The more security-conscious the network is, the less security-conscious the software applications running on it need to be. Possibly the greatest advantage of using network-level security rests in the network's indifference to the end-user. It works whether they know it or not. Where companies begin to rely on the Internet for the first time, network-level security can also help to protect the company from itself and its own inexperience.

Network-level security controls which applications within a system may receive and process data. Customer order information, for example, should be viewed by specific departments within a company, and not by just anyone. Whereas access is typically controlled at the application level through the use of security tables, the network can also protect how data are disseminated within an organization via the use of routing controls.

SET, in fact, addresses several aspects of security at the network level. SET supports authentication to identify consumers to merchants, merchants to consumers, and payment acquirers to both. All parties can feel secure not only in knowing with whom they are dealing, but also that their data are not modified in any way. SET *guarantees* that only intended recipients can view and make sense of the data.

Using Firewalls

In automobiles, a firewall prevents a fire in the engine compartment of the car from spreading to the passenger compartment. In a computer network, a firewall protects a secure portion of the network from intrusions by other parts of the network.

To build a firewall on a computer network requires not only software acquisition and configuration, but policy setting and standards definitions as well. Firewalls typically control which internal applications can receive traffic from the Internet. Internal servers, for example, receive incoming file transfer requests only if the server has been explicitly enabled (both technically and administratively) to do so.

A firewall can also act as a security gateway, encrypting and/or checking the integrity of traffic over the Internet backbone or from another security gateway (sometimes referred to as a Virtual Private Network or VPN). In this scenario, groups of network sites can communicate with each other via the backbone *knowing* that they are not susceptible to outside attacks. A firewall can encrypt data at one site so that only the firewall at the receiving site can decrypt and route the data through the internal network as defined by internal security procedures.

Application Security

Application-level security addresses the issue of access control—those aspects of data security not covered at the network level. In some instances, an application may duplicate some security measures that are also performed at the network level.

Electronic purchasing requires additional safeguards for data as the process moves across multiple networks of unknown reliability and security. SET addresses the problem of protecting confidential information, such as account numbers, from disallowed viewing. For example, the Payment Gateway needs to see this information to complete a transaction, but the Merchant does not. In the SET Authorization Request/Response message, the Merchant sends data about a customer's purchase, signed and encrypted using the Merchant's key, and separately sends Cardholder payment instructions, signed using the Payment Gateway's key. Each piece of data contains the hash of the order description and the amount, thus assuring the Payment Gateway that the Merchant and Cardholder agree upon what's being purchased and how much should be charged. The Merchant, however, never sees the Cardholder's payment instructions. He only knows that the Cardholder is who she says she is and the type and amount of purchase.

Web servers also play an increasing role in application-level security through the use of dynamically created Web pages that are based on a user's specific needs. Once a user has been authenticated, he will be provided only those choices that apply to his domain of use. Again, these forms of access control increasingly rest upon the applications themselves. The network simply cannot handle all the specifics of security control at the application level. While SET is responsible only for protecting payment-related information, it works within the context of systems that can customize a shopping experience, as described in detail in Chapter 20 on "Commercial Purchasing and Open Buying on the Internet (OBI)."

Securing the System

This third area covers those aspects of security not addressed at the network or application level. In this case, network administrators and company managers must implement policies and procedures to reduce the risk of attacks on their systems. Specifically they should be aware of and understand the weaknesses of vendor-supplied security software and verify that it is properly installed, operated, and maintained. Systems should be configured so that they listen for Internet traffic only on the designated ports for each type of application. Dutiful network administrators can reduce the threat of attacks by keeping all access control data current. By requiring frequent changes to system passwords and disallowing obvious passwords, systems administrators can reduce the threat factors significantly. Furthermore, all system accounts should be monitored, and those that expire should be removed immediately. Finally, network administrators should impose self-audit procedures in addition to any other audits that outside groups may perform. A more complete list of factors to consider in building your own policies may be found toward the end of this chapter.

Intranets and Extranets

Just as intranets and extranets have different purposes and characteristics, they also have different security requirements. Since these terms have entered the Internet vernacular, they often come with conflicting or vague definitions. A brief discussion of their similarities and differences is in order before discussing their security concerns.

According to Steve Guengerich in his book *Building the Corporate Intranet* (Wiley 1997), "An intranet is a corporate network and the business applications that run on it that shares the 'DNA' of Internet computing technologies (e.g., Internet Protocol, browsers, Web servers) and exists behind the corporate security 'firewall.'"

Intranets allow a company to easily publish business information in forms that make the most sense for the type of information. They frequently house sensitive corporate information that's not intended to be viewed by anyone outside the company.

In a typical intranet, a local area network (LAN) is built, and a special device, called a proxy server, is established to offer one-way (outgoing) access to the Internet by serving as a third party between you and the sites you want to visit. Sometimes called firewalls, proxy servers trust those on the local network side but don't trust anybody on the Internet, thus disallowing requests from the outside. Most proxy servers require those on the trusted side to log in as proof of their authorization to use it. It's possible, however, to open the access to those on the Internet side with adequate security controls to ensure its safe use. Through Access Control Lists (ACLs) on the server and router configuration settings, you can limit those who enter through the Internet to tightly controlled resources that can be defined as narrowly or as broadly as you desire.

IDs and passwords can be assigned in whatever ways work best for you. You might ask those who wish access to your site to complete a profile that gathers any information you'd like to have about them. Once they complete the profile and submit it, you can review it to decide if it is acceptable, and return the ID and password via e-mail. By gathering this type of information yourself, you can use it to your advantage. Building profiles of your visitors helps you focus your advertising costs and the products that you offer in ways no mass-marketing approaches can begin to match. Customer profiles help you build demographics on your clients, help you understand how your click-through advertising is working, and might serve as the foundation for data warehousing applications or Customer Information Systems.

Using combinations of stored profile information and CGI scripts, you can customize the user experience especially to each visitor's preferences and in ways that target individual interests and maximize the chances that visitors will buy something from you. Once they do, they'll not only perform the order entry work you'd otherwise have to pay someone to do, but they'll thank you for it and walk away happy. Now you've not only saved on marketing costs but you've also saved on other operating costs and built levels of customer goodwill that might never be possible with a storefront.

Even though it uses Internet and Web technologies, an intranet does *not* necessarily need to be connected to the Internet. This does not mean, however, that security should be less of a concern. Some experts believe that the greatest threats to a company's information do not come from outside hackers but from company insiders, perhaps a disgruntled employee whose annual increase wasn't quite what he had hoped for. Intranets require strict internal security policies and procedures to control the access to sensitive corporate data from within. Who sets up each department's intranet? Who decides upon the content? Who maintains and controls access to each department's intranet? Intranets clearly illustrate how challenges to security are not so much technical as they are procedural.

According to Julie Bort and Bradley Felix in their book *Building an Extranet* (Wiley, 1997), an extranet is "A bridge between a company and its most important business contacts, its partners."

A company builds an extranet to share information with whoever it deems its most strategic business partners, whether they be other companies working on a joint business project, an outsourcing firm, or a supplier of goods or services. The difference between an extranet and an intranet is one of audience. Whereas the intranet addresses the needs of the company as related to its employees, the extranet looks outward to its key business partners, establishing vital links in what might be a supply chain.

Who's Using Extranets?

When the Web became popular, the industry predicted that middleman distributor organizations would become obsolete, since direct connections between consumers and suppliers are possible. What's happened instead is a renaissance of the distribution industry, where stronger ties between consumers, distributors, and manufacturers are forged in the form of value-added and consulting services.

"The selling chain is about integrating customers and distributors into your company. You build channel loyalty because you make it easier to do business with your company than with anybody else in the industry," says Sameer Dholakia, a product manager at the Web-based sales management tools company Trilogy Development Corp.

SELine on the Web

Merisel Inc., a leading distributor of PC products to resellers, was thought of as one of those companies that would become extinct. In 1996 they launched an extranet called SELine on the Web that offers resellers product support information, order information, technical support, price quotes, and even updates to Merisel stock prices.

Some of the features and benefits of SELline on the Web include:

- Free freight on all orders

- RSA encryption for secure transactions

- Daily custom pricing downloads

- Links to FedEx and UPS tracking sites

- Off-line order building and storing of partial orders

- Real-time inventory availability

- Real-time custom pricing

- Enhanced technical product descriptions and product photos

- Robust search engine for searches by manufacturer, keyword, product name, UPC code, product category, and Merisel or manufacturer SKU

- Customer Service form downloads

- Daily product promotions

- Red tag and excess inventory promotions

- New and discontinued product lists

The Big Three's Network

An extranet's primary benefit is in its ability to wring out costs in the supply chain. Extranets can help companies to finally realize the benefits of Just-In-Time (JIT) inventory systems, a goal that Electronic Data Interchange (EDI) failed to achieve.

Today, the Big Three automakers, Chrysler, General Motors, and Ford, are building a collaborative extranet that links them to their suppliers through designated ISPs via a managed, virtual private network (VPN) called the Automotive Network eXchange (ANX). It's estimated to save billions of dollars in costs in the supply chain. ANX replaces 50 to 100 direct-dial connections to the automakers, reducing telecommunication costs (up to 70 percent) and complexities, but the real payoffs are in speeding communications between suppliers and manufacturers. ANX will be used to electronically route product shipment schedules, order information, CAD files for product designs, purchase orders, and other financial information. The improved exchange of information should result in new business practices between vendors and manufacturers. "They'll be holding information rather than inventory," states Laura Migliore, a Chrysler process control specialist.

> **HOPS for the Web**
>
> Heineken USA began rolling out its Heineken Operational Planning System (HOPS) extranet last year to tighten the links between the brewer and its network of regional suppliers. With HOPS, resellers can log in, post their monthly forecasts for sales, and place product orders. "Now, beer from our brewery in Europe can make its way through the U.S. retail channel in just about the same time it takes Anheuser-Busch to ship from its domestic breweries. We can react faster than ever before," states Heineken's vice president Dan Tearno.

Regardless if you're building an intranet or an extranet, security is imperative. As Bort and Felix point out, when a company builds an extranet, it typically risks the exposure of highly sensitive corporate data to unauthorized viewing. Furthermore, trust between partners might be compromised should a breach in security occur—a situation potentially far more expensive than a loss of data. For this reason, corporate applications built for strategic partners follow the e-commerce model using protocols such as SET instead of business-to-business models such as Electronic Data Interchange (EDI).

The point is, both intranets and extranets require higher levels of security than a Web site on the Internet does. Their intent is to communicate with a select and targeted audience. Here the company must weigh the importance of establishing communications with employees and business partners against the risk of losing sensitive corporate data. The company should *never* compromise on security practices and procedures.

Basic Threats to Intranets and Extranets

John Wylder, a senior vice president for information technology at SunTrust Service, one of the larger banks in Atlanta, has said, "The key to making sure you have the right security is not so much knowing the features of all the products. It's really just understanding what kind of Internet use creates what kinds of threats—and matching products to those threats."

Following his own advice, Wylder along with other IT executives developed a list of nine basic threats to Web sites as part of the Open User Recommended Solutions (OURS) Task Force, a Chicago-based committee of 60 corporate users and computer vendors. These threats are identified as:

Data destruction. The accidental or malicious loss of data on a Web site and the interception of data flowing from or to the Web site, whether these data be encrypted or not.

Interference. The derailing of a Web site by rerouting data intended for a site or overloading a site with data not intended for it, thus crippling the server.

Modification. The altering of incoming or outgoing data for a particular Web site, whether intentional or not. A particularly pernicious hazard, since modification is difficult to detect in large transmissions.

Misrepresentation. The kind of electronic posturing that is the source of so many stories about bogus Web sites, where the perpetrator hands out false credentials, perhaps creating a counterfeit Web site to siphon off traffic intended for a legitimate destination.

Repudiation. The denial on the part of a consumer or customer that an on-line order was ever placed or the goods ever received.

Accidental use. The inadvertent misuse of a Web site by a bona fide user.

Unauthorized altering or downloading. The inappropriate use of data, whether copying or updating, by someone without the proper security rights.

Unauthorized transactions. Any use of a Web site by someone without approval.

Unauthorized disclosure. The viewing of data without the appropriate permissions.

Most experts in the field of electronic security agree that before a company rushes out to purchase firewall software or invests heavily in encryption services, it should first assess the sensitivity of its various data and consider the potential loss of these data to any of the threats listed above.

SET's Role in Intranets and Extranets

The OURS committee states that Web usage falls into one of three categories, Vance McCarthy's "Web Security: How Much Is Enough?" article in *Datamation* reported. These types are:

- Advertising (brochure-ware)
- Secure Internet/intranet
- Electronic commerce

Obviously, SET focuses on concerns of electronic commerce and the handling of credit card payments on the Internet, but a company will often see a blurring of the borders between these uses. What companies should do then is evaluate their data, determine how much that data is worth to them, and implement the appropriate levels of security for each type of data.

For example, a company that has put its catalog of parts on the Internet where customers can order them on-line should understand what SET is about and how to implement it. Another company that simply advertises its presence on the Internet for the purpose of entertaining its audience will care little about who enters the site. In the latter case, illegitimate users don't really exist.

Sound security strategies are based not on what the market has to offer in the way of security software packages but on what a company has to secure and from whom they need to protect it. To this end the OURS guidelines identify six best weapons against security threats. They are:

User ID/Authentication. Anything from the use of simple passwords and callback systems to one-time passwords and challenge/response tokens. User authentication is something that should be found in all but the most open Web sites.

Authorization. Identifying the user to be who he says he is through the use of privilege tables, authorization (digital) certificates, and directory services. OURS considers authorization to be a second-level protection against unauthorized access to a company's intranet or modification of Web content.

Integrity control. This focuses on the integrity of the data rather than the user. Integrity control is extremely important to the kind of security features found in SET. Here, messages are verified and receivers can be assured that the data has not been altered in transit. Again, integrity control is of utmost importance to e-commerce and SET.

Accountability. The use of audits and Web server logs to enforce security policies. Whereas these technologies by themselves do little to protect a Web site from threats, they can aid in researching security violations.

Confidentiality. From forms of cryptography to the use of Virtual Private Networks (VPNs) that provide end-to-end encrypted links that can shield a site from the public Internet. Key escrow also falls in the category of confidentiality.

Availability controls. How quickly can a Web site be restored in the event of catastrophic failure such as hardware failure? Solutions here include fault tolerance, backup/recovery plans, and capacity management systems.

Even with these safeguards in place against security threats, many companies are reluctant to allow outsiders the ability to communicate using Web technology. Even MasterCard, one of the joint authors of the SET protocol, keeps its sensitive corporate data on a separate network domain, far from the prying eyes of the public Internet.

MasterCard's manager of IS, Bob Perrey, states that each company must assess how sensitive each piece of its data is and determine how long it will remains sensitive. Only then, Perrey feels, can a company decide how tough its encryption needs to be. It only follows that the longer a company's data remains sensitive, the tougher its encryption must be. Items of data with a shelf life of weeks or even months only give hackers that much more time to steal and plunder. Perrey's rule of thumb is, "If a piece of data is only valid for a week and you encrypt with a certain strength that you figure takes two weeks to break, then it is protected in your eyes."

SET and Intranets

On an intranet, SET may not offer too much help keeping your system secure from rogue employee attacks, but it may help in other ways.

If you're operating a Company Store for your employees on your intranet that accepts payment cards, you may want to require SET on the Merchant Server for employee uses of their personal payment products. A more likely use, however, might be for corporate card purposes, especially if you encourage employees to use their company-supplied Internet connection for business-related purchases. You might, in fact, use your intranet to handle any or all aspects of corporate card uses, including issuance, bill presentation, payment via department expense reports, management, and reporting. While these SET Cardholder Certificates won't help you better secure your intranet, they will help you to better control the uses of your corporate cards.

To better secure your intranet, you might consider using SET's cousin—Authentication Digital Certificates. Like SET certificates, X.509 authentication certificates replace user IDs and passwords, as the means to access *internal* resources, and make perfect sense where business applications (mainframe access, distributed (e.g., X-Window)) are available through an intranet browser–based user console.

With these X.509 certificates, you can restrict or permit access to whatever degree serves your interests best. Furthermore, you can incorporate these certificates into SmartCards to provide still tighter security. Recently, IBM, Netscape, Network Computer Inc., and Sun Microsystems announced a SmartCard standard for use on corporate personal computers outfitted with SmartCard readers. The OpenCard Framework permits users to roam freely from PC to PC with their SmartCards. With these, users have the authority to access network information, databases, and services for such purposes as using e-mail, running Internet applications, and running company applications.

The OpenCard Framework defines the means to download from the Internet all SmartCard device drivers needed to enable SmartCard use.

With a high-level interface that supports multiple SmartCard types, the OpenCard Framework enables the cards to be used on PCs from different manufacturers. After you insert your SmartCard into the reader, you use a personal identification number (PIN) to identify yourself further. Once authenticated, you can access everything you're authorized to access. Figure 19.1 illustrates the OpenCard Framework as an architecture to support different SmartCard operating systems, different SmartCard terminals, and different SmartCard functions, all through the use of Java classes that are customizable.

Figure 19.1 The OpenCard framework.

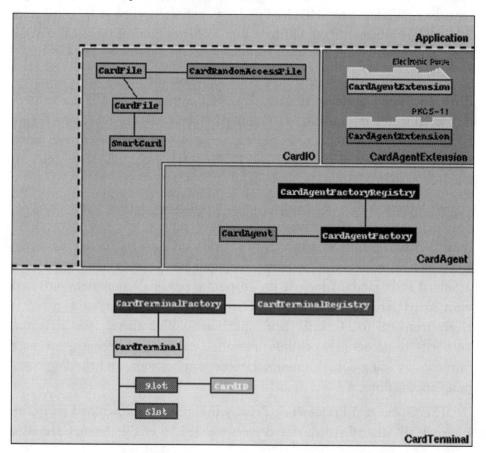

SET and Extranets

More than any other type of system, extranets are natural candidates for supporting the uses of SET. This is especially true where commercial transacting is present. Since an extranet primarily supports business-to-business trade, you can control its uses far better than you can with a consumer-based site. A well-engineered extranet could well prove to be the *killer application* that reduces phone, customer service, and order entry costs throughout your company.

Many commercial catalog-related shopping problems are addressed by the Open Buying on the Internet (OBI) protocol (discussed in Chapter 20), but OBI does nothing to help assure you that authenticated users are presenting legitimate forms of payment. By combining SET with OBI, you increase the success of your extranet (through frequent user visits and purchases) as well as reduce your potential losses through fraudulent payments. Together, OBI and SET offer a more complete solution to otherwise extremely messy problems.

E-Commerce Raises the Stakes

As companies continue to move to the Internet and begin to merge private intranet data with electronic commerce applications, the situation will only grow more complex. The best approach a company can take is a practical and realistic one. First, it must realize that there is *no* such thing as absolute security. With this in mind, savvy IS managers should conduct a thorough inventory of their company's data and formulate clear and consistent policies regarding the use of its data. This includes the management of both intranets and extranets. A firm commitment to the use of the SET protocol whenever Internet card payments are involved adds to these practical solutions.

Finally, security policies must be reviewed regularly and updated when needed. Just as a company's business changes in response to business demands, so too does the world of security. In the rapidly accelerating game of electronic commerce, nothing stands still for very long.

To help you construct those policies, here's some factors you may wish to consider.

Roll Your Own Policies

Policy creation is not the exclusive domain of technical experts. In fact, many of the policies you need should come as directives from upper management and clearly spell out which activities will be tolerated and which won't. Any organizational policies you develop should cover as many of these topics as possible.

Planning

Planning an intranet or extranet environment should include an evaluation of current work flows to determine how improvements can come about through automation and investments in other technologies.

Desktop Standards

Desktop systems standards should be defined to provide the framework needed to improve information sharing among employees, external partners, vendors, and customers.

Systems Development Standards

Development standards define the processes governing the design, development, and maintenance of software. Management often uses software for decision making, and the software development processes must be appropriately established and controlled.

Distributed Systems Support and Other Support Functions

Reliability and availability should be assured for support functions and should include plans for connecting to outside organizations as well as to the Internet. In many cases, the maintenance work on PCs that prevents people from continuing to work can be eliminated by using "information appliances" instead.

Information Security

Policies regarding information security govern the access to sensitive or critical data crucial to company operations. The development of such standards is challenging, since the lack of security features where they're needed often restricts the ability to properly protect information. Critical information must be secured regardless of where it's stored and who accesses it. Should you elect to use them, policies that govern the use of SmartCards (see above) should be included.

Device Security

Portable computer use increases daily. Laptop and portable computer theft is prevalent—thieves steal these devices because they're small, expensive, and easily fenced. To help minimize this threat, you need to protect these assets as much as possible. Policies here will include reporting thefts to company security personnel and basic training for employees regarding the protection of computing devices.

If laptops also store any types of digital certificates (e.g., SET Corporate Card certificates), make certain you're prepared for identifying and revoking those certificates before they're used for unintended purposes.

Work-at-Home Users

You might espouse telecommuting for your employees, but you need guidelines to ensure that they use the equipment you send home with them in acceptable ways. You want to help ensure that the purposes for working at home are not being defeated through abuses. The same considerations for laptops and digital certificates apply to work-at-home equipment—perhaps even more so.

Inventory and Tracking

Asset inventory tracking policies should address the processing that accounts for hardware, software, licensing, financial records, reporting, and management.

Training Policies

Training policies need to address how you will train your personnel. Policies should also cover training for employees who have never had to use computers and now need to use them for e-mail and for Internet access.

Disaster Planning and Recovery

Disaster planning and recovery defines the procedures that protect the organization from losing valuable data by maintaining the reliability and availability of data systems. It also includes disaster recovery processes for data and critical systems that day-to-day operations depend upon. Plans in this category will include backup schedules, off-site storage of backups, and immediate replacement of PCs and servers that fail, and may even specify remote computing facilities where the organization's work can continue in the event of a building fire or other casualties.

Policy Compliance

Compliance refers to the usage and monitoring of policies and standards. You may decide to require employees to sign a form (Acceptable Use Policies) that states their intent to comply with such policies and spells out the consequences of their noncompliance. Periodic auditing will indicate whether policy compliance is at an acceptable level. Figure 19.2 provides an example of an AUP form for employees of a public school.

You cannot develop policies in a vacuum. Formulation must include those who will be expected to abide by the policies. Once you have developed the policies, you must also disseminate them. With an intranet in place, you can publish the policies rapidly and efficiently.

Continuous Improvement

Policies developed, approved, and put into action must be revisited regularly. Things change—especially activities based on digital technology—and the policies that govern them must change too. To help aid in continuous improvement, it's important for people to know that their opinion counts for something. With an intranet, it's easy to obtain the feedback and involvement needed from the employees to help ensure that policies aren't considered a waste of time and effort.

Figure 19.2 An Acceptable Use Policy example.

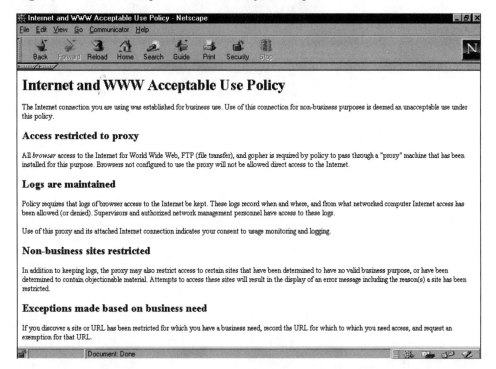

Judicious uses of intranets, extranets, and the combination of the two can help accelerate building corporate bridges into the 21st century in ways no other technologies can match. Infrastructure development is no small matter, but once in place, the possibilities and speed of new system development are nothing short of astounding.

In the next chapter, we take a look at some practical e-commerce uses for intranets and extranets, and we'll see how SET fits in the corporate world of payment card uses.

S ET is helping to spawn new vocabulary in the global marketplace. While some expressions like *supply chains* and *procurement reengineering* are being redefined, wholly new phrases like *virtual enterprise* and *OBI* are finding their way into the lexicon of purchasing managers.

Here we explore the complexities of business-to-business electronic commerce, how a sister Internet-based commercial purchasing protocol addresses many of these complexities, and what the synergy of OBI and SET means to the future of business buying. Topics we cover include:

- An overview of commercial buying

- Problems that require answers

- Open Buying on the Internet (OBI)

An Overview of Commercial Buying

We now move beyond the understanding and implementation of SET to business concerns about the e-commerce marketplace and its relationship to SET. So far, the emphasis has been on consumer-related shopping experiences on the Internet.

Now let's consider the business-to-business purchasing environment.

The employees at the Albatross Corporation complain steadily because the supply room is always empty of critical supplies: ballpoint pens, paper clips, and business envelopes. The purchasing department is obligated to control procurement of these essential supplies, so they have managed to strike a deal with their suppliers, committing to an entire year's supply of goods at a hefty volume discount. This business model, while appearing straightforward to an outsider, introduces several problems that involve internal procedures, controls, and technology.

- Who does the ordering? Obviously, the purchasing department doesn't want a thousand employees placing thousands of different purchase orders. How does a company control the purchasing of supplies via the Internet?

- Once a purchasing department has struck volume discount deals, how do they guarantee that their commitments will be honored? How can they know that the individuals making the purchases will go to their preferred suppliers and nowhere else? If an unwitting employee buys from an "off-contract" supplier, companies might end up paying higher prices and risk weakening their established supplier relationships.

- Who stores the catalog and buyer information? Corporate purchasing card users need information from the supplier for line-item reporting. Unfortunately, not all suppliers provide the same information in the same way. Data may be incomplete. Without additional manual processes, buyers will have incomplete purchasing logs and insufficient audit trails. Not only will this cause inconsistency in data, but reconciliation will require much more time. In addition, do you want your suppliers maintaining information about your employees on their systems? Doing so only seems to beg for trouble.

- How can purchasing departments know that the right products are purchased at the right price by the right people at the right times? Abuse of authority is certain to run rampant without adequate controls in place to prevent it.

- How will companies integrate business-to-business electronic commerce processing into their back-office systems that meet the requirements for themselves and all their suppliers? How will the new business models fit into existing accounting procedures and systems?

Where SET may work perfectly to help pay for purchases conducted on-line, the business-to-business model does not map well into the phases of on-line payment card processing that we've discussed throughout the book—yet the needs of companies cannot remain unsatisfied.

Open Electronic Commerce

In the 1980s, one of the more dominant ways in which companies electronically transacted business with each other was through the use of Electronic Data Interchange (EDI). Still in use today, EDI allows companies, typically manufacturing giants in the auto and aerospace industries, to transact with a finite number of suppliers. After weeks of technical effort, organizational changes, and process modifications, these companies established nearly permanent relationships based on high-volume buying and selling.

These relationships became long-term due to the high costs of establishing them. Some of these costs include dedicated communication lines, and dial-up and mainframe services, all of which are usually administered by Value-Added Network (VAN) service providers, requiring significant investments. The Internet has given EDI users more options and a far less expensive medium to transport messages without jettisoning existing back-office systems. However, what the Internet also provides, and SET enforces, is a dynamic and "virtual" business marketplace where buyers and sellers can engage in temporary or one-time relationships based on current needs and market conditions.

Some experts believe that SET-compliant Internet-based technologies will eventually supplant EDI as the forum for business-to-business electronic commerce. According to a new report by the Aberdeen Group, Inc., *The Dollars and Sense of the New Electronic Commerce in Transition,* firms will increasingly turn to the Internet as a cheaper and more responsive medium for conducting business with other companies while slowly abandoning the more costly and entrenched solutions such as EDI. EDI won't disappear overnight, Aberdeen states, but reliance upon this technology will diminish over the next decade.

This new electronic marketplace, termed by many experts "open electronic commerce," leverages the high speed and low cost of the Internet to find the best deal possible for supplying and meeting the needs of commercial customers. Business-to-business transactions are becoming, in a sense, more ad hoc. Many companies, for example, are redefining their more traditional roles of "middlemen" or resellers in light of this emerging electronic marketplace.

Buyers Be Wary

Until recently, software vendors have focused on systems that cater to the sellers in electronic transactions. Putting suppliers' catalogs on-line, for example, has attracted the development efforts of several major software companies. Little attention has been paid, however, to the needs of the corporate buyer. The increase in the number of companies using corporate purchasing cards as a way to reduce costs and simplify paperwork simply hasn't attracted the kind of attention it deserves.

Payment is typically easier with purchasing cards, reducing the number of invoices from hundreds or thousands to one consolidated bill. And consider this: According to Jesse Berst, automating business-to-business buying could theoretically create huge savings for a company. If the cost of a single purchase order were cut by $25 to $150, multiply that number by the estimated 100,000 annual purchase orders a major corporation places. The challenge is to integrate purchasing cards with electronic procurement systems, reaping all of the benefits with few of the drawbacks.

So Why the Reluctance?

Since technology is often a solution looking for a problem, what prevents the software moguls from carving out a new empire? Jesse Berst, editorial director of *ZD Net AnchorDesk,* has several explanations:

> **Two by Two.** Purchasing has resisted automation thus far because two clients are involved, the employee who needs the supplies, and the buyer, the person authorized to make the purchase. Furthermore, pur-

chasing has two aspects, the purchasing (i.e., the placement of the order), and the procurement (i.e., requisitions, approvals, purchase orders, accounting, etc.). Four agents are involved, not two as in most early systems.

Side Buy Side. Suppliers sell products by distancing themselves from the pack. They need products and pricing that distinguishes them from their competitors. How, then, do they prevent their catalogs from getting pulled into enormous, consolidated catalogs where they lose their distinction? Furthermore, how can they maintain control of not just content but form? The buyers, on the other hand, don't want to master the fine art of keyword searches just to find the best price for a widget. How do you balance these two competing needs?

Step by Step. Slowly, smaller companies are developing procurement systems that tackle the hefty problem of automating the procurement process. Elekom (www.elekom.com), for example, indexes products by a company's top suppliers, providing links to the supplier's Web page for additional detail. The system integrates the procurement process by electronically processing an order and interfacing it with back-office systems (e.g., accounting). Berst feels that although electronic procurement is harder than it sounds, neglected buyers will soon see their day.

MasterCard Joins In

What better endorsement of the importance of the procurement system than to see MasterCard pilot the use of Elekom's on-line purchasing system. Jim Cullinan, vice president of global purchasing, began streamlining MasterCard's central purchasing group in 1995 when he joined the company. MasterCard deals with hundreds of suppliers globally, and Cullinan wanted to focus less on the ordering process and more on strategic issues.

Standardizing its procurement practices in 1996 with a single purchase order system, Cullinan pushed for an interactive system of electronic commerce for use in MasterCard's global purchasing group. Elekom's system supports electronic catalogs and on-line requisitioning along with approval processing. The fact that MasterCard has a high stake in the SET protocol gives tremendous visibility to the pilot and the results.

The system allows approximately 50 buyers and requisitioners at two sites to order office supplies, services, and promotional items once the buying team has negotiated the contracts. Elekom's system, an intranet system housed on one of MasterCard's local servers, allows approved users to search the system's master catalog of products and services. Future plans include performing catalog searches over the Internet with direct links to the suppliers' Web sites.

Prospects for procurement systems look bright. By consolidating the buying activities and streamlining operational procedures, these kinds of systems allow purchasing departments to focus on long-neglected aspects of the business. The integration of on-line payments is the logical next step for procurement systems—once again putting SET in the spotlight.

Another phenomenon that's made possible through the Internet and has attracted the attention of software makers is that of "on-line auctions."

Going Once, Going Twice, Sold—to the Man with the Digital ID

OnSale, a California-based firm, has generated more than $70 million in gross revenue in the first three quarters of 1977, through its proprietary auction software that generates e-mail bid confirmations, automatic credit card billing, and an EDI link to the warehouse. Manufacturers and distributors for companies like IBM and Hewlett-Packard sell unwanted inventory without sabotaging their primary sales channels. On-line auctions have attracted businesses of all sizes looking to acquire needed equipment at significant savings, with some buyers estimating an average savings of 50 percent off the best resale prices.

Auction buyers can only pay with their credit cards, again underlining the increasing significance of on-line payments and the need for SET.

Although on-line auctioning does not guarantee that a specific quantity is available and does not follow typical purchase order models, electronic commerce software vendors like WebVision have already begun to develop auction applications for sales and legacy database integration.

Purchasing systems won't ever be the same.

Open Buying on the Internet

The Internet Purchasing Roundtable, a group of Fortune 500 companies and their leading suppliers, created the Open Buying on the Internet (OBI) Standard to eliminate some problems with today's systems and processes. According to Thayer Stewart, vice president of Marketing for American Express Corporate Services, "The OBI Standard should break through the gridlock that has prevented corporations and suppliers from transacting business over the Internet. Having a common standard will facilitate Internet commerce and should deliver significant savings for users."

In this section, we take a close look at the OBI Specification in the light of SET as an enabling technology for OBI's payment mechanism. Topics include:

- A background on the need for OBI

- OBI requirements

- OBI standards

- Commercial piloting of OBI

Who Needs OBI?

We've looked at institutional buying systems, processes, and their associated problems. In forging some solutions to these problems, managers must consider a variety of viewpoints.

Business transactions for low-dollar goods and services presently account for over 80 percent of institutional buying, yet don't directly contribute to a company's profits. These types of purchases include:

- Maintenance, Repair, and Operations (MRO) materials
- Office and laboratory supplies
- Indirect materials (those not used in production processes)

With centralized purchasing processes in place to help control costs and limit the number of outside supplier relationships, today's purchasing managers must also deal with diverse and disparate sets of requisitioners of goods who may be spread across the country or even the globe.

For simplification reasons, corporate purchasing departments often reduce their base of suppliers to achieve a tighter integration of the supply chain. As a select group, these providers are expected to be highly responsive to customer demand or face losing their "preferred status." Some of the demands include:

- Custom catalogs
- Custom products
- Custom pricing
- Value-added service offerings

In response to these demands, companies have developed a slew of highly customized, *one-off* electronic catalogs and purchasing systems, creating maintenance nightmares. These systems often use proprietary software and mechanisms that lack standard processing or systems support. Interoperability among these systems is rare.

While SET helps to solve the problem of payment processing with payment cards and corporate purchasing cards, it fails to address the problem of the *three-way relationship* that exists in organizational buying. Consumer payment cards tie a person to a Brand, but in the case of tying a person to a company which in turn is tied to a payment card, SET can't directly provide support.

The OBI Standard

OBI represents an architecture that includes:

- Detailed technical specifications and guidelines
- Compliance and implementation information

Just as organizations can obtain the SET specifications, any organization or individual can obtain a copy of OBI specifications to build a product, a service, or a complete solution.

OBI's underlying design relies on the notion that buying organizations are responsible for the profiles of those who request goods and services, accounting procedures, tax status information, and internal approval processes. Selling organizations are responsible for electronic catalogs, pricing, order entry and fulfillment systems, and inventory systems.

Rather than require the selling organization to maintain profile data on potentially thousands of different buyers, OBI requires the use of authentication digital certificates that store those unique user profiles. These digital certificates, similar to SET digital certificates, are based on the X.509 Version 3 Standard. OBI uses these certificates to authenticate buyers, describe their roles and permissions within the buying organization, and offer selling organizations the highest level of assurance that they're dealing with the businesses and individuals whom they think they're dealing with. OBI certificates also benefit sellers by helping them test the integrity of purchase order information through cryptography.

Where the Secure Electronic Transaction (SET) Standard governs the security of payment cards on the Internet, it does not govern any of the processing or customization of the user's shopping experience, which OBI does. OBI's intent is not to standardize the payment methods that may be used, but it does encourage the use of SET for card payments, and it also supports any other means specified by the Payment Authority within each buying organization. As we saw in Chapter 19, a corporate intranet can offer the infrastructure to implement such a system.

OBI's ultimate goal is the establishment of a common ground for what the OBI Consortium refers to as the "Trading Web," where OBI adopters establish trading relationships with other OBI adopters through secured access to extranet facilities connected via the Internet (see Chapter 19 for some examples of extranets). These companies, in turn, establish further relationships with others, and the Trading Web expands, forming dynamic groups of interoperable systems.

Software support for OBI from various e-commerce solution providers has already appeared on the market. Open Market's Transact system offers OBI-compliant order management, on-line customer service, security services, authentication services, flexible payment processing, and secure transaction processing. Transact is intended to aid in the movement of on-line product catalogs to complete end-to-end Internet commerce systems that form the core of the Trading Web. A view of the Trading Web is illustrated in Figure 20.1. Figure 20.2 shows the interface to Open Market's Transact 4 system.

Other systems, like the one from Elekom described earlier, expand the horizon for standardized corporate purchasing systems and build an even more compelling case for SET.

Solving the Needs of Businesses

At its highest level, the OBI architecture describes the interaction of four entities:

Requisitioner. Represents end-users of the system—the ones who place orders. Requisitioners are typically employees of the Buying

Figure 20.1 The Trading Web.

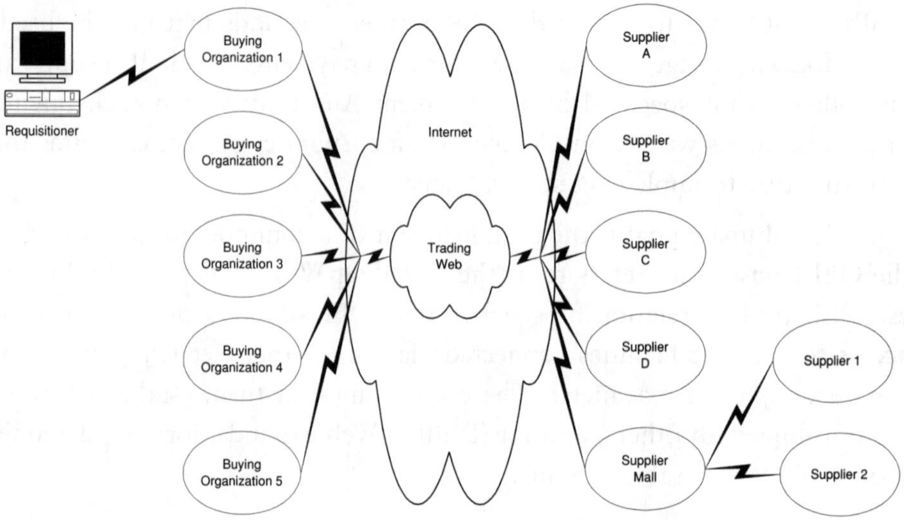

Figure 20.2 Open Market's Transact 4 interface screen.

Organization. They're assumed to have access to a PC with a World Wide Web browser, a corporate intranet, and access to the Internet. Requisitioners also have OBI digital certificates, issued by a trusted OBI Certificate Authority.

Buying Organization. Represents purchasing management and the information systems that support the Purchasing Department. Components of these systems include

- OBI server for receiving OBI order requests and returning OBI orders

- Processing and storage to handle Requisitioner profile information, trading partner information, workflow, approvals, account and tax status information

The buying organization is also responsible for negotiating and maintaining their contractual relationships with preferred Selling Organizations.

Selling Organization. Maintains dynamic electronic catalogs that present current product and price information—information that's tailored to the affiliation of the Requisitioner to the buying organization as determined by the Requisitioner's digital certificate. The catalog information reflects the effective contract between the buyer and the seller. Selling organizations can also authorize certain transaction types through the appropriate Payment Authority.

Payment Authority. Provides authorization for the payment types presented by the Requisitioner. Payment authorities reimburse selling organizations and indicate those payments to the buying organizations through rapid exchange of invoice or debit information. Payment authorities include banks or other financial institutions. Depending on how the Payment Authority is established, support for purchase order processing with later remittance is also possible. OBI supports a variety of payment options, including SET that handles all types of payment cards, personal and corporate.

These four entities, working in cooperation with one another, represent the cornerstones of a single instance of the Trading Web (described earlier). With their roles and responsibilities defined, OBI outlines those system and technical requirements that pave the road to OBI partners' common utility.

OBI System Requirements

OBI is rooted in a host of rules and protocols that govern all business and technical aspects for its operation. The Purchasing Roundtable outlines those requirements OBI is intended to satisfy. The requirements are summarized in the following section (taken from the OBI Version 1.0 Specification).

Sourcing and Pricing Catalogs

These high-level requirements describe certain aspects of what we called Phase 1: Browsing and Shopping. Dynamic and private catalogs differentiate commercial from consumer shopping, for which a more generic catalog serves the purpose.

- Buying Organizations *must* have the ability to configure a "Purchasing Home Page" which provides a custom buying environment for the Buying Organization and which can be used to channel Requisitioners to the catalogs of preferred Selling Organizations.

- Requisitioners *must* have access to Selling Organization product and service catalogs containing current product descriptions and illustrations, pricing, and links to ordering systems and other related value-added information and services.

- Product and service catalogs *must* be customer-specific in terms of specific product sets and contract pricing.

- Selling Organization catalogs need not be standard or consistent in terms of their "look and feel." Selling Organizations *must* be able to provide unique value-added services through their catalogs, services that might enable them to differentiate themselves.

- Selling Organizations *must* provide searching capabilities for their catalogs.

- An OBI solution *must* provide access to product availability information as defined by the agreement between trading partners and wherever it is applicable.

- Catalogs *must* offer "frequently ordered item" shopping lists.

- Sensitive catalog information, such as contract pricing, *must* remain confidential to all knowledgeable parties.

- Selling Organizations or their Agents *must* be responsible for the maintenance of product or service catalogs.

- In most cases, the catalog will be stored at the Selling Organization site. In some cases, the Buying Organization may want to store one or more Selling Organization catalogs at its site. A solution *must* be flexible enough to support either approach.

OBI catalog-specific requirements are defined to enable the most flexible yet predictable shopping experiences between businesses.

User Profiles

The database required for user profiles forms a cornerstone for OBI. Its presence may lead to the elimination of unnecessary, wasteful, or redundant work within the purchasing process.

- OBI-based solutions *must* include a User Profile database containing information on authorized Requisitioners (e.g., name, user account, purchasing authorizations, shipping address, electronic mail address, etc.).

- Buying Organizations *must* maintain the User Profile database and have administrative tools to maintain the data. Buying Organizations *must* also be responsible for the "Purchasing" servers.

User profiles are required to implement OBI's principle that process owners are responsible for the management and maintenance of information associated with their processes.

Ordering

Order forms should appear consistent for buyers across all the suppliers with whom they deal. The following requirements ensure that this occurs.

- Buying Organizations *must* be able to specify the appearance of order forms so that they can be consistent across Selling Organizations.

- Order forms *must* be autofilled with standard user profile information regarding the authorized Requisitioner to minimize data entry errors and speed the ordering process.

- Buying Organizations *must* be able to specify accounting information that passes through the system at either line item or order (header) level.

- There *must* be a default tax status code in the User Profile that can be overridden at the order level and/or the line item level at the time of order. The tax status code will be passed through to the Selling Organization.

- Selling Organizations *must* provide Requisitioners with receipt-of-order acknowledgments and the capability of turning this feature on or off.

- Requisitioners *must* have the opportunity to specify special instructions at the time of order. Examples of special instructions include unusual shipping information, or willingness to accept partial payments.

- Selling Organizations *must* be able to determine whether an order they have received has been "authorized" by the Buying Organization.

With standard order form "look and feel," efficiencies for affected personnel are maximized and chances for error are minimized.

Payment

Payment flexibility through OBI ensures that OBI may be used with any type of reimbursement model. SET is a natural candidate to handle some of this processing.

- The standard *must* support a variety of payment options including bulk invoices and checks, EDI invoices and electronic funds transfer, and procurement cards.

The Payment Authority charged with this process within each organization will dictate the methods it supports. If SET with purchasing cards is an option, the PA will provide the structure under which digital certificates are issued and managed.

Approval and Authorization

OBI supports a variety of purchase authorization and approval processing methods to help streamline transaction processing.

- Buying Organizations *must* be able to preapprove authorized Requisitioners for transactions under specified limits.

- The OBI Standard must support approvals and authorization at the time of order.

- Selling Organizations *must* only ship to valid, preapproved "ship-to" addresses.

- The Standard *must* not impose constraints on existing shipping and receiving processes.

OBI is intended to be incorporated into any existing processing that permits employee-initiated purchases.

Information Access

Trading partners require information to negotiate, measure, and analyze the performance of their processes. OBI specifies that such information be available when it's needed.

- OBI-compliant systems *must* provide the Buying Organization with the data necessary to generate information for evaluation criteria such as the order status, order history, dollars spent per Selling Organization, and Selling Organization performance.

- Requisitioners *must* be able to access order status and order history information. For the purposes of Requisitioner information, access should be maintained for a minimum of 90 days and should be user defined. This requirement may be met through traditional reports from Selling Organizations. Electronic access is not required, but is desirable.

- OBI solutions *must* accommodate active (sent by Selling Organization) or passive (looked up by Requisitioner) shipment notification.

Flexible access to system information yields the highest degrees of adaptability and success for all Trading Partners.

Internal Controls

OBI meets the needs of accounting controls that prevent problems and abuses of authority. While it does not state specific internal control solutions, it defines the environment for the implementation of any required ones.

- OBI supports the principle of risk-based controls and relies on an integrated internal control framework involving nontraditional control techniques currently deployed by various progressive organizations.

- The control techniques used within an OBI solution will vary depending upon the degree of integration with legacy systems and/or the payment method. For example, with an OBI approach involving bulk invoices, the following factors should be used in evaluating the controls/risks:

    - Front-end controls embedded in the user profiles (e.g., spending limits, accounting information, ship-to address, etc.)

    - Risk level of the order request, so that it can be routed for approval prior to release

    - Back-end budgetary controls (i.e., review of completed transactions by cost managers to detect issues/irregularities)

    - Capability of Requisitioners to reconcile order history to invoices

OBI adopters are expected to have simplified their internal control processes for low-dollar, high-volume purchases prior to their implementation efforts.

OBI Technical Requirements

The following sets of requirements deal with the environment under which OBI operates.

Security

OBI security requirements are intended to protect private, confidential, and sensitive information from unauthorized access or use.

- An OBI solution *must* maintain the confidentiality of sensitive data.

- The OBI Standard recognizes that information has varying degrees of sensitivity. An OBI solution *must* be capable of protecting business information on multiple levels of security.

- OBI-based solutions *must* provide a strong authentication component to prove that all parties, users, and systems involved in a transaction are who or what they claim to be.

- The solution *must* provide an authorization component that restricts access to sensitive information and limits transaction authority to specified parties.

- Solutions based on the OBI Standard *must* protect sensitive data as they are transmitted from one party to another. In particular, OBI solutions should guarantee that data have not been intercepted or falsified by a third party.

- The secure transmission of orders directly to Selling Organizations *must* include authentication of parties and encryption of sensitive data. Payment data *must* be transmitted securely at all times.

The security requirements for OBI, much like those for SET, enhance the environment for secure and well-protected operations.

Interoperability

Like SET-compliant products, OBI-compliant products must be able to work across differing vendor product lines.

- OBI solutions *must* use existing or emerging industry standards as the basis for architectural design. The OBI architecture *must* allow the same functionality to be implemented in different ways and enable integration of products from different vendors. This will be accomplished through the use of standard and/or open data formats, access protocols, and system interfaces. Key components and subsystems (catalog, payment, approval, etc.) provided by different technology partners *must* be able to interoperate to form an end-to-end solution.

- All data exchange formats *must* leverage existing standards—for example, ANSI X12.850 (and/or related EDIFACT standards) for purchase orders, Hypertext Markup Language (HTML) for content display, Secure Sockets Layer (SSL) for secure Internet communications, X.509 for digital certificates, and Secure Electronic Transactions (SET) for Internet transfer of payment data.

- Interoperable security systems *must* be maintained by Selling Organizations, Buying Organizations, and financial institutions.

- OBI-based solutions *must* follow a standard database layout that includes required, optional, and site-defined fields. Also, mechanisms for accessing and modifying this information through on-line, batch, or archive methods *must* be provided.

- OBI-compliant solutions *must* follow the data formats and transport methods specified for purchase orders, and employ existing methods for Internet security. It is *recommended* that OBI-compliant solutions follow the guidelines established for the display and format of user profiles, catalogs, order status, and order history.

Interoperability testing will be required for all aspects of OBI compliance. That testing appears far more complex than what's needed for SET alone.

Ease of Use

These *soft* requirements appear based on the principle that if end-users perceive that the on-line system is easier to use than traditional methods, they'll not only be more encouraged to use it, but the organization's goals to eliminate errors and reduce transaction costs will be met.

- The user interface *must* be designed and implemented to allow Requisitioners with minimal information technology skills to quickly become productive. The user interface should therefore be simple, consistent, intuitive, predictable, and responsive.

- The effort it takes to complete an order using OBI-based solutions *must* be less than or equal to the effort to complete an order using traditional methods. Specifically, it must take little effort to find the catalog, identify the goods and services desired, place the order, etc.

- Central administrators at Buying Organizations *must* be able to delegate maintenance of purchaser profile information to local administrators.

- Requisitioners *must* be able to electronically modify some information in their purchaser profile, such as password, e-mail address, or office location.

- It is *recommended* that OBI-based solutions require no more than three "clicks" for the Requisitioner to perform some meaningful action.

The overall intent of these requirements is to eliminate any steep "learning curve" requirements for rapid and effective use of the system.

System Interfaces

These OBI requirements describe a recommended approach to developing interfaces with legacy back-office systems to support processing. The OBI specification encourages a loose integration into systems via open interfaces to systems and data.

- OBI-compliant solutions *must* provide some capability to interface with external applications or legacy systems. Interfaces to legacy systems such as workflow, financial, purchasing, and HR systems for Buying Organizations, and order entry, inventory management, and catalog systems for Selling Organizations, *must* be accommodated. Workflow functionality in an OBI-compliant solution is optional. However, the solution *must* be capable of interfacing with workflow systems. Interfaces between such systems *must* not be complex.

- Orders *must* be transmitted to Selling Organizations in such a way that they can be automatically entered in a Selling Organization's order management system.

While not mandating direct integration into back-office systems, OBI supports any types of interfaces that will best serve company interests.

Architecture

By specifying the Internet as the minimum network, OBI assures Trading Partner communications without any reliance on private networks.

- OBI-compliant solutions *must* provide the ability to purchase goods and services and transmit buy-pay related information over the Internet.

- OBI-compliant solutions *must* allow companies the option of using public or private network transport for transmission of orders, order acknowledgments, payment transactions, etc.

- The user interface and presentation *must* be delivered via Hypertext Markup Language (HTML) and follow the current standards supported by the World Wide Web Consortium (W3C).

- OBI-compliant solutions *must* support international use.

- OBI-based solutions *must* not require the use of U.S.-restricted software or hardware components.

- Components of the solution *must* be modular and distinct, allowing a company to implement partial solutions at a pace that suits their business objectives and evolving business needs.

- With the exception of some minimal downtime for routine maintenance, OBI-based solutions *must* be capable of operating 24 hours per day, seven days per week. OBI-based solutions *must* be highly reliable.

- Solutions must not require, nor preclude, the involvement of third-party service providers.

- The overall system *must* be capable of scaling to thousands of Buying Organizations and Selling Organizations. The architecture and design *must* not limit the potential for growth in numbers of users, transactions, or organizations. OBI-based solutions *must* put no restrictions on the number of Buying Organizations, Selling Organizations, or value-added service providers. The design *must* ensure that performance and reliability expectations can be met as use of the system increases. As the number of users accessing the solution increases, the cost to maintain and support the solution *must* not dramatically increase.

- Systems *must* recover gracefully from user, system, or network failure.

- OBI-based solutions *must* provide the ability to complete a temporary or partial implementation, or roll out subsets of a redesigned business process.

- Systems *must* be usable over standard dial-up phone lines.

With a flexible, yet predictable operating environment, OBI is adaptable to suit all types of intercompany communications and processing.

Systems Administration

Administration requirements are based on the principle that any system's continuing operations costs remain reasonable.

- On a day-to-day basis, the OBI-solution *requires* a minimum of operational and administrative effort. The solution should be easy to maintain and administer from the standpoint of both IT and business organizations.

- OBI-compliant solutions *must* install at the desktop with minimal effort and expertise.

- System updates and upgrades *must* be transparent to end-users and require minimal deployment of software to desktops. Routine software updates or maintenance releases should be deployed using tools that allow updates to many desktop computers at once. Software upgrades *must* be backward compatible with previous releases of the OBI solution.

- OBI-compliant solutions *must* not make assumptions about the underlying information technology infrastructure beyond some basic Web capability for the Requisitioner. Solutions *must* rely on user-specified configuration parameters to capture site-specific information.

- OBI-compliant solutions *must* have the ability to capture system performance metrics.

OBI encourages the use of modern systems technology to help keep operating costs to a minimum.

With the full set of requirements, anyone interested in developing solutions may rest assured that all aspects of the system have been fully considered. Provided that the specific implementations meet the stated requirements, OBI is achieved.

Piloting OBI

In August 1997, the Motorola Space and Systems Technology Group in Tempe, Arizona ran the first pilot test of OBI using the Intelipro System. Employees at Motorola accessed Office Depot's on-line catalog in the first business-to-business electronic commerce pilot program compliant with the OBI standard. Intelipro was developed by Intelisys Electronic Commerce, LLC (www.intelisys.net), a joint venture between Chase Manhattan Bank and software developers, BVR, LLC. According to Peter Roden, executive director of the OBI Consortium:

> *This pilot will prove the viability of the OBI standard from both a technical and business standpoint. It is the first tangible example of how the OBI standard streamlines the online purchasing process so that companies and technology providers can transact business in a seamless fashion.*

Executives from both Motorola and Office Depot were pleased with the results of the pilot and plan on continued use of the system as issues of OBI compliance by software developers are being resolved. "The only way standards become useful is with commercial applications like Intelipro," states Scott LaForce, vice president and Intelisys product manager at Chase Manhattan.

Commercial purchasing is complicated. No single solution can possibly meet all the needs of all businesses. When companies are able to reduce their costs on nuisance-type purchases, they're well advised to so do.

With its comprehensiveness, OBI-based extranets are certain to wring out many of the costs in commercial supply chains. These same extranets can finally help companies to realize the benefits of Just-In-Time (JIT) inventory systems. As more companies participate in the types of information sharing that OBI encourages, added to a tight integration of SET, consumers, merchants, and commercial enterprises alike are sure to benefit and prosper.

In the last chapter, we wrap up with a look at how SET affects and is affected by the future, including how SET will find its way into the global marketplace of consumer and business shopping and buying.

SET for the Future

To best understand the future of SET, a fortune teller's crystal ball would be most helpful. Specifications have yet to be published for any future versions, but lively discussions about it continue unabated. Thus far, it's clear that SET will play a major role in global e-commerce, but the when and the how are still up for grabs.

In this final chapter of the book we'll conclude with a discussion of the following questions as they relate to the future of SET:

- What exactly is elliptic curve cryptography and why is it an improvement over RSA cryptosystems?

- How do European SmartCard initiatives affect the future of SET?

- What are other international implications for SET?

- Is interoperability truly achievable for SET?

Elliptical Curveballs?

Elliptical Curve Cryptography (ECC), a cryptosystem developed in 1985, uses the algebraic system defined on the points of an elliptic curve to create public-key algorithms. Mathematicians have studied this kind of system for many years. In 1985, Neal Koblitz and V. S. Miller proposed using elliptic curves for public-key cryptosystems.

The mathematics of how such systems work are complex and far beyond the scope of this book. Simply put, ECC produces strong security with 56-, 84-, and 96-bit keys, compared with the 512-bit and 1,024-bit keys used within RSA. Its prime feature is smaller keys that yield strong encryption but at much faster processing speeds.

The framers of SET are considering using ECC in the SET 2.0 specification for several reasons. Some experts are very concerned that the current implementation of SET requires extensive processing speeds and may impair its acceptance. ECC operations can occur more quickly than RSA's and smaller key sizes make it a natural candidate for SmartCard technology (discussed later in this chapter).

ECC appears most beneficial where computational power is low (e.g., SmartCards, PC Cards, and wireless devices), where memory space is restrictive (SmartCards, PC Cards, and wireless devices), where faster processing speeds are needed than what can be achieved using larger keys, and where bandwidth is restricted (e.g., wireless communications).

. . . Or Maybe a Sinker? . . .

Not everyone, however, is ready to take a swing at the ECC pitch. "They have to prove it's secure through rigorous testing, and that takes time," said Forrester Research Inc. analyst Carl Howe. "Users of cryptography and security have to be sure there are no unknown holes or back doors."

Industry reaction to ECC ranges from a wholehearted embrace to a more skeptical distancing from its touted advantages. At its January 1998 Data Security Conference, RSA announced that its BSAFE Version 4.0 toolkit will include ECC algorithms in mid-1998, but some analysts quickly point out that RSA's patent on its popular encryption technology will expire in the year 2000.

Also at the RSA conference, an IBM spokesperson said they'll participate in the beta testing of BSAFE 4.0, since they already license RSA toolkits for their eTill components. However, Nev Zunic, program manager for IBM's Cryptography Center of Competence, added, "It will take a while before the public is comfortable with this new technology." Sun Microsystems also has their share of doubts, calling ECC a "theory thing" and saying they are "agnostic on this issue."

Still, the potential for ECC in SmartCard technology and its potential for use in SET 2.0 have garnered enough votes to give it serious consideration by industry experts. While users care little which cryptosystem is used, they do indeed care that their electronic transactions remain secure.

SmartCards and ECC

A SmartCard closely resembles a regular plastic payment card but also contains a semiconductor chip with logic and nonvolatile memory. Sometimes compared to an electronic safe deposit box, the card stores software that detects unauthorized tampering or intrusions. Millions of these cards are in the wallets of users in Asia and Europe, and they are slowly gaining in popularity in the United States.

Some of the various uses of smart cards include:

- Stored value cards which a consumer carries instead of cash to use in retail stores, public phones, and vending machines

- Health care cards which carry an individual's medical history and emergency and insurance information

- Security and access control cards which monitor an individual's entry to and exit from secured buildings such as offices and hotels

- Ticketing cards which accelerate the process of buying transportation tickets and checking baggage as well as making these tasks more convenient

- Stored traveler profiles that speed up check-in processing at hotels that support their uses

Smart cards offer other advantages: lower replacement costs than cash, greater flexibility as they can be read remotely by microwave or infrared signals, and greater security than cash. The latter point—greater security—is where SET enters the picture.

Smart, Set, Secure

SmartCards (sometimes called Chip Cards) typically use a combination of digital signatures and public-key cryptography for their security. Using write-once memory that cannot be modified once it has been stored, Smart-Cards contain unique identification numbers. They can be used with many different algorithms for security, but two French pilot programs are combining two technologies with SET. e-COMM and C-SET appear to be on the horizon for e-commerce, at least in France.

The Reference Standard EMV, internationally known as the SmartCard Reference for "Europay, Mastercard, and Visa," offers the following advantages for electronic payments:

- Controlled access to the SET payment software

- Authentication of SmartCard information by the card reader

- Support for nonrepudiation through the use of high-level encryption and digital certificates

- Cardholder protection through verification of the confidential PIN number

- Familiarity and the feel of a plastic card along with superior security via SET

Currently 27 million bank cards circulate around France. Some experts there see SmartCards as the means to wean consumers off traditional payment methods and onto electronic commerce. SET + EMV will soon be the standard in France for payment transactions—combining the best of consumer authentication, familiarity of the card itself, and the increased security of SET.

How e-COMM Works

The e-COMM pilot, conducted in two phases, will initially enable consumers to use their existing SmartCards for banking applications. During the second phase, e-COMM will begin testing an EMV card capable of performing cryptographic functions and permit the storage of SET digital certificates. The hopes are that EMV SmartCards will allow consumers to take their cards from one Internet payment terminal to another, à la kiosks or self-service devices.

e-COMM is actually an implementation of the SET protocol, using SET software with SmartCards, shown in Figure 21.1. It incorporates all of the same features as SET does:

- Prerequisite certification of the participants

- Digital signing of messages

- Encryption of payment information

e-COMM commerce will allow all SET Cardholders, including those not associated directly with e-COMM, to make payments directly to e-COMM Merchants.

The actual steps in conducting a transaction are as follows.

Customer

- The customer requests a Visa/Carte Bleue bank card issued by one of the e-COMM Consortium banks. She presents this card initially at registration time and any time thereafter when she makes a payment.

- The customer must have access to an IBM-compatible PC with standard Internet access (e.g., Microsoft System Network), a standard Internet browser (e.g., Netscape Navigator), and an approved SmartCard reader with the requisite e-COMM software.

Figure 21.1 e-COMM SmartCard.

- Next, the customer registers with her bank to make payments. The bank provides access to a Web site for this purpose.

- The customer can now make purchases at all e-COMM Merchants and any other Merchant accepting Visa cards using the SET payment protocol.

Merchant

- Using industry standard software such as IBM's NetCommerce, the Merchant builds a commercial shopping Web site on the Internet.

- The Merchant installs a standard application from one of many software providers that support the SET protocol. This software is not proprietary to e-COMM.

- Next, the Merchant must establish a relationship with one of the Consortium banks and sign an agreement indicating that he will accept card payments over the Internet. Likewise, the Merchant must register with his bank, which will provide Web site access for this purpose.

- The Merchant can now accept Visa Internet payments from e-COMM participants and from any other cardholders using the SET protocol. The card they use can be issued from anywhere around the globe as long as it supports the SET protocol.

Banks

- The bank sets up a Web site that allows it to register clients and issue digital certificates. It must also have a Merchant server that accepts Internet card payments using the SET protocol.

- The bank also maintains the traditional financial interfaces for authorization, clearing, and settlement of payments.

How C-SET Works

C-SET, or "Chip-Secure Electronic Transactions," represents another French pilot combining the technologies of SmartCards with SET. Developed by the Groupement des Cartes Bancaires, C-SET launched in December of 1996 with the backing of Credit Agricole, Credit Mutuel, Banques Populaires, CIC, Caisse d'Epargne, and La Poste. Europay France meanwhile coordinates the technical details needed to ensure the success of the pilot.

Like e-COMM, C-SET merges the physical security of the SmartCard with the SET protocol to create a technology touted as being even more secure than SET. In October of 1997, 2,000 Eurocard MasterCard cardholders received a SmartCard reader terminal from their banks that enabled them to make SmartCard purchases from their PCs at home. In 1998 C-SET will extend its reach across the globe, wherever a consumer can reach a SET-enabled Merchant.

C-SET addresses the problem of the initial issuing of the certificate to the customer, an event that takes place on-line. Since the customer must identify himself before receiving his certificate, the backers of C-SET feel that their system will offer a physical level of security that SET has expressly left out. Proponents believe the card readers simply offer an important level of security sorely lacking in the current nonphysical implementation.

More specifically, C-SET intends to prevent the following kinds of fraud which SET also addresses:

Invalid card carrier. The customer presents a bogus or pirated card number. Although he may be tracked down, the merchant will incur substantial costs investigating the case.

Invalid merchant. The hacker sets up a bogus Web site for a few weeks, sells nonexistent goods or services, collects card numbers, and vanishes after a few weeks.

"Trojan Horse" viruses. Their name comes from the fact that they can lie dormant in the system until triggered by an event, possibly a sequence of numbers entered from a keyboard.

"Non-WYSIWYG" viruses. These create discrepancies between the data displayed on the screen and the actual data transmitted as part of the payment transaction. For example, the true price of an item may display on the screen while a sum significantly higher is sent to the merchant.

C-SET claims to be as much an architecture as a protocol—a physical implementation of SET that offers yet another level of security. The distinguishing features of C-SET include:

- A bank card with an embedded chip, offering a physical level of security.

- Secure card readers that use an RSA encryption module to verify or sign messages and also check the authenticity of the software.

- Electronic Commerce Black Boxes that are secure encryption units adapted for use with TCP/IP networks and with RSA encryption.

- Internet Remote Payment controllers that act as Internet Payment Gateway and Remote Payment Controllers. The first is a firewall that controls the C-SET protocol the same way a payment gateway operates under SET. The latter devices are currently used in France for on-line services.

- Translators that control the flow of data outside of France by acting as secure bridges between France and other countries, converting C-SET transactions in SET and vice versa.

The operation of C-SET resembles the e-COMM model. Customers download the C-SET software and install it into their PCs. At this time, the Web browser activates the C-SET software and prompts the customer to insert his SmartCard into the card reader. A SmartCard reader acts like a POS card reader at a merchant establishment. The device displays the payment amount and prompts the customer to enter his PIN number. The encrypted data contained in the SmartCard chip is activated and sent to the merchant along with other data calculated by the SmartCard chip. Unable to decode this information, the merchant routes it to the Internet Remote Payment Controller (IRPC), which carries out the security checks, issues an authorization request on the Cartes Bancaires authorization network, and sends a response to the Merchant, positive or negative. During this time, the screen displays the current status of the transaction; if the transaction is successful, a payment slip bearing the transaction information results.

Beyond those advances in technology and infrastructure improvements that aid in SET's adoption, other issues related to the law, politics, and human special interests appear to attenuate some of SET's momentum.

Applying SET Internationally

The success of global electronic commerce depends upon the unfettered acceptance of SET. Actually, many factors will determine whether the Internet moves beyond the "gift economy," as some skeptics call it, to become an international marketplace. But SET raises issues about international electronic commerce in two main areas:

Regulatory Agreements. What part, if any, should governments play in controlling how electronic commerce is conducted within their borders and across borders?

Interoperability Agreements. How can governments agree between themselves upon standards in networking and encryption when many of them (the United States included) can't agree on this within their own borders?

In order for the Internet to become the 21st century agora, business and technology leaders must agree upon the standards that will offer each country—and each business within a country—an equal slice of the e-commerce pie. Are the two goals of an equal opportunity but yet a still secure global medium compatible?

Get Your Own (White) House in Order

The U.S. government for one has had a difficult time loosening the grip on the security noose. The National Security Agency (NSA) has keen interests in controlling "communication intelligence activities" in the name of protecting national security. Spawned by Cold War politics, the NSA, created by President Harry Truman in 1952, remained a secret for many years. Today, its budget, estimated by some to exceed $13 billion annually, is still unknown. NSA's charter is to listen to and decode all foreign communications which the U.S. government deems vital to its national security.

The NSA allegedly is the single largest employer of mathematicians in the world and buys more computer hardware than anyone else on this planet. It uses its clout to restrict the public availability and use of cryptography, believing that by doing so it makes it more difficult for enemies of the United States to get their hands on cryptography that the NSA can't crack. As Bruce Schneier points out, the NSA undoubtedly has cryptographic expertise years ahead of what is known in the public sector, and it has shown little interest in relinquishing that control.

Decades of U.S. policy to control who can develop and use cryptosystems has resulted in strict export laws governing the sale and shipment of products overseas, a policy seen by many opponents as a *serious* obstacle to global electronic commerce. At the heart of the matter is a distinction made between "weak" and "strong" encryption. Weak encryption technology, simply put, uses what are known as 40-bit keys, whereas strong encryption uses 56-bit keys and higher. As the law currently stands, Bill Gates can send a 128-bit encrypted message to a colleague in Amsterdam, but Microsoft cannot sell 128-bit encryption software to his customers unless the U.S. government is given a copy of the keys to break the codes. This policy, known as "key-escrow," is thought to ensure that enemies of the U.S. government won't be able to send messages that NSA agents can't read.

Although SET is not about selling encryption software, it does use strong public cryptography for securing card payments on the Internet. That has many government watchers concerned about how heavy a regulatory hand the United States will have in global e-commerce. Opponents of strong governmental control in this area feel that in order to stay competitive with the rest of the world, the United States must support the open architecture of the Internet.

The U.S. government is starting to show some signs of relaxing its grip. Vice President Al Gore has proposed a compromise on the matter of strong encryption, advocating that a third party, with no interest in the data, would hold copies of the keys to 128-bit encryption. More significant motivation to solving the stand-off may rest in the fact that users can already download 128-bit cryptosystems from the Internet; many of them for free.

The Global Information Infrastructure (GII)

This relaxation of governmental policy may also be evidenced in the White House's set of principles in support of the Global Information Infrastructure (GII), namely:

- The private sector should lead. Although the U.S. government initially developed the Internet as a secure communications channel for national security, it now recognizes that it must allow the private sector to be the innovators and lead its development. Furthermore, the government should support self-regulation of the industry wherever appropriate.

- Governments should avoid unnecessary restrictions on electronic commerce. Consumers and businesses should be able to buy and sell on the Internet with minimal government involvement or intervention. The government simply moves too slowly to keep up with the breakneck speed of the rapidly evolving business model of electronic commerce.

- Where governmental involvement is needed, it should support a simple and consistent environment for electronic commerce. Government agreements undoubtedly will be necessary to promote electronic commerce in some areas. Even then, it should decentralize its effort to ensure competition, prevent consumer fraud, protect intellectual property and copyrights, and generally support commercial transactions and help resolve disputes.

- Governments should recognize what makes the Internet the Internet. The Internet by nature is decentralized and has a tradition of "bottoms-up governance." These qualities run counter to existing regulatory models. Governments should adapt their policies accordingly and not the other way around.

- Electronic commerce over the Internet is not a parochial concern. Governments should facilitate it globally. The legal framework supporting electronic commerce should transcend state, national, and international borders, leading to predictable results no matter where a particular buyer or seller lives.

To its credit, the United States continues to strive to find the ideal balance between government power and Internet commerce. Clearly, much work lies ahead.

Europeans and the United States at Odds over Encryption

Europeans are particularly concerned about the fifth principle of the U.S. government's Framework for Global Electronic Commerce, namely its continued ban on the export of strong encryption. A meeting of executives from Deutsche Telekom AG and Microsoft called for a relaxation of encryption policies. At that meeting, Ron Sommer, CEO of Deutsche Telekom, stated, "There's one thing I want to make clear on our view of electronic commerce. Electronic commerce will only become a reality if the users have absolute security when they send off data." Some officials in Europe believe that influencing the United States to lift its ban on 56-bit and 128-bit encryption is their top priority.

However, U.S. Secretary of Commerce William Daley states that governments "must also make sure national security is safeguarded by applying those rules sensibly, so that potential terrorists ... cannot hide their work behind encryption technology."

In mid-1997, the House Committee on International Relations passed a bill that would lift nearly all restrictions on the export of data-scrambling software. The reality of global electronic commerce may be hitting home, according to Rep. Sam Gejdenson, D-Conn., a supporter of the bill as well as of Security And Freedom through Encryption (SAFE). "You may as well try to control geometry flash cards," Gejdenson told FBI Assistant Director James Kallstrom. "The reality is there is very high quality encryption available globally."

Representatives from U.S. and European businesses who met at the Global Business Infrastructure 2000 Conference in The Hague voiced the same need for not only highly secure encryption protocols, but also a global base of security standards that work across international borders. Conference attendee Antti Lahtinen, a security consultant at Finland Post Ltd., said that until standards are set that involve government policy and technological collaboration among businesses, users will turn away from electronic commerce.

In order to create electronic commerce networks, businesses and banks must choose encryption tools and protocols from a number of vendors, keeping in mind governmental encryption policies. SET is regarded as one of those standards because of its ability to meet external standards.

SET's Standards Compliance

As previously discussed in Chapter 5, Version 1.0 of SET design is based on industry standards, the Internet, and international organizations as defined in ISO, IETF, PKCS, and ANSI standards.

Furthermore, the scope of SET for Version 1 intentionally includes the minimal functionality required to support Cardholders and Merchants on the Internet. Because SET cannot anticipate all business practices of every national market of every Acquirer, the design allows the kind of openness and flexibility needed. For example, the design allows a way to extend SET payment messages. In Japan, issuers have options for payment that the consumer selects at the time of purchase. Since the SET message has no place for this information in Version 1.0, the designers allowed for an extension to the protocol. This is just one example of how SET allows for different business functions through the use of protocol extensions.

Open Trading Protocols (OTP)

Since the encryption standard is just one aspect of global electronic commerce, a consortium of companies with significant plans for commerce on the Internet have established the Open Trading Protocols (OTP), a global standard for all forms of trade on the Internet. Among those who support the standard are British Telecom, CyberCash, Hitachi, IBM, Oracle, Sun Microsystems, and VeriFone, joining the founding partners AT&T, Hewlett-Packard, MasterCard International, Mondex International, and Open Market Inc.

The partners involved in the creation of the standards recently made the open specifications available for view and comment (www.otp.org). Freely available to developers and users, the standards belong to everyone, not to any one organization. Understanding the importance of estimates that the Internet marketplace will exceed $200 billion in revenue by the year 2000, the creators of OTP undertook the task of defining global standards that allow Internet trading transactions to occur easily and safely for all parties, regardless of the method of payment.

SET focuses on how a payment is made; the OTP complements but does not replace SET or other protocols in supplying a set of rules that cover the following:

- Offers for sale

- Agreements to purchase

- Payment (using existing payment protocols such as SET)

- Transfer of goods and services

- Receipts for purchases

- Multiple methods of payment

- Support for problem resolution

OTP will give consumers a consistent method of trading on the Internet and creation of records useful for tax purposes, completing expense claims, feeding financial management software, or sending a claim back to a Merchant for problem resolution. Steve Mott, former vice president of electronic commerce of MasterCard International, said:

> We consider OTP to be a significant opportunity in the arena of electronic commerce. These proposed protocols have been designed as an open standard and offer a secure trading environment which cooperates with and potentially enhances other payment protocols including SET and EMV96 for debit and credit.

OTP also recently garnered the support of DigiCash and SIZ, two leaders in retail electronic payment systems. DigiCash is one of the leaders in

SmartCard technology, using public-key cryptography in its products. This company has used this technology in a wide array of applications including CAFÉ, the SmartCard-based payment system run by the Headquarters of the European Union in Brussels.

SIZ Computer Science Center of the German Savings Bank, a German leader in SmartCard introductions, expressed its pleasure about a framework that handles the entire business transaction while supporting different payment systems. This is particularly significant as SIZ sets standards for the German Savings Bank Organization (GSBO), including architecture and methodology. Also, the German federal cabinet recently approved the German Information and Communication Services Bill (IuKDG), which includes an act on digital signatures, requiring public-key encryption for the generation and verification of documents. The IuKDG, however, does *not* accept Internet-standard PGP for the public-key scheme. It does demand the establishment of trust centers to handle the public-key directories of valid certificates and the certification of encryption products used.

With this digital-signature act, Germany has become the leader in creating a legally binding electronic communications infrastructure. Critics are upset over the exclusion of PGP and the impossibility of retrospective invalidation of certificates, but for now any country wanting to join the electronic commerce marketplace in Europe will have to be, at the least, familiar with the IuKDG.

As protocols like OTP and Open Buying on the Internet (OBI) evolve, mature, and integrate more tightly with SET, many of those loud concerns heard from voices across the world will be appropriately quieted.

Further European Initiatives

Europe currently is forging a European Initiative in Electronic Commerce, leveraging its technological strengths and cultural diversity for the take-up of Internet commerce. Its success is based in part on the fact that it represents the world's largest single market, bolstered by the acceptance of a single currency, the Euro. Members of the initiative feel that not only will the Euro bolster e-commerce, but conversely, e-commerce will bolster the Euro.

To understand the importance of the SET protocol in particular and electronic commerce in general, one need look no further than the Netherlands, one of the most developed electronic commerce markets in the world. According to International Data Corp. (IDC), the Netherlands has a high PC penetration (38 percent of households), high use of the Internet (22 percent of PC users have access to the Internet compared with 16 percent in the United States and 12 percent in Germany), and a high use of electronic commerce (33 percent of Internet users use it to buy on-line versus 22 percent in the United States).

The European Initiative in Electronic Commerce emphasizes the importance of both interoperability and consistent regulation by governments (or lack thereof). It makes a strong case for the use of strong encryption and is evident in ways most Europeans express their discontentment in sole dependence on the Americans and *their* SET Specification. Consequently, European banks and financial institutions are working on their own Internet banking schemes. SIZ, along with a consortium of German savings banks, have developed the Home Banking Computer Interface (HBCI), deploying RSA for message verification and encryption as does SET. The Europeans simply feel too uneasy about the indecision in the United States over the exporting of encryption software to sit around and wait forever.

Japan and China

The two major partners in the Asian e-commerce market, Japan and China, have set up systems incompatible with SET, although Japan is working to make its JSET Specification (Japan SET) compatible with SET Version 1.0. JSET evolved for a couple of reasons. First, credit card commerce in Japan is regulated by the Ministry of International Trade and Industry (MITI) rather than the Ministry of Finance. Second, Japan uses a different security algorithm for credit card commerce than for its interbanking commerce.

China currently has no interbanking standard at all, further proof of the need for an international standard. For example, a Bank of China customer in Beijing cannot use his ATM card at a Bank of China branch in Shanghai, much less another bank's ATM. The Golden Card project in Shanghai, China's electronic commerce joint venture between Pu Dong Development Bank and Bull of France, began five years ago and currently has 350,000 CP8 transaction cards in circulation. This system uses proprietary Pu Dong interbank settlement software, which is incompatible with SET. This has prompted Bob Hepple at Visa International to say, "We are currently negotiating with several banks in China to introduce a SET/EMV system in China. Our and MasterCard's plan is that this system should be internationally universal, not proprietary."

The Next Tower of Babel?

The success of global electronic commerce depends on geopolitical, not geotechnical solutions. Today, we see a picture where technology continues to narrow the gap between economies and cultures, hopefully ushering in an age of peaceful economic coexistence.

What do symmetrical or asymmetrical, private key or public key, weak or strong encryption have to do with the price of tea in China or a round of cheddar cheese in Wisconsin? Directly, probably little. However, in order for this new world economy to grow, buyers, shoppers, consumers, merchants, suppliers, and everyone else who purchases services or goods on the Internet *needs* to know that their transactions are secure.

SET is that security standard. Many global initiatives are taking place at this very moment with the purpose of ensuring a uniform, open, and consistent set of rules for conducting commerce electronically on the Internet. Other issues such as currency exchange and language still need to be addressed by the international community. Above all, one point should be clear: the need for security is universal, whether in Hong Kong or Peru, Canada or New Zealand, New York or Newfoundland.

Still, a thorny problem perches on the horizon. Globally, people wonder how a worldwide electronic commerce community based on a single set of standards will be realized.

I'm OK. You're Not OK. Or Are You?

In Chapter 17, we discussed SET interoperability at some length to stress its importance for any serious acceptance of SET. It's importance truly cannot be overemphasized.

In the United States, NationsBank of Charlotte, North Carolina conducted the bank's first SET transaction in early 1998. What is significant about this "first" is NationBank's use of the SET 1.0 production specification and software from different technology suppliers, demonstrating full interoperability. NationsBank worked closely with IBM, MasterCard, GlobeSet, and GTE to create a system for purchasing items from the MasterCard Emporium, an initial Web site built by the association to help consumers make small initial purchases and overcome their fears of shopping electronically. NationsBank used IBM's CommercePOINT Wallet and the IBM Registry for SET certificate services. MasterCard , working with GlobeSet, supplied the Merchant Server software and Payment Gateway software. Steve Mott pointed out, "While there has been a lot of worry lately about SET interoperability, efforts like these with leading banks like NationsBank go a long way to showing the path forward to secure and efficient Internet commerce."

Further efforts are still necessary.

Challenges and Beyond

Although SET is the de facto standard for secure card payments on the Internet, more work awaits. The United States and Europe continue to wrangle over U.S. encryption export policy. Critics claim that SET will prove too slow and costly to ever succeed because it is simply overkill. Every day a new software vendor enters the fray, offering what it claims is *the* suite of software tools.

From the outset, you've understood that the road to SET needed solid pavement. Hopefully, through this book we've aided in that effort.

While the world's future for SET is far from certain, your individual contribution to success with your now-operating SET-enabled site is a model that others may follow. Wear that contribution as your badge of honor.

Best of luck to you all!

WEB RESOURCES APPENDIX

Organization	URL	Description
@BRINT: E-commerce and E-markets Information	www.brint.com /Elecomm.htm	Research material for electronic commerce.
Aberdeen Group, Inc.	www.aberdeen.com	Research reports on commercial electronic commerce.
ActivMedia Inc.	www.activmedia.com	Internet market research reports and services.
AIM Technology	www.aim.com/	Product information on network management tools.
American Banker Financial Services Newspaper	www.americanbanker .com/	On-line magazine for the banking community.
American Express Company	www.americanexpress .com/business/ merchservices.shtml	Information about SET and Merchant Services.
ASN.1 Homepage	www.inria.fr/rodeo/ personnel/hoschka/ asn1.html	Technical information about ASN.1.
Atalla Corporation	www.atalla.com/	Product information for hardware-assisted cryptography.
Bank of America	www.bofa.com/ b-banking/bbmerchov .html	Merchant Services from Bank of America.
BankGate (CompuSource LTD South Africa)	www.bankgate.com	One implementation of SET from South Africa.
Banking Technology Resource Center	www.amarshall.com/ resix/	Various links to information about banking technology.

BBN Planet (GTE Internetworking)	www.bbn.com/	SafeKeyper product information.
BMC Software Inc.	www.bmc.com/	Product information on network management tools.
BYTE Magazine	www.byte.com/	Various articles on electronic commerce topics.
Cert-Talk at Structured Arts Computing Corp.	mail.structuredarts .com/cert-talk/	X.509 discussion group (majordomo service).
CommerceNET Home Page	www.commerce.net	Information about the industry consortium for companies using, promoting, and building electronic commerce.
Computer Crimes and Investigations Center	www.ovnet.com/ ~dckinder/crime.htm	Links to information related to computer crimes and security issues.
Computerworld Magazine	www.computerworld .com	Various articles on electronic commerce topics.
Cryptography Research	www.cryptography .com/	Research information on computer security and cryptography.
Cybercash Inc.	www.cybercash.com	Information on CyberCash payment systems.
Diners Club	www.dinersclub.com/	Information about Diners Club International and the Diners Club payment card.
Discover Card (Novus)	www.discovercard.com/	Information about Discover Card services.
Elekom Corporation	www.elekom.com/ home.htm	Information about ELEKOM Procurement, an enterprise-wide intranet application for corporate electronic commerce.
First Data Corporation	www.firstdatacorp.com/	Information about First Data Corporation and First Data Resources company for bank card processing.
First Union Bank	www.firstunion.com/	Information about First Union Bank in Charlotte, NC.
Forrester Research	www.forrester.com/	Research material on all topics related to electronic commerce.
GartnerGroup Interactive Home	gartner12.gartnerweb .com/public/static/home/ home.html	Research material on all topics related to electronic commerce.

GlobeSet Inc.	www.globeset.com	Information about GlobeSet's suite of SET products.
GTE CyberTrust Home	www.cybertrust .gte.com/	Information about GTE's Certificate Authority services.
IBM CommercePOINT Information	www.internet.ibm .com/secureway/ commercepoint.html	Information about IBM's suite of SET products.
IEEE Computer Society	www.computer.org:80/ cshome.htm	Technical information related to standards-setting work for computers.
Information Week	www.informationweek .com	Various articles on electronic commerce topics.
Intelisys Electronic Commerce, LLC	www.intelisys.net	Information about OBI-enabling products for commercial purchasing systems.
Interactive Week	www.interactive-week .com	Various articles on electronic commerce topics
International Data Corp. (IDC)	www.idc.com	Internet market research reports and services.
Internet Engineering Task Force	www.ietf.org/	Information about Internet standardization efforts.
Internet Guide To Cryptography	www.enter.net/ ~chronos/cryptolog1 .html	Various links to all topics related to cryptography.
Internet.com	www.internet.com/	Various articles on electronic commerce topics.
Japan Commerce Bank (JCB) Company, LTD.	www.jcb.co.jp	Information about JCB, a sponsor of SET.
Journal of Internet Banking and Commerce	www.arraydev.com/ commerce/JIBC/	An on-line journal from Ottawa, Canada about issues related to electronic banks and banking services.
Maithean Incorporated	www.maithean.com/	Information on the NetPay SET-compliant System.
MasterCard International - SET Info	www.mastercard.com/ set/	General information about MasterCard and links to SET materials.
Mercantec Inc.	www.mercantec.com	Information about SoftCart and StoreBuilder products for Merchant Commerce Servers.

Microsoft Site Server E-Commerce	www.microsoft.com/ siteserver/commerce/ default.asp	Information about Microsoft's products for electronic commerce.
National Fraud Information Center	www.fraud.org/	Internet and general fraud information compiled by the National Consumers League.
National Institute of Standards and Technology (NIST)	www.nist.gov/	Information about standards-setting work by the U.S. government.
Netscape Communications	www.netscape.com	Information about products and services for electronic commerce.
NIST Computer Security Resource Clearinghouse	csrc.ncsl.nist.gov/	NIST site for computer security information and resources.
OBI Information from Supplyworks	www.supplyworks .com/obi	General information and downloadable specifications for Open Buying on the Internet.
Object Management Group (OMG)	www.omg.org/	Information about standards-setting efforts for distributed computing.
OnSale	www.onsale.com	Information about on-line auctions and in-progress auctions.
Open Market Inc.	www.openmarket.com/	Information about the Transact System and related e-commerce topics.
PKCS Information at RSA Data Security Corporation	ftp://ftp.rsa.com/ pub/pkcs/	Downloadable documents on Public Key Cryptography Standards.
Rainbow Technologies	http://isg.rainbow.com	Information about CryptoSwift hardware-assisted cryptography products.
Rational Software Corp.	www.rational.com	Information about Rational Rose Unified Modeling Language (UML) CASE tools.
Science Applications International Corporation (SAIC)	www.saic.com/	Information about consulting services related to secure electronic commerce.
Secure Electronic Transactions, LLC (SETCo)	www.setco.org	Information about SET's governing body and certification programs.
SET Central RSA Data Security	www.rsa.com/set/	Comprehensive collection of material relative to SET and Internet security.

Spyrus	www.spyrus.com	Information about Spyrus hardware-assisted cryptography products.
Tenth Mountain Systems	www.tenthmtn.com/	Information about SET compliance testing for SETCo.
Terisa Systems Inc.	www.terisa.com	Information about SecureWeb developer toolkits for SET implementation.
Trintech Ltd.	www.trintech.com	Information about Trintech's suite of SET software products.
U.S. National Security Agency (NSA)	www.nsa.gov:8080/	U.S. government information about cryptographic technologies and use within the U.S. and abroad.
Verifone Corporation	www.verifone.com	Information about Verifone's Internet commerce POS devices and services.
Verisign Digital ID Center	www.verisign.com	Information about Verisign's Certificate Authority services and general information about digital certificates.
Webreference.com E-commece	http://webreference.com/ecommerce/payment.html	On-line journal for all topics related to electronic commerce of particular interest to Webmasters.
Wells Fargo Bank	http://wellsfargo.com/home/	Information about Wells Fargo Bank and Merchant Services.
World Wide Web Consortium (W3C)	www.w3c.org/	Information about standards-setting efforts for World Wide Web uses.
Ziff-Davis Internet Magazine	www.zdimag.com	Various articles on electronic commerce topics.

GLOSSARY

Abstract Syntax Notation One (ASN.1) A standard, flexible method that (a) describes data structures for representing, encoding, transmitting, and decoding data, (b) provides a set of formal rules for describing the structure of objects independent of machine-specific encoding techniques, (c) is a formal network-management Transmission Control Protocol/Internet Protocol (TCP/IP) language that uses human-readable notation and a compact, encoded representation of the same information used in communications protocols, and (d) is a precise, formal notation that removes ambiguities.

Account number A unique number assigned to Cardholder accounts that identifies the specific financial institution, type of card, etc.

Acquirer *See* **Acquiring Bank**.

Acquiring Bank Bank that does business with Merchants who wish to accept credit cards. Merchants are given an account to deposit the value of a batch's card sales. The bank acquires batches of sales slips and credits their value to the Merchant's account. The bank then submits the charges destined for the other banks in the open loop to the interchange network, either directly or through third parties.

Acquiring financial institution *See* **Acquiring Bank**.

Acquiring processor Transaction processing company that offers card processing services, billing, MIS reporting, settlement, and other work to banks and card companies. Since operating these systems is rather complex and highly expensive, many banks outsource this work to third parties who specialize in such services.

Application Program Interface (API) A standard method for programmers to access the features and functions of commercial software using custom-written routines that "call" these services through the interfaces provided to the programmer.

Asymmetric key cryptography When one key is used to encrypt a message and a second key is used to decrypt the message, the key-pair indicates the use of asymmetric key cryptography.

Authentication *See* **Message authentication.**

Authorization A process whereby transactions are approved or declined by the card issuers. Successful authorizations reduce the amount of available credit but do not actually charge the customer, nor move money to the seller. Authorizations can be performed via telephone, POS terminal, or the Internet.

Authorization code An enumerated code that's returned with a successful authorization response to a payment card charge request.

Authorization reversal The process of reversing a successful authorization in the event a consumer changed his mind about an order or an order was canceled for other reasons within a short period of time following the purchase request.

Baggage A mechanism whereby encrypted data is appended externally to a SET message that links to the information contained within the message itself. Baggage is used in several SET message pairs to avoid super-encrypting already encrypted data, yet still provides the linkage necessary to tie both components together.

Bank Identification Number (BIN) A three- to five-digit code, defined by ISO 8663, that assigns ranges for account number assignments that are explicitly tied to a specific brand or card company.

Batch settlement An accumulation of card transactions awaiting settlement processing. Batches can be submitted for processing throughout the day or continue to grow until their value is sufficiently large enough and worthwhile to process.

Bolt-on application A "helper type" of application software that extends the functionality of another program. SET is bolted on to existing Merchant Commerce Servers and consumer Web browsers using POS functionality and E-wallet functionality, respectively.

Brand Certificate Authority A trusted party that serves on behalf of a payment card brand (Visa, MasterCard, etc.) to perform the services of brand digital certificate management.

Branded payment card A credit or charge card that bears a company brand name (Visa, MasterCard, American Express, etc.).

Brute force attack Attempt to crack a cryptosystem by trying every combination of a key and subsequent inspection of the decryption process to determine if any sense can be made of it.

Capture reversal The process of reversing a previously successful capture response in the event of returned goods within a (short) period of time following the completion of the sale.

Card association Cooperating banks that support the franchise for a particular payment card brand (e.g., Visa) and establish the by-laws that frame the uses of the franchise and the products within it.

Card issuer A bank or card company that issues branded cards to its customers.

Card-not-present A transaction using payment cards where the physical plastic card is not present for the Merchant to see. These are considered riskier transactions than card-present transactions, and typically describe Mail Order/Telephone Order (MOTO) purchasing scenarios.

Cardholder The user (typically a consumer) of a credit or charge card issued by an Issuer Bank.

Certificate Authority Trusted party that operates on the behalf of SETCo and payment card brands to manage the distribution and currency of SET digital certificates. Each layer in the Tree of Trust is represented by a well-defined Certificate Authority.

Certificate chain Ordered group of digital certificates that are used to validate a specific certificate within the chain.

Certificate Practice Statement A named set of rules that indicates the applicability of a certificate to a particular community and/or class of application with common security requirements.

Certificate renewal The act of renewing a certificate pending an expiration date to ensure continued use for transacting.

Certificate revocation The act of canceling a certificate in response to theft or suspected theft of the associated private key. Revocation is performed by the CA that issued the certificate, and once revoked, the serial number for the certificate will be placed on a Certificate Revocation List (CRL).

Certificate Revocation List (CRL) A mechanism that SET uses to ensure that revoked certificates are not used in transactions. CRLs contain revoked certificate serial numbers, their date of revocation, the date the CRL was generated, its expiration date, the issuer name, and the serial number of the CA certificate used to sign it. The CRL is distributed with each downstream SET message during an in-process transaction. The CRL is checked by the Payment Gateway with each message received.

Certification The process of attesting to a person or entity's proof of identity and right to use a payment card relationship via the issuance of a signed certificate bearing the entity's public key.

Charge card Contrasted to a credit card, a charge card carries no preset spending limits, and charges are due in full at the end of the month, are not tied to revolving lines of credit, and do not accumulate interest or finance charges under normal uses.

Ciphertext The output from an encryption algorithm after plaintext is passed through it.

Clearing The process of exchanging transaction details between the Merchant Bank and the Issuer Bank. Clearing posts charges to Cardholder accounts and reconciles the Merchant's settlement position.

Closed loop Processing arrangement where a single company or bank owns both the Cardholders who use their products and the Merchants who accept their products. American Express and Discover (Novus) are examples of closed loop systems.

Commercial Data Masking Facility (CDMF) Used as a data-scrambling technique that relies upon DES to mask rather than encrypt data. Its use is primarily for passing messages between the Acquirer Payment Gateway and the Cardholder as they move through the Merchant Server.

Confidentiality Protecting private, personal, or sensitive information against attacks or disclosures.

Credit A transaction that returns money to the Cardholder when goods are returned to a Merchant for restocking.

Credit card Describes a payment card that carries a preset spending limit established by the issuer based on a line of credit obtained at the time of issue. Some are signature lines of credit, while others are secured lines of credit. In addition, the balance revolves around the line of credit and may be paid in full or financed over time.

Credit reversal A transaction that reverses a previously granted credit in the case where it was incorrect or where a credit should not have been granted.

Cryptanalysis The science (or art) of breaking a cryptosystem.

Cryptographic key A series of data bits that are used to control a cryptographic process, such as encryption, decryption, or message authentication testing.

Cryptography The science (or art) of designing, building, and using cryptosystems.

Cryptology The umbrella study of cryptography and cryptanalysis.

Cryptoperiod The span of time in which a given key is authorized for use or considered to be in effect.

Cryptosystem Refers to both the algorithm used in cryptography and the means in which the algorithm is implemented.

Data Encryption Standard (DES) SET's default symmetric key encryption algorithm, defined by the Federal Information Processing Standard (FIPS) 46-2 and published by the National Institute of Standards and Technology (NIST).

Dictionary attack Attacks on a cryptosystem using a dictionary of common possible keys. Brute force attacks on a key often start out with an attacker using the easiest keys first (English words and names, etc.).

Digital certificate The binding of an entity's identity with a public key, performed by a trusted party. Required for PPK cryptography purposes.

Digital envelope When a digitally signed message is further encrypted using the receiver's public key, the message is said to be contained in a digital envelope.

Digital signature Created using PPK cryptography and message digests. Encryption allows a message sender the ability to digitally sign messages, thus creating a digital signature for the message. When a message digest is computed and then encrypted using the sender's private key, and later appended to the message, the result is called the digital signature of the message.

Discount rate Merchant fees are determined through the discount rate set by the Merchant Bank as a privilege fee for using their account services. Fees are based on the value of each transaction, and typically range from 1 percent up to 5 percent, depending on a number of factors, including charge volumes, risk models, size of the business, methods of submission, bank policies, etc.

Distinguished Encoding Rules (DER) Distinguished Encoding Rules provide *exactly one* way to represent ASN.1 values as an octet string. DER is intended for use in applications where unique, unambiguous values are required, as with security-conscious applications such as SET.

Dual signature Used under special circumstances within SET, like authorization requests, to hide information between two sending parties but reveal the information to the processing party.

Electronic commerce (e-commerce) Electronic forms of communication that permit the exchange of sale information related to goods and services purchasing between buyers and sellers.

Electronic wallet (E-wallet) The Cardholder's component for SET that implements the protocol necessary from his end and helps to acquire and manage Cardholder digital certificates.

Encapsulation Encapsulation combines the uses of encryption and signatures to ensure the highest degrees of message integrity and end-entity authentication.

Encryption The hiding or masking of information through cryptography such that only those permitted can see through the disguise.

Financial institution Any bank or card company that supports the use of payment cards as an alternative to cash for the payment of goods and services.

Freshness challenge A technique to test the freshness of a message by generating a random number, placing it within a sending message, and looking for it within a return message from the message's recipient.

Geopolitical Certificate Authorities Those optional levels of the SET Tree of Trust that permit Card Brands to further control how they wish to manage digital certificates across geographical or political boundaries.

Hash A mechanism to reduce a large domain of possible values to a smaller range of values. Hash values and message digests are created using hashing functions. SET uses the Secure Hashing Algorithm (SHA-1) as the default for hashing operations.

Idempotency A property of a SET message where the operation may be repeated over and over each time yielding the same result (e.g., an inquiry message pair where no changes have occurred with a transaction).

Integrity A quality metric that describes information and processes that are free of defects or errors.

Interchange The banker's interchange exists to exchange information, data, and money between the banks connected to it. The interchange systems are managed by Visa and MasterCard to standardize the network's use across the globe.

Interchange fee An amount charged to a Merchant Bank by an Issuer Bank to compensate the Issuer Bank for the time it needs to wait for payment between settlement time and actual receipt of bill payment from the Cardholder.

Internet Engineering Task Force An open international community of network designers, operators, vendors, and researchers concerned with the evolution of the Internet architecture.

Interoperability The virtue of software products to work correctly with counterpart software produced by other developers with access to the same sets of specifications.

Issuer *See* **Issuer Bank.**

Issuer Bank The bank that extends credit to its customers (Cardholders) through bank card accounts. These banks enter into contractual agreements with Visa or MasterCard to issue their respective products.

Key-Exchange Certificate One type of digital certificate that's used to share the public key with those intending to send messages to the certificate owner. Contrasted with Signature Certificate.

Mail Order/Telephone Order (MOTO) Situation where a charge is requested in a card-not-present scenario that carries greater risk to Merchants and the Card Issuers.

Member bank A bank that is a franchisee of a payment card brand.

Merchant Any business operation that accepts payment cards for goods or services. Merchants establish the privilege of accepting payment cards through relationships with Acquiring (Merchant) Banks and card companies.

Merchant Bank *See* **Acquiring Bank**.

Merchant number The unique identifier assigned to a Merchant that identifies the Merchant's account at the Acquiring Bank.

Merchant Services The department within a bank that serves the needs of Merchants, including the establishment of Merchant accounts for payment card acceptance and processing.

Merchant SET POS System The "bolt-on" application for Merchant Commerce Servers that carries out the work necessary for on-line payment card acceptance using the rules and messages defined by SET.

Message authentication The process of authenticating that a message received came from the entity whom the recipient believes to be the sender.

Message digest A unique fingerprint of a message that's calculated based on the contents of the message using a hashing algorithm. The original message cannot be recovered from the message digest, but is used to verify that no changes to the message took place while en route to the recipient.

Message pair SET message pairs are used to implement the POS and certificate management processing that's defined by the specification.

MessageWrapper All SET-related processing begins with the MessageWrapper, a top-level ASN.1/DER encoded data structure that presents information to the receivers of messages upon receipt. MessageWrapper structures do not involve any cryptography but do identify both the type of message being received and its unique ID, which aids in the detection of duplicate messages.

Nonrepudiation In the context of on-line payments, nonrepudiation is a legal term that dictates that if a message is decryptable using a person's public key, the message *must* have originated with the holder of the private key. Under nonrepudiation, a private key holder cannot deny having signed the message if the decryption process succeeds. SET does not support nonrepudiation.

Nonce A randomly generated string of bits (nonsense) that's used to check the freshness of return messages from other entities.

Open Buying on the Internet (OBI) A protocol that's intended to standardize the commercial purchasing environment for Maintenance, Repair, and Operations (MRO) goods and services.

Open loop In contrast to a closed loop, in an open loop Merchant and Cardholder relationships are maintained by separate banks, but transacting with payment cards can still take place.

Open Trading Protocol (OTP) Sets of rules that cover processing out-of-band to SET, including:

- Offers for sale
- Agreements to purchase
- Payment (using existing payment protocols such as SET)
- Transfer of goods and services
- Receipts for purchases
- Multiple methods of payment
- Support for problem resolution

Open-to-buy A piece of information on every credit card account that indicates the difference between the line-of-credit amount and the balance currently owed by the Cardholder.

Optimal Asymmetric Encryption Padding (OAEP) Developed by Bellare-Rogaway and used in conjunction with SET's encapsulation operators to securely pad public key encrypted data.

Order inquiry A pair of SET messages used to check on the status of an open or pending order.

Out-of-band Any activity that's performed outside the definition of the SET Specification. For example, the exchange of order detail information is conducted out-of-band to SET.

Payload Information contained within a SET message that comprises business-related information (sale details, etc.).

Payment Account Number (PAN) The account number found on the front of plastic payment cards and card statements.

Payment authorization *See* **Authorization**.

Payment Card Describes credit cards and charge cards for use within SET. In the future, payment cards (under SET) may include ATM or debit cards.

Payment Gateway The front-end processor computer to Acquirer authorization and settlement systems that translates SET messages to and from standard bank financial processing record formats.

Payment instructions The portion of a SET Purchase Request that includes card information for processing by the Acquirer Payment Gateway that cannot be decrypted by the Merchant POS System.

Plaintext The input to an encryption algorithm for the intent of producing ciphertext and the output from an decryption algorithm after ciphertext is passed through it.

Point-of-sale (POS) The technology (devices and systems) that carries out the work of authorizing and settling payment card charges wherever goods and services are exchanged.

Pretty Good Privacy (PGP) A distributed key management approach that does not rely on Certificate Authorities. Users can sign one another's public keys, adding degrees of confidence to a key's validity. Someone who signs someone else's public key acts as an introducer for that person to a third person, with the idea that if the third person trusts the introducer, she should also trust the person who's being introduced.

Privacy Enhance Mail (PEM) An encryption standard for electronic mail, developed in the late 1980s by the Internet Engineering Task Force (IETF).

Private key The half of a key-pair that's retained on the computer which generated the key-pair. Private keys are used to encrypt messages that can be verified as legitimate if the associated public key is able to decrypt them.

Processing fees Fees that are charged to Acquirer Banks and Merchants for the privileges of using the interchange network or for using Merchant Account services. Typically processing fees are built into the discount rates.

Pseudo-random numbers Numbers output from computer-based random number generators that begin to repeat a pattern over time. The challenge for cryptography is to build random number generators that won't repeat sequences of bits predictably often. Some of the pseudo-random number generators available today show randomness through 2^{256} bits, making them more suited for cryptographic purposes than were earlier generators.

Public key The half of a key-pair that's shared with message recipients to use in sending encrypted messages back to the private key holder.

Public Key Certificate *See* **Digital certificate**.

Public Key Cryptography Standards (PKCS) A family of public-key cryptography standards used by SET which include:

- RSA encryption for the construction of SET digital signatures and digital envelopes

- Diffie-Hellman key agreements that define how two people, with no prior arrangements, can agree on a shared secret key that's known only between them and used for future encrypted communications

- Password-based encryption to hide private keys when transferring them between computer systems, sometimes required under Public-Private Key Cryptography

- Extended certificate syntax to permit the addition of SET extensions to standard X.509 digital certificates, in order to add information such as certificate usage policies, other identifying information, etc.

- Cryptographic message syntax describing how to apply cryptography to SET-related data, including digital signatures and digital envelopes

- Private-key information syntax describing how to include a private key along with algorithm information and a set of attributes to offer a simple way of establishing trust in information provided

- Certification request syntax describing the rules and sets of attributes needed for a SET certificate request from a SET Certificate Authority

Public/private key-pairs A required component for Public-Private Key (PPK) cryptography whereby two mathematically related keys are used to encrypt and decrypt communications between two or more parties.

Random number Any number within a set of numbers that has an equal chance of being selected from the population, and the selection of which is considered unpredictable.

Receipt A hard-copy document that represents the fact that a transaction took place at some point in time.

Record of charge (ROC) *See* **Receipt**.

Referral A condition upon the return of an authorization request where the Merchant is requested to call the Issuer for further instructions regarding a charge request.

Replay An attack in which a message is repeated over and over by either the true originator of the message or an attacker posing as the originator.

Request-Response Pair *See* **Message pair**.

Rivest, Shamir, Adelman (RSA) Cryptosystem A public-key cryptography system named after its inventors—Rivest, Shamir, and Adelman.

Root Certificate The highest level in a Tree of Trust that's used to sign subordinate certificates. The SET Root Certificate is used in signing the Brand Certificates.

Root Key Authority The managing organization that's responsible for the generation, maintenance, and distribution of root certificates. For SET, SETCo is that managing body.

Sales Transaction A payment authorization option under SET that permits a Merchant to both authorize and capture a sale using a single message pair. These types of transactions are only possible where goods are delivered immediately following authorization (e.g., downloaded software, clip art, etc.).

Secret-key cryptography *See* **Asymmetric key cryptography**.

Secure Electronic Payment Protocol (SEPP) A predecessor payment protocol to SET, developed by MasterCard, Netscape, IBM, CyberCash, and GTE.

Secure Hash Algorithm (SHA-1) Used for hashing all data under SET. It is defined by Federal Information Processing Standards 180-1.

Secure Sockets Layer (SSL) A security protocol that sits on top of a reliable transport protocol to encapsulate other higher level protocols. The SSL Handshake Protocol authenticates the client and server to each other and enables them to decide upon an encryption algorithm and cryptographic keys before the higher level protocol sends or receives data.

Secure Transaction Technology (STT) A predecessor payment protocol to SET, developed by Visa and Microsoft.

Secure/Multipurpose Internet Mail Extensions (S/MIME) Based on technology from RSA Data Security, it offers another standard for electronic-mail encryption and digital signatures.

SET Consortium A group that formed following the joint Visa and MasterCard announcement of SET that included support from GTE, IBM, Microsoft, Netscape Communications Corp., SAIC, Terisa Systems, VeriSign, and RSA Data Security. Their goal was to resolve the differences and conflicts between STT and SEPP and develop a new unified standard.

SETMark Visible proof of successful SET certification for vendor software, providing consumers with a comfortable knowledge that they're transacting using SET.

Settlement A process that occurs when the Acquiring Bank exchanges financial information in return for funds from an Issuer Bank.

Signature Certificate A type of digital certificate that is used by the message recipient in authenticating the origin of a signed message. Contrasted with Key-Exchange Certificate.

SmartCard Credit-card size device with embedded programmable chip that can store enhanced information for special purposes. Applications of SmartCards include storage of digital certificates, e-purse (stored value of cash for small purchases) applications, and traveler preferences.

Split shipment Occurs when an entire order cannot be shipped at once (back-order conditions) and previously successful authorization information must be changed accordingly to reflect what can be shipped and what will wait for a later authorization.

Split-dial A feature built into most POS terminals that allows Merchants to accept several card products without requiring them to use separate POS devices.

Symmetric key cryptography When the same shared, secret key is used to both encrypt and decrypt messages.

Third-party processor Company that enters into contractual agreements with Issuer and Acquirer Banks to process authorizations and settlement operations on their behalf.

Thumbprint A hash value calculated over items of data to generate or verify a digital signature.

Thumb An instance of a thumbprint. A chain or more than one thumbprint would be called Thumbs.

Tree of Trust The hierarchy established for SET to manage the issuance, maintenance, and currency of SET Digital Certificates.

Tuple Zero or more components of data arranged in a sequence.

Virtual Private Network (VPN) A tunnel through the Internet that uses cryptography to hide the contents of messages as they traverse public networks

X.509 Defines the most widely accepted format for digital certificates, as specified by the CCITT. SET's version of X.509 digital certificates are a special "flavor" designed exclusively for payment cards.

INDEX